Missing, Presumed

Alan Bailey

LIB
ERT
IES

Contents

The Vanishing Triangle

1. Body of Phyllis Murphy located at Ballinagee, Wicklow Gap, on 1 January 1980.

2. Body of Antoinette Smith located at Glendoo Woods, Kilakee, Dublin Mountains, on 3 April 1988.

3. Body of Patricia Doherty located at Feather Beds, Glassamucky, Dublin Mountains, on 21 June 1992.

4. Last sighting of Annie McCarrick, Enniskerry, Dublin, on 26 March 1993.

5. Body of Marie Kilmartin located at Barnanaghs, Portlaoise, on 10 June 1994.

6. Site of rape, Powerscourt/Enniskerry, Dublin, 30 December 1994.

7. Last sighting of Jo Jo Dollard, Moone, County Kildare, 9 November 1995.

8. Last sighting of Fiona Pender, Tullamore, County Offaly, 23 August 1996.

9. Last sighting of Ciara Breen, Dundalk, 12 February 1997.

10. Last sighting Fiona Sinnott, Broadway, Wexford, 9 February 1998.

11. Last sighting of Deirdre Jacob, Newbridge, County Kildare, 28 July 1998.

12. Body of Layla Brennan, located at Kilakee Road, Dublin Mountains, on 3 March 1999.

13. Abduction of female in Carlow town by Larry Murphy on 11 February 2000.

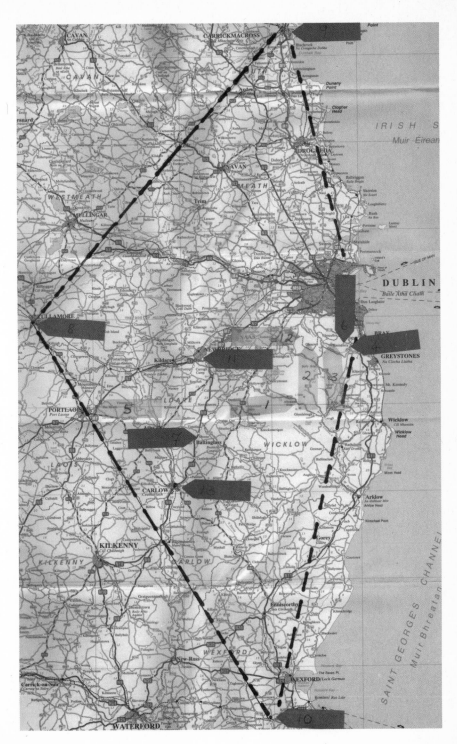

A Note from the Author

All names marked by asterisks have been changed,
either for discretion or safety.

Introduction

Those friends and neighbours who met and greeted the young teenager, as she strolled homewards down the tree-lined road on that balmy July afternoon, could not have known that theirs would be the last verifiable sightings of her alive. Within six hours, her distraught parents would report her missing at their local Garda Station. Neither could they have imagined that, within eight hours, some of them would be hastily grouped together within search teams, combing the fields and roads near her home, desperately looking for some sign of the missing girl.

By the following morning, her disappearance was being linked, by both media and public, to other cases where females had disappeared, and had either never been seen again, or whose badly decomposed bodies had been accidently found months later. Fears were openly expressed that a serial killer was operating, either alone or with other like-minded predators, in an area of the country where instances of female disappearance had become so common that it had been dubbed the 'Vanishing Triangle'.

This was the second disappearance of a teenager within the space of a few months. In February of that same year, a young girl had gone missing after leaving her local pub in the south-east of the country, to make the short journey to her rented home. She bid her friends goodnight as she walked out the door, and was never seen alive again.

Although these disappearances would account for just two of some six thousand missing-person reports filed with Gardai that year, the circumstances surrounding them were considered worrying enough to warrant the setting up of a specialised taskforce, to investigate both these and a number of other cases involving the disappearances of females.

The taskforce, codenamed Operation TRACE (an acronym for Tracing, Reviewing And Collating Evidence), were given – among others – six disappearances to investigate: American national Annie McCarrick, on Friday 26 March 1993; Kilkenny girl Josephine 'Jo Jo' Dollard, on 9 November 1995; Tullamore native Fiona Pender, last seen on 23 August 1996; Dundalk teenager Ciara Breen, last seen alive on 12 February 1997; Fiona Sinnott, a young

Wexford mother, last seen alive on 8 February 1998, and Deirdre Jacob, who went missing from Newbridge in County Kildare on 28 July 1998.

★

The taskforce would eventually reopen investigations into a number of other similar cases, including instances where bodies had later been located. These included the disappearance of Phyllis Murphy, who was last seen alive as she stood at a bus stop in Newbridge, on the evening of 22 December 1979, laden down with Christmas shopping. Her naked body was located on 18 January 1980, hidden in a forest in the Wicklow Mountains.

Housewife and mother Antoinette Smith disappeared on 12 July 1987, after a night out in Dublin city. Her body was located in the Dublin Mountains on 3 April 1988. There was a plastic bag wrapped tightly around her head.

The murder of another female, whose body was located less than three weeks after that of Antoinette's, was also under examination. On this occasion, however, the body was located outside of our jurisdiction, in a national park in North Antrim. German tourist Inga Hauser had last been seen alive getting off the ferry at Larne, on 6 April 1988.

Prison officer Patricia Doherty left home on the evening of 23 December 1991, to do some last-minute Christmas shopping. Her body was located on 21 June of the following year, by a man cutting turf in the Dublin Mountains. The body dump site that had been selected was less than a mile from where Antoinette's body had been located some three years earlier.

There was also the case of agoraphobia sufferer Marie Kilmartin, who disappeared on a dark winter evening, in December of 1993, after inexplicably leaving her house. Her body was accidentally located in June of 1994, in bogland outside Portarlington.

Arlene Arkinson, a native of Caslederg, Northern Ireland, was last seen alive shortly after leaving a discotheque in Bundoran, County Donegal, in August 1994. What the carefree young teenager could not have known was that her escort to the dance that night was, and is, one of Ireland's most prolific and vicious sex offenders. Her body has never been located.

The conviction of two settled travellers for the violent rape of a young sex worker on 30 December 1994 would also form part of our investigation. Though the culprits had been brought to justice and their victim, in this instance, had survived her ordeal, their crime was nevertheless considered relevant, if only because of the area where they brought their victim. Whether by accident or design, this rape occurred within walking distance of the body dump sites of both Antoinette and Patricia.

★

Shortly after TRACE began its work, the body of a young girl would be located in the Dublin Mountains, after a convicted rapist called to Rathfarnham Garda Station with his wife, and casually admitted to her rape and murder. The crime had, until then, gone unreported. Again, the body dump site selected by him was considered relevant to our enquiries.

Months later, Wicklow man Larry Murphy would be arrested for the abduction, multiple rape and attempted murder of a young woman within the area of the 'Vanishing Triangle'. There would be no further disappearances following his arrest, a fact which led to him being linked by both media and public alike to the abduction of a number of the other missing-female cases.

Our investigations would bring us into almost daily contact with Irish society's underworld; one occupied by rapists, paedophiles and other criminals.

A convicted serial killer, serving time in a high-security prison in Canada, would claim to have in his possession naked images of some of the missing females, taken both before and after their murder.

We would meet with and interview men who, outwardly, seemed as if they were doing everything they could to assist in the search for their loved ones. We would become aware, while talking to these same people, that they themselves had questions to answer, in relation to their involvement in the missing person's disappearance or death.

There would be family members, lovers and friends who would all supply detailed alibis, knowing, deep down, that they were, though perhaps misguidedly, allowing someone to get away with murder.

It is now sixteen years since the establishment of Operation TRACE. The investigations into all these various cases continue. The families of the missing still spend every waking moment hoping and praying that, some day, their loved ones will be returned to them. The family of Phyllis Murphy received some closure, with the conviction of a trusted neighbour for her murder. For the rest, the wait continues.

These are their stories.

Annie McCarrick

During her inaugural address to the nation on 3 December 1990, President Elect Mary Robinson spoke of the various roles she would take on during the course of her presidency. One of her key tasks, she told the crowds gathered at Dublin Castle on that historic day, would be to reach out to the vast Irish diaspora, that is, to the descendants of those Irish who had, through economic necessity, been forced, over the years, to emigrate in search of a better life, both for themselves and for their families. She spoke of placing a lighted candle in the window of Áras an Uachtaráin, as a welcoming sign to these travellers. In those heady days, little did we realise that this welcoming light would ultimately lure one of our diaspora to her death.

Annie McCarrick's parents, Nancy and John, were very proud of their Irish heritage. They inculcated this love of all things Irish in their only child, Annie Bridget McCarrrick, born in March of 1967. Their family weekends were filled with visits from like-minded friends and relatives, with regular trips to the Irish shows and *fleadhs*, that were a feature of everyday life in the Bayport area of Long Island, New York City, where the family lived. Bayport was home to thousands of descendants of Irish emigrants. A blue-collar area, many of its citizens worked for the city as policemen, fire fighters, garbage collectors and in other services. Like their neighbours, the McCarricks were practising Catholics, and attended the service at the local church every Sunday.

Annie's first visit to Ireland came in December of 1987, when she spent a week in the country as part of a school tour. At the time, she was attending Skidmore College in New York. She fell in love with the country immediately, and on her return home announced to her parents that she wanted to return to Ireland as soon as she finished college, and take up further studies there. At just twenty years of age, Annie possessed a maturity far beyond her years. Her parents, though heartbroken at the thought of their only child leaving home, did not, at the same time, wish to stand in her way.

Between 1988 and 1990 Annie attended teacher training courses in Ireland, initially at Saint Patrick's College in Drumcondra, and then at Saint Patrick's in

Maynooth. During her time in Drumcondra, she would meet and fall in love with Dublin man Phillip Brady. Though their romance ended amicably after a number of months, Annie and Phillip would remain friends. She was also friendly with the rest of his family, particularly with his brother, Hillary, and Hillary's fiancé, Rita Fortune.

During her time in college, Annie – always an independent spirit – financed her studies by taking on any job that came her way. She worked for a while as a teachers' assistant in a school in the Ballymun area of Dublin. Her work there convinced her that she was indeed cut out for the role of teacher. That summer, during school holidays, she travelled with friends to Germany to find part-time employment.

A bright, personable and friendly girl, Annie had a wide circle of friends and acquaintances. If she was swept off her feet by their quaint Irishness, they, equally, were enamoured by this pleasant girl. One friend said she was 'like a ray of sunshine'. Far from feeling out of place in the Dublin of the nineties, she fit right in, and actually could not get enough of Irish culture and tradition. She would regularly drag her friends to the many Irish music and dance sessions in the city.

Love would once more find Annie, while she was attending Maynooth College. Her new boyfriend was Dermot Ryan, a fellow sociology student. The couple would go everywhere together. However, when she graduated in 1990 with her BA in Sociology and English Literature, Annie announced that she wished to return to New York, to finish up her studies at Stonybrook University. Before parting, the young couple had agreed to remain in touch, and Dermot had even gone out to New York and stayed for a number of weeks in the McCarrick home. However, after his return to Ireland, Annie would diligently apply herself to her studies, and their relationship gradually petered out.

While in college, though totally immersed in her studies, Annie had continued to pine for the life she had left behind her in Ireland. It came as no surprise to her parents when, towards the end of 1992, she announced that she intended to return to live in Dublin, to take a Higher Diploma course which would then qualify her to teach in the country. She was unable to teach before completing the course, as she had, of course, not learnt Irish in school.

In January 1993, Annie, now almost twenty-six years old, once again left her family home. This time, before leaving, she prevailed on her mother to come and visit her, and arrangements were made for mother and daughter to meet in Dublin on 2 April 1993, where she would stay until Annie settled down. As she boarded her plane, little did Annie's parents think that they would never again see their daughter.

Upon her arrival in Dublin, Annie immediately renewed her old acquaintances. She stayed with Hillary Brady and Rita Fortune for a few nights, until she secured accommodation for herself in an apartment in Saint Catherine's Court in Sandymount, a quiet suburb on the south side of Dublin. She shared this apartment with two other girls, Jill Twomey and Ida Walsh, with whom she built up an immediate and lasting friendship.

★

Initially, Annie secured work at the Courtyard Restaurant in Donnybrook, Dublin. Although she only worked there for a few short weeks, it would eventually provide a vital clue to her last known movements on the day she disappeared.

She enjoyed working in the Courtyard, but because they could not guarantee her full-time employment, she started looking for work elsewhere. Though she knew that her parents would afford her every financial support if she needed it, Annie refused to be a burden on them. She would much rather pay her own way through college. In the short time that she had been working, she had quickly established a reputation for being a reliable hard-worker, and had no trouble securing another job at the well-known Café Java on Leeson Street. There, she proved herself to be very popular with staff and clientele alike. During the subsequent Garda investigation into her disappearance, a number of the customers would describe her, when interviewed, as 'the pretty American with the heart of gold'.

★

Saint Patrick's Day, and the days that followed, would pass in a flurry of excitement and anticipation, as Annie prepared for the visit of her mother. Everyone around her was swept up in her enthusiasm. Given all the arrangements she was putting in place for her visit, her mother was certainly not going to have much time to sit around on this particular holiday!

Annie finished work at Café Java at 3 PM on Thursday 25 March 1993. She was asked by Jean*, the manageress, to wait for ten minutes while she prepared the wages. The lunch trade had been particularly busy, and Jean had not had the opportunity to get them ready. Annie, seeing the pressure that Jean was under, told her not to worry, and that she would call in to collect her wages the next day (Friday). Although that was due to be her day off, she also told Jean that she would prepare some deserts at home on Friday morning, and bring them into the restaurant with her desserts when she called in that afternoon. This was an additional job for which Annie did not receive any payment, but one that she actually enjoyed doing. Officially, she was not due back at work in the restaurant until Saturday 27 March.

Annie had spent the evening of Thursday 25 March visiting a friend's home. After dinner, they had sat around talking. Once again, the main topic had been her mother's visit, and she arranged to bring her mother over to introduce her when she arrived. The friends parted around 10 PM, and the husband and teenage son drove Annie home to her apartment in Sandymount. There, she spoke briefly with her flatmates before going to bed.

The following morning, Friday 26, both Jill and Ida were up early packing their suitcases. They were travelling home to their families after work, and planned to be away for the weekend. They spoke to Annie before leaving the house. She was sitting in bed knitting, a skill she had developed during her time in Ireland. She told Ida that she planned to go for a short walk in the Enniskerry area that afternoon with a friend. She still had a number of last-minute preparations to make for her mother's visit. She also invited Hillary and Rita over for Saturday-night dinner.

★

Annie may have been delighted with having the time to herself, but there was a downside to her 'home alone' weekend. When Annie failed to return home on that Friday evening, there was no one in the apartment to notice that she was missing. Her friends would call on Saturday night to find that she had not returned. Though this was totally out of character, it would be another forty-eight hours before she would be officially reported missing.

At 11 AM on Friday morning, Annie visited the local Quinnsworth supermarket, where she purchased the ingredients needed to make the desserts for Café Java. Realising that she would have very little time to shop for the meal she planned to serve her guests, she also bought ingredients for that. This was to be a special meal, one of the first she would prepare and serve in her new home, and meant as a 'thank you' to Hilary and Rita for their kindness. Her purchases included a number of perishable items, such as cream, meat and butter, all of which required refrigeration.

After leaving the supermarket, Annie called into her local Allied Irish Bank branch. When she arrived in Dublin in January, she'd opened a bank account at the AIB bank in Clondalkin, a short walk from Hilary's house. During her visit to the bank, she arranged for the transfer of her account from the Clondalkin branch to Sandymount.

Annie's visit to the bank was captured by the in-house closed circuit television system. Annie was well known there, and can be seen on the footage to be relaxed and cheerful, chatting, as usual, with staff and customers alike. There was nothing in her demeanour or attitude that would give any indication of the events that were to follow. This is the only footage available of Annie, as there were no other security cameras in operation in the area, unlike modern-day Ireland, where almost every shop has their own security cameras. Sandymount, at that time, was considered to be one of the lowest crime risk areas in Dublin city.

On her way back to her apartment, Annie stopped to make a brief phone call from the public telephone kiosk on the Green in Sandymount. The phone in her apartment was only working intermittently at that time. She first rang Hillary Brady at work to confirm their dinner date for Saturday night, and she told him how much she was looking forward to their company.

Annie then rang another friend, Anne O'Dwyer, to ask if she was free that afternoon to accompany her on a short walk in the Enniskerry area, just outside the city. Enniskerry, derived from its original Gaelic name meaning 'rugged ford', was a place that held a special attraction for her. Situated beside the Powerscourt Gardens and waterfalls, it was one of the most picturesque areas in the Dublin Mountains. The two of them regularly walked in the Dublin Mountains together. Unfortunately, Anne had injured her ankle some days earlier, and could not go. Annie ended their conversation by saying that she might go out alone for a short walk.

★

Her decision to take this walk alone is a classic example of one of those random, seemingly harmless choices, made by so many people on a daily basis, little knowing that they were about to put in motion a series of events that would, ultimately, cost them their life. These 'spur of the moment' choices are reflected in a number of the cases that we looked at in the TRACE taskforce.

The call to Anne would be the last contact that Annie had with any of her friends. Our enquiries show that she then headed back to her apartment in Saint Catherine's Court.

Sometime after 1 PM on that same date, plumber Bernard Sheehan, who was doing some repair work in a separate apartment in the complex, observed Annie leaving the building through the front door. They had exchanged a brief greeting, and he watched her leave, heading in the direction of nearby Newgrove Avenue, where the public-bus terminus was located. If she wished to travel to Enniskerry, Annie would first have to get the Number 18 bus from Sandymount across the South City to Ranelagh. Once in Ranelagh village she could then take the 44 bus into Enniskerry village. Shortly after returning from America, Annie had bought herself a car. She had not, however, mastered the use of the stick shift and right-hand drive, and the car was left sitting outside Hillary's home.

As Annie approached the 18 Bus Terminus at Newgrove Avenue, the bus was just beginning to pull away from the stop, and she broke into a run, shouting at the driver to stop. Bruno Borza, the owner of the Borza take-away in Sandymount, later told Gardai that he had observed Annie running to catch the bus, which had stopped in response to her shout. He watched as she boarded the bus, which then drove away.

It is almost certainly the case that, had Annie missed this bus, she would not have gone to Enniskerry on that fateful day. The next available bus would not have left for almost an hour, at which stage, it would have been getting dark as she arrived in Enniskerry, and would certainly have been too late to set out walking.

Events such as catching or missing the bus, Anne hurting her ankle, the apartment being empty over the weekend, are all those imponderable 'if onlys' that, in their own way, each contributed to Annie being in the wrong place at the wrong time that day, thereby putting her in a situation which, undoubtedly, contributed to her death. This, as I have said, is a recurring theme that can be found in a number of the other cases.

All the witnesses who recalled seeing Annie that afternoon would describe her as wearing a tweed jacket and jeans, dark red boots, and carrying a distinctive tan shoulder bag. Given her statuesque bearing and height of 5 foot 8 inches, Annie would stand out in any crowd.

★

Annie was due to work at the Café Java on the morning of 27 March. By noon of that day, she had not arrived, nor had she contacted any of the staff. This was totally out of character for her; she was a stickler for punctuality, and her absence was commented on by other staff members, who had expected her to call in with her home-made desserts. She had also not turned up to collect her wages on Friday afternoon.

At 8 PM on that same Saturday evening, Hilary and Rita arrived at Saint Catherine's Court to keep their pre-arranged dinner date with Annie. Both of them were looking forward to the night ahead. As well as being good company, Annie was also an excellent cook. To their amazement, there was no response to their knocks on the apartment door. This was not something you expected from Annie.

They waited outside the flat for about twenty minutes, and then went to a nearby pub, where they stayed for half an hour before returning to Annie's flat. Once again, they did not receive any response, and Rita suggested that they should go home to Clondalkin and ring Annie from there. When they later attempted to ring the apartment, they realised that they did not, in fact, have the phone number. They rang Nancy in New York City and she gave them the number. In a brief conversation they mentioned the broken dinner date, but thought no more of it.

On a number of occasions throughout that Sunday, they rang Saint Catherine's Court. They received no response. Rita then rang Café Java, and was told that Annie had not turned up for work that day. As the afternoon progressed, their concern for her well-being began to grow.

Later that same evening, Jill and Ida returned to their apartment. They were surprised not to find Annie waiting there to greet them, full of questions about how their weekend had gone. They were equally surprised to find a plastic Quinnsworth shopping bag propped against the wall just inside the front door. The bag was full of food that should have been refrigerated. Gardai later established that the bag contained all the shopping that Annie had purchased on Friday morning.

This can be interpreted as a clear sign that, on arriving at the apartment that Friday morning, Annie had merely opened the door and left the shopping propped just inside, with the full intention of returning later to put it all away.

Rita and Hilary had checked with both Jill and Ida, and also, once more, with Annie's place of work on the morning of Monday 29. At this stage, they decided that there was something seriously wrong, and rang Nancy in New York to ask her if she'd had any contact from Annie. When she heard that they had not been able to contact her daughter all weekend, Nancy immediately changed her travel arrangements, and flew to Dublin that evening. It would be nearly two months before she would once again return to America.

★

Nancy was met by Rita and Hilary at the airport and, on hearing that there still had been no contact from her daughter, immediately went to Irishtown Garda Station, and formally reported her missing. It was now almost eighty hours since anyone had last had contact from Annie. An investigation under then Detective Inspector Martin Donnellan was immediately launched.

By the end of that week, Annie had been missing for seven days, and it was decided to make a formal appeal to the public for assistance. Her photograph was published in the media, with information being sought in relation to her whereabouts and well-being. The appeal elicited two very important responses.

The first response came from a most unlikely source. A Sam Doran contacted Irishtown Garda Station, and told Detectives Tom Rock and Val Smith that he worked as a doorman at Johnny Foxes, the famous traditional Irish music pub situated on the Ballybrack Road, in the tiny village of Glencullen nestled high in the Dublin Mountains. It is a thirty-minute drive from Dublin's city centre, and about three miles from Enniskerry village. Established in 1798 and touted as the 'highest' pub in Ireland, Johnny Foxes was and remains one of those 'must-see' places on the itinerary of most visitors. Indeed, it was one of the places that Annie was considering bringing her mother to see when she arrived on holidays.

Sam said that he had been working on the main door of the function room attached to the pub on the night of 26 March 1993. The traditional folk group, The Jolly Ploughmen, were playing a concert there that night with the doors due to open at 8 PM. They were a very popular group, and normally drew a huge crowd of trad fans. There was an admission fee of £2.00 (about €2.50). As part of their duties, Sam and fellow security man Paul O'Reilly supervised the collection of monies from patrons as they entered.

He said that some time after 8 PM that Friday evening, a young female had walked into the function room. She paused briefly inside the door and looked around, as if trying to find a seat. She had then strolled past the pay kiosk desk without paying the entry fee. From her demeanour he believed that she seemed to be unaware of the fact that there was an admission fee being charged, and she appeared surprised when he stopped her. A short queue formed as he spoke with her. Sam said he told the female that she had to pay, and she immediately apologised and put her hand into her pocket. Just then, a man standing directly behind her in the queue addressed Sam, saying 'I'll get that'. She had turned and smiled at him, acknowledging his generosity, and then walked on alone into the room. The stranger paid £4 (€5), to cover the entry fee for the two of them, and followed her in.

Sam Doran was of the opinion, from her reaction to this offer, that the girl did not appear to either be in the company of or to know the identity of her 'benefactor'. His intervention had appeared to take her by surprise. It looked to him like it had been a chance encounter. He was, in his words, 'certain' that the girl was Annie. It had been a particularly busy night in the pub and, with it being so close to St Patrick's Day, there had been a large number of visitors and tourists in and out all week. Nevertheless, he vividly recalled the tall and attractive American he had spoken too, and was adamant that it was indeed Annie.

His colleague, Paul O'Reilly, could only vaguely recall some of the episode as described by Sam, as he had been dealing with another customer at the time. He was not as certain that the visitor had been Annie. More significantly, neither of them could recall seeing either the female or her 'benefactor' again during the course of the night.

In one of those coincidences that often bedevil investigations, there was an American tourist at the show that night who bore a passing physical resemblance to Annie, and even dressed in a somewhat similar style. In fact, their dress sense was so similar that investigating Gardai would subsequently ask her not to wear certain items, as they became inundated with calls about sightings of Annie, that would turn out to be this other woman. As recently as 2010, myself and Christy Mangan, the Superintendent then in charge of the Garda Cold Case unit, would interview a witness who claimed to have met Annie a few days after the sighting in Johnny Foxes. From the location given to us and the description of the clothing, we were satisfied that this had, in fact, been another sighting of Jane. On the night of 26 March, Jane had been accompanied by her mother, and had definitely not been involved in any incident as described by Sam Doran.

Witness recollection being an imprecise science, Gardai had to carefully scrutinise Sam Doran's story. After all, given the sheer number of persons he must have met on a daily basis at the pub, they had to consider that he might have been wrong. However, what is significant about this encounter is the fact that, if he was mistaken, and if the couple he described had not included Annie, then surely at least one of the persons involved would have come forward, given the publicity that surrounded this claim. Even allowing for the fact that one or other of the couple may not have wanted it to be known that they had been there on the night for personal reasons, it is considered highly unlikely that both of them could have remained silent for so long, especially when one considers the importance that has been attached to the sighting.

Doran described the man as being about five foot eight inches tall, and of average build. He estimated his age at somewhere between twenty-five and twenty-eight. He was clean-shaven, with dark brown hair cut short, in an almost military style. He was wearing a green wax jacket, similar in style to the 'Barbour' brand. A photofit was created from the description given by Doran, and was widely circulated in the media. Although photofits are notoriously unreliable as a tool in identifying people, it is nevertheless the case that no one answering that description has ever come forward to say that it might have been him that Doran was describing.

The publicity that greeted the news of a missing American also generated a second, extremely important, piece of information. Eimear O'Grady, who had worked with Annie in the Courtyard restaurant, contacted Gardai, and told them that shortly before 3 PM on Friday 26 March, she had been standing in line at the 44 bus stop opposite the Ulster Bank in Ranelagh village. Just as the bus pulled into the stop, she saw Annie coming around the corner from the direction of the 18 bus terminus, that same bus that Bruno Borza had seen her catch in Sandymount some twenty-five minutes previous. She stood at the rear of the queue.

★

The 44 bus was, by that stage, beginning to load. Eimear, who had previously worked with Annie at the Courtyard Restaurant, was one of the first in the queue boarding the bus. She tried catching Annie's attention, taking a seat at the rear of the bus, but Annie went directly upstairs before Eimear had the opportunity to greet her. The bus reached Eimear's stop in Milltown minutes later, and she got off without having spoken with Annie.

This is a very important sighting as it clearly puts Annie on the route to Enniskerry, somewhere she had told Anne O'Dwyer she intended to go. The fact that the sighting was made by someone who knew her lends it greater weight. We would revisit Eimear some years later, and she remained adamant that she had seen Annie on that day. She could recall it vividly, she told us, because she herself was actually returning home that same day, having spent a week visiting family members down the country.

The bus driver, Paddy Donnelly, could only confirm the time the bus left, and the route it had taken to its terminus in Enniskerry. Unfortunately, given the sheer number of passengers he carried on a day-to-day basis, he was unable to recall any one individual. Unlike all modern Dublin buses, this bus was not fitted with internal security cameras.

The sightings of Annie made by Sam and Eimear changed the focus of the Garda enquiries entirely. Up to this, enquiries had been concentrated on the Sandymount area. This new evidence effectively moved the investigation some fifteen miles further south.

After her first few days here in Ireland, Nancy had been joined by her husband John, her brother Tim and her brother-in-law. The family gradually grew frustrated at the lack of progress in the Garda investigation, and decided to start making their own enquiries. They would remain in Ireland for almost two months, staying in a bed and breakfast in the Rathgar area, each day visiting the area in and around Enniskerry, in the hope of finding some trace of their daughter.

As the days progressed, they become increasingly convinced that they would never see their daughter alive again. They hired an Irish-based private investigator to help them in their search, recommended to them by the American Embassy. The group visited the village of Enniskerry and, armed with photographs of the missing Annie, canvassed every house and shop in the area. They visited all the houses on the possible routes she could have taken between the village and the pub three miles away.

It was actually the family, and not the Gardai, who visited the small sub-post office in the picturesque village square, and there met a female assistant who recalled a lady with an American accent coming into the shop on that Friday afternoon, and buying three postage stamps. This was an area they had been told had already been canvassed – without success – by Gardai. This certainly did nothing to improve the couple's confidence in Gardai capability in locating their daughter. John, an ex-Parks policeman himself, offered a substantial personal reward for any information they received which could assist in locating his daughter.

Unfortunately, there were no CCTV facilities fitted in the post office in Enniskerry, nor in any of the other nearby buildings on that day. Armed with the new information, though, Gardai could now prepare a timeline and movement chart based on both verified and unverified sightings of Annie McCarrick, on the day she disappeared. Everything now appeared to suggest that she had, as planned, visited Enniskerry village on the day in question. The one major gap that has never been accounted for is the period between 4 PM and 8 PM, that is, the period between her alleged sighting in the post office and her arrival at Johnny Fox's pub. A regular walker, it certainly would not have taken her four hours to walk the three miles between village and pub. Where – and with whom – she had spent those few hours, has remained unestablished to this day.

We can only speculate as to what exactly happened during that period. The indications of Annie's unusual behaviour that evening were clear. She had abandoned her food shopping just inside the front door, not even bothering to refrigerate it. It included the ingredients for the meal she planned to cook for her visitors on Saturday night. She hadn't even called to her workplace to collect her wages. Undoubtedly, she had left Catherine's Court in a hurry, anxious to fit a short walk in before dusk fell on that March afternoon. Had she intended to stay out late she would almost certainly have rung work, or at least put the cream into the refrigerator!

No one since has ever actually been arrested in connection with Annie's disappearance, though a large number of people have been treated as 'Persons of Interest' (POI) to the investigation. Each POI necessitated a full 'Trace, Implicate or Eliminate' (TIE) process to rule them in or out of any involvement in her disappearance. These included males who had been nominated by others, whose account of their movements did not ring true, or who had surfaced either through investigative work or through their involvement in similar types of crimes.

For instance, in the first few weeks of the investigation it emerged that Annie had had a brief liaison with a former associate on the Saturday before she disappeared. She had shared this information with one of her friends, expressing huge regret at having 'let things get so out of hand'. The incident in itself was not of huge significance, until it was vehemently denied by the male she had named when it was put to him by Gardai. He even attempted to supply an alibi for that particular night!

In turn, this was considered to be a very important development, and his denial led investigators to wonder what else he was attempting to cover up. He had previously supplied an account of his movements for the Friday of Annie's disappearance, but his story and alibi were revisited, and subjected to more careful scrutiny. Eventually, he admitted that Annie's version of the story was correct, and added that his denials were based on the wish that his then girlfriend not find out about it. It was one such incident where a little lie could have had major consequences all around!

During the course of carrying out routine enquiries at the Quinnsworth supermarket where Annie had purchased her groceries on the Friday morning, Gardai also checked the public noticeboard there. Nestled amongst the hand-written advertisements for local babysitters, gardeners and van rental, was one particular ad that caught their eye. It was addressed to females seeking employment in the beauty industry, and offered the services of a professional photographer who would compile a portfolio of their photographs.

What was especially interesting about this advertisement was the fact that it specified that applicants must be foreign nationals. Further enquiries led Gardai to a grotty little bedsit off the South Circular Road, one part of which was cordoned off as a 'studio'. The 'professional photographer' and his male 'assistant' turned out to be two perverts, whose only interest lay in trying to get wannabe models to take off as much clothing as possible. Judging from their own 'portfolios', they had not been very successful in their appeal. Luckily for them, they could provide cast-iron alibis for 26 March, and that line of enquiry was shut down immediately.

There is, however, one further person of interest to the investigation, who has yet to be eliminated. This person is the man who walked into the pub behind Annie that Friday night. Repeated requests and appeals were made, but without success. Years later, important information was received that opened a whole new field of enquiry into this matter.

We learnt that the benefactor who told Sam Doran that he would pay for Annie's admission at Johnny Fox's was, in fact, a named 'hit man' for the west Belfast brigade of the Irish Republican Army (the IRA), who was on the run from the North after carrying out a particularly savage murder. At twenty-eight years of age, Manus Dunne* had built up a reputation for himself as a cold-blooded assassin without equal, in an organisation that boasted many such killers. On 26 March he had been staying with some friends in a safe house in the Rathfarnham area and, though maintaining a low profile to avoid being nabbed by Special Branch officers, had gone for a night out to the pub, believing it unlikely he'd be seen so far off the beaten track.

★

According to our source, who is considered to be extremely reliable, he was completely smitten by the tall, attractive American, and they spent an enjoyable evening together in the pub. It is suggested that, on realising how interested in all things Irish Annie was, he had tried to impress her by divulging some stories about his activities in the Northern Ireland conflict.

There is no doubt that, initially at least, he found in Annie an audience that clung to his every word. She had been steeped, since birth, in the history of Ireland. As the night wore on and drink continued to flow, he may have spoken openly of his personal involvement in acts of atrocity, and began to cause her disquiet. Dunne could have reached a stage of drunkenness where her obvious, growing revulsion only encouraged him further. If we are to follow this line of reasoning, he could have spoken not only of the crimes he himself had committed, but also of crimes carried out by his colleagues. He may even have committed the ultimate betrayal, and referred to them by name.

Our source tells us that, by the end of the night, the enormity of what he had done began to dawn on him. He quickly sobered up, realising the damage that he might have done, both to himself and to the organisation he claimed to support. At this stage, Dunne realised what the only way open to him was. To ensure that Annie would never repeat what he had confided in her, he had to kill her. The taking of an innocent life to mask his own weaknesses presumably caused him little, if any, concern. What was more important to him was that he secure his own freedom.

Earlier in their conversation, Annie had told him that she lived in the Sandymount area of the city. Using all his charm, he convinced her to accept a lift from him back towards Dublin. He told her that he would drop her at a taxi rank in the Rathmines area, from which she could get a taxi home. Dunne was shrewd enough to realise that she would not have allowed him to know her actual address. He then told her that he needed to use the bathroom, and they agreed to meet in the car park at the rear of the pub. What the unsuspecting Annie did not realise was that, by making this arrangement, he avoided them being seen leaving the pub together.

Dunne had earlier that night parked the non descript Ford Sierra, which had been made available to him during his time in Dublin, towards the rear of the car park, where it couldn't be seen from the pub and where, equally, any security cameras fitted at the back of the building could not pick up on it. Such precautions would have come as second nature to him, considering his line of work. At the back of the car park, street lights did little to brighten up darkened areas. Annie left the pub, and walked towards where he had told her that his car was parked. He had followed at a safe distance, to ensure that she was alone, and did not stop to speak to anyone. It is unclear what he would have done had Annie chosen to avoid him, or had refused his offer of a lift. It has been suggested that he had a firearm concealed in the car, and that he would have used it if he had to. He knew that the car could not be traced back to him if he needed to make a run for it.

After driving out of the car park, Dunne had turned right and headed back up the mountain, instead of taking the left turn that would have brought him back towards the city. We are told that, at this stage, Annie realised that she was in trouble and had attempted to open her door. He then used his fist to strike her face, temporarily stunning her. About a mile above Johnny Fox's, he had pulled off the road into a lay-by, where he had strangled his still semi-conscious victim. He concealed her body in a nearby ditch, marked the spot and then drove home to Rathfarnham.

When he arrived back at the safe house, Dunne told his 'minders' that he had met an American in the pub who had spent the night trying to elicit information from him in connection with his activities on behalf of the movement. He told them that she had approached him the moment he walked in, and that she appeared to know who he was. Dunne said that he suspected she was a Special Branch plant and, fearing that his and his colleagues' safety could be compromised, had tricked her into leaving the pub with him, and had then killed her. At first light, he and a number of his colleagues had driven in two separate cars to the area where he had left Annie's body. One of the cars would be used to run 'interception' in case they met any Gardai, while the second car would transport the body.

Shortly after this incident, Manus Dunne returned to active service in Northern Ireland. Some months later, an allegation was made against him by the teenage daughter of a prominent Republican, in connection with an incident of serious sexual assault. An internal investigation was held. Both Dunne and the young girl's father were considered to be powerful men within the organisation, and it was feared that a ruling in favour of one before the other could lead to a significant rift. Exile seemed the best alternative, and it was decided that Dunne would leave Ireland altogether. Work was secured for him in a pub owned by an IRA sympathiser, in one of the larger cities in America. He was expressly ordered, under threat of death, not to return to Ireland.

This story only came to the attention of the Gardai within the last few years. It is a highly plausible explanation for Annie's disappearance, and one that is the main avenue of investigation.

Annie's family would return to Ireland again in August of 1993, and continue to carry out their own enquiries. In the years since her disappearance, either one or both of them would make the long journey over to meet with the investigators, and be filled in on the progress, if any, that had been made in the investigation. Nancy herself travelled over in 2001 to meet Assistant Commissioner Tony Hickey, the man in charge of Operation TRACE.

★

The never-ending search for their daughter would ultimately take its toll on John and Nancy's marriage. In 1998, the couple divorced. John died a heartbroken man in 2007. Nancy now sits alone in her apartment, still waiting for the phone to ring with the news that her daughter's body has been located. This is never information any parent wants to hear, but being able to bring her child home, and having a grave at which to mourn, would provide the mother with some limited solace.

In the year 2010, I gave evidence by deposition before the New York City Civil Court, in connection with Annie's disappearance. I cited Annie's out-of-character actions as grounds for the assumption that she did not disappear voluntarily, and had, I believed, been murdered. I also presented a brief synopsis of the extent and scope of the Garda investigation into her disappearance. The case had been brought by lawyers acting on behalf of Nancy, who were seeking an order of 'death in absentia', that is, a legal presumption of her death. The court, on hearing my evidence read into the record, issued a death certificate. It was, at that time, some seventeen years since Annie disappeared.

I spoke by telephone with Nancy in May of 2011, the week before I retired from *An Garda Síochána*. I was calling to pass on the contact details of my successor. During our conversation, she told me that, even now, eighteen years after her daughter's disappearance, all she wanted was to have her remains returned, to afford her daughter the dignity of a proper burial. This was, she said, far more important to her than knowing the identity of the person who killed her daughter.

The search for Annie has, over the years, been raised to government level by a number of prominent people, including Al Gore, then Vice President of the USA, and Jean Kennedy Smith, the American Ambassador to Ireland, and herself one of the Irish diaspora.

Jo Jo Dollard

Like Annie, Josephine 'Jo Jo' Dollard worked as a waitress. Where Annie had come to Ireland from America and fallen in love with all things Irish, Jo Jo had been equally smitten by Mike, an American she had met while working in Dublin. Mike was on a gap year travelling around the world and, after a few months, broke her heart by continuing on his travels. This would be one of the chief influences leading to Jo Jo's departure in late 1995, when she returned to live near her home town in Callan, County Kilkenny, with her friend and flatmate, Mary Cullinane. It would be this same move that would, ultimately, cost her life.

Both girls had spent the previous two years living in the city. They initially attended a beautician course, but the cost proved too expensive. They lived in various flats in the Rathmines and Phibsborough areas of the city, and secured temporary waitressing work in a number of pubs. When they eventually managed to secure work at Dawson's pub in Callan, they decided to leave the city, and return to live nearer to home. Jo Jo rented a small flat for herself in the centre of town, and quickly settled down.

Returning to live in Callan meant a great deal to Jo Jo, as it brought her nearer to her siblings, with whom she was very close. Just twenty-one years of age, her young life had already been marred by tragedy. Her father had died suddenly in the weeks before her birth, leaving behind his pregnant wife, their three daughters and one son. This sad blow had united the family. However, when Jo Jo was just ten years old, the family suffered another huge loss with the death of their mother. Her elder sisters tried to fill the gap left by her untimely passing. Jo Jo would live for a number of years with her sister Kathleen and her husband Seamus, before leaving for Dublin to move in with her sister Mary and Mary's husband, Martin. They were all delighted at her decision to leave the city and to return to live nearby.

On Thursday morning, 9 November 1995, Jo Jo took the early-morning bus to Dublin. Prior to moving back down the country, both girls had been drawing their social-welfare payments at the sub-post office at Harold's Cross, in Dublin. Their last such payment was due for collection on that particular Thursday.

Having collected her money, she was left with a number of hours to wait around for her bus, which was not due to leave until shortly after 6 PM that evening, from the Busáras terminus in the city centre. She decided to look up some former acquaintances, and spend the time catching up with them on all their news.

★

While living in the city, the two girls had regularly frequented Bruxelles, a pub in the south inner city area. Jo Jo went there that Thursday to see if any of the old gang were still around. She was delighted to find that her friend Anthony* was still working behind the bar. The two youngsters were soon deep in conversation, catching up on all the gossip. Other friends joined and left their company at different times during the course of that early afternoon.

Sometime around 2.30 PM, they were joined by Roman*. Jo Jo had had a brief affair with him some months earlier, and they were still very close. As the evening wore on, they found their old flame being rekindled. After sharing a few drinks, they decided to spend the night together. A quick phone call was made to the North Star hotel in Amiens Street, and a room was booked in their name for that night. A twist of fate would, however, prevent this from happening.

Shortly after 6 PM that evening, incidentally, at about the same time that Jo Jo's bus was pulling out of Busáras and heading for Kilkenny, the friends were joined by a girl called Angela*. After breaking up with Jo Jo, Roman had met Angela, and the two of them had been living together for a number of months. Needless to say, Angela was not happy to find Roman and Jo Jo together. An argument ensued and, after some time, Roman left the bar with Angela. This meant that Jo Jo, who by this time had had a number of drinks, was now, effectively, stranded in Dublin.

Had she perhaps been a little more sober, or maybe not quite so annoyed with the way Roman had led her on, Jo Jo might have decided to call it a night, book herself into one of the hostels scattered throughout the city centre and get the bus home the following morning. As with Annie, this was one of those life-altering decisions that, on the face of it, appear innocuous enough, but would actually have fatal implications. Impulsively, she headed towards Busáras, hoping to find a late bus heading for Waterford or Wexford, that would bring her in the right direction for home.

When she arrived at an almost deserted Busáras shortly after 9 PM, she found that the last bus out of the terminus that night was about to leave, but was only travelling as far as Naas. She decided to take it, and then to hitch a lift from Naas to Callan. In those days, it was a common sight to see hitch-hikers on our roads. Seldom, though, would they be alone, and out so late.

By the time the bus arrived at its terminus just opposite Naas Garda Station, the long day had taken its toll on Jo Jo, and the driver had to wake her up to tell her he was not going any further. As she alighted from the bus, it was almost 10 PM, and a further choice now presented itself to her. She could have gone into the Garda Station and asked to sit in the public area until daybreak. That was a common practice in those days, too. She decided, though, to continue on her journey, and walked towards the main road, heading in the direction of Kilcullen, the next town on her road home.

Jo Jo had been standing on the side of the road for just a few moments with her thumb crooked, when a car pulled in. Disappointingly, the male driver who offered her a lift told her he was only going as far as Kilcullen. She accepted his offer, knowing, at the same time, that it was just a fraction of the journey that lay ahead of her. As they drove the twelve kilometres between the towns, she informed him of the length she still had to travel and, prophetically, he advised her to be careful about whom she took a lift with. He even advised her to book into lodgings, and wait until the morning to continue. However, as far as she was concerned, she was now well into her journey, and decided to press on.

At Kilcullen, her apparent luck would, once more, hold out. She had no sooner started hitching when a car pulled in beside her. The driver, a much younger man than the previous one, told her that he was only going as far as the village of Moone which, at that stage, the old Dublin/Waterford main road still passed through. In 1995, the main road also passed through both Kilcullen and Naas, and the bypasses created by the new N10 motorway were still a long way off.

Knowing that Moone would leave her with over half the journey still to cover, she nonetheless decided to take the lift. They arrived in the village shortly before 11.30 PM, and Jo Jo got out of the car by a telephone kiosk, halfway down the main street. The next town on her journey, if she was lucky enough to get another lift, would be the somewhat larger town of Castledermot, which would leave her with some fifty kilometres to travel.

As she stood there in the dark on the side of that deserted street, the enormity of the journey that still lay ahead of her must have begun to weigh heavily. It would be natural, at that stage, for some sense of desperation or panic to set in. One of the only bright spots on the darkened street was the light shining from the telephone kiosk, and Jo Jo was drawn to it. She decided to ring her friend Mary back in Callan, and fill her in on her plight, in case Mary was worried that she had not shown up on the last bus from Dublin. The thought must have struck her that her brother lived not too far away, on the other side of Athy. If all else failed, she could even ring him.

As she stood in the telephone kiosk, she kept the door partially ajar so as to be able to keep trying to hitch a lift. A number of cars passed her while she stood there. Indeed, years later, when we on Operation TRACE were checking statements that had been taken during the original investigation, a number of motorists told us that they recalled seeing the girl standing just inside the kiosk and attempting to thumb a lift, with the door held partially open. They would also tell us that they felt guilty for not stopping; if they had given her a lift, they might have saved her life.

When Mary Cullinane answered the phone, Jo Jo explained her predicament to her. She told her that she was in Moone attempting to get a lift home. She then began to fill Mary in on all the gossip she had heard that day about their former friends. Suddenly, she asked her to hold on for a moment, and had then put down the telephone. Mary could hear the sound of the kiosk door closing, and then there was a silence, which had lasted for about thirty seconds. Then Jo Jo had picked up the phone and, in a breathless voice, told Mary, 'I have a lift. I'm off.' She then terminated the call. This would be the last ever contact received from Jo Jo Dollard.

Investigators have, over the years, speculated on what might have been had Jo Jo supplied even some basic details about either the car, or the driver, to Mary. Even knowing the make of car would have been of some assistance to the enquiry that followed. Equally, though, if we are to believe that she met her death at the hands of the occupant (or occupants) of this car, then they were also taking a risk, not knowing whether she had passed on any details to whomever she had been speaking with.

One witness later told Gardai that she had observed a woman, running from the telephone box to a car, that had pulled up a short distance from it. She stated that, as she drove past, she observed the girl open the car door. All she could offer by way of a description of the car was the fact that it was a four-door and darkly coloured, and may have been a Toyota Carina, a very popular model of car during the nineties. What was, however, more significant about this sighting, is that the witness claimed that she believed that the girl had actually opened the rear passenger door. This would suggest that there were at least two other persons in the car at the time, both of whom were in the front seats.

It has been central, to media reports over the years, that the last reported sightings of Jo Jo were those made in Moone village. However, a number of people told Gardai that they had seen a strange female walking along the main street in the village of Castledermot, just before midnight that Thursday. Castledermot is the next town to Moone, and the times of these purported sightings corresponded roughly with the travel times between the two locations. The sightings were made by people leaving local pubs and restaurants, and by others working in local late-night shops. One of the witnesses claimed to have actually crossed in front of the girl as he walked into a chipper. He reported that she had walked along the Main Street and past the local school, heading towards the main road leading to Carlow – the same route that Jo Jo would have followed as she headed towards Kilkenny.

The following Friday, the evening of 10 November, Mary Cullinane arrived into work in Dawson's pub. She had not heard from Jo Jo at all that day, and was growing increasingly worried. On learning that she had not shown up for her shift, Mary told the bar owner about the late-night call she had received. They decided that they would ring her sister, Kathleen, to see if she had heard from Jo Jo. When told that her sister had been out hitch-hiking so late at night, Kathleen immediately began ringing around a number of Jo Jo's acquaintances and their other family members.

When she realised that there had been no contact from her younger sister throughout that day, she rang the local Garda Station to report Jo Jo missing. This would be the first of a number of calls that an increasingly desperate Kathleen would make to the station. She eventually called over in person, as she felt that her report about her missing sister was not being taken seriously. Kathleen would, years later, tell me that she had been very disappointed with the initial Garda response to her frantic telephone calls. She stated that the attitude she was met with was a near-blasé dismissal of her concerns.

Undoubtedly, it is the case that it was only by the following Monday, four days after the last contact was received from Jo Jo, and three days after the first missing-person report was made, that any serious investigations commenced. There is no doubt that the longer it took for the Garda operation to swing into gear, the greater was the chance of evidential opportunities being lost. Given that the last contact from the young girl had been received as she was hitch-hiking alone on a public road, late at night, alarm bells should have been ringing earlier.

After it was established that the call from Jo Jo had been made from the kiosk in Moone, it was decided to concentrate all search efforts on the roadway leading from there onwards, towards Castledermot. The call to Mary from the telephone box was verified through telephone records. A further check of these same records would show that the next call made would not be for several hours.

Gardai, assisted by Army and Civil Defence personnel, together with hundreds of volunteers, combed both sides of the main road as far as Castledermot, in the hope of finding some trace of Jo Jo. Media appeals were made, which resulted in a number of motorists who had been driving through that area the night coming forward. As a result of this appeal and the publicity that followed, the two drivers who had taken her from Naas to Kilcullen, and then onwards from there to Moone, would both contact Gardai.

It was not long before the identity of both drivers became public knowledge. One of the drivers, a member of a very prominent local family. quickly came to be seen as a prime suspect by some media outlets, the rumour machine stopping just short of actually naming him. Subsequently, rumours circulated suggesting that Jo Jo's body was buried on land belonging to this man's family.

★

At the time that Operation TRACE first began its investigations, speculation had taken on a life of its own. We were met, during the course of our enquiries in the Moone area, with the suggestion that 'the dogs in the street' knew who had abducted and killed Jo Jo, and were later accused of all being party to a government conspiracy to cover up the suspect's identity. Equally, it was claimed, everybody knew where her body was buried, yet the Gardai had done nothing about it.

There were two main rumours circulating about the location of the body. Both suggested that the dump site was on the farm owned by the aforementioned popular suspect's father, a politician. The first story held that Jo Jo's body had been hidden in newly poured foundations for a cattle byre. Others suggested that the body had been hidden in drainage ditches that were being cleared around the same time. It quickly became apparent that there would be no progress with our enquiries until we laid these issues to rest.

We obtained the name of the builder who had erected the byre, and established that the building had been in place for some time prior to Jo Jo's disappearance. Records at the firm who supplied the ready-mix concrete confirmed this. We also spoke with the contractor who had worked at digging, maintaining and filling the various drainage ditches. He could tell us that the work had been completed at least a year before the disappearance. This very basic information had been readily available all along, and could have been used to allay the concern, suspicion and fear felt by so many in the local community.

Despite the various claims that a female had been seen walking along the main street in Castledermot that same night, no driver has ever come forward to say that they picked up a female hitch-hiker either in Moone or later on in Castledermot. In particular, the failure of any driver coming forward to say that he had given Jo Jo a lift on this part of her journey, is one of the main reasons why doubt has been cast on all those sightings.

In Operation TRACE, we felt that it was a mistake to just dismiss these sightings out of hand. We believed that insufficient credence had been given to the possible sightings in Castledermot. This was because, if the sightings were to be accepted, then the assumptions being made about the behaviour of certain individuals in the Moone area had to be ruled out. We worked on the basis that all evidence, including contradictory evidence, must be accepted until proven otherwise.

As the days turned into weeks and the weeks into months, the search for Jo Jo continued. Each and every reported sighting and nugget of information received was carefully checked out. In an unprecedented move, every ditch and opening on the major roads and intersecting by-roads between Moone and Castledermot was searched. This search was later extended to take in all roads between Castledermot and Carlow town. It was hoped that some of her property, which may have been dumped on the roadside, would be located. However, nothing of evidental value was found, nor were any further clues given as to her whereabouts.

Early on in the investigation, Gardai learned that a number of men, all speaking with pronounced English accents, had been seen drinking in a pub on the night of Jo Jo's disappearance, in a village not far from Moone. The local who alerted Gardai felt that the strangers were acting suspiciously. A check of bed and breakfast outlets in the surrounding area turned up the five strangers, all of whom had come to Ireland on a fishing holiday. However, it quickly emerged that, by 11.30 PM on that Thursday night, they were all safely tucked up in their beds, under the watchful eye of their landlady.

From the outset of the formal investigation, it had been recognised that the case could not be solved without the assistance of the public. Jo Jo had disappeared from a very public place, and had last been seen by a number of passing motorists, taking a lift that may have carried her to her death. A massive campaign to keep the case in the public mind was mounted. This included a full-scale, staged reconstruction of her movements, both prior to and whilst in Moone village. The reconstruction was intended to form part of a television appeal that, it was hoped, would jog the memory of any person who had not already contacted Gardai.

On the night of the planned reconstruction, an actress, who bore a passing resemblance to Jo Jo, walked the short distance from where she had been dropped off, along the Main Street of Moone and onto the telephone kiosk. On this occasion, however, the female pedestrian was not alone, but flanked by a film crew, Gardai and onlookers. After a number of takes, the director was satisfied by the footage of the actress entering and exiting the kiosk. They then moved on to the next scene, which would show the actress standing on the roadside, with the lights of an approaching car in the distance. To lend authenticity to the scene, traffic was let flow. Once cameras started to roll, one passing driver even pulled up beside the stunned actress, lowered his window and asked if she needed a lift. The shocked driver found himself surrounded by an irate film crew and Gardai. He turned out to be a local elderly man, who had not noticed the crowd.

On the night of Friday 10 November, an incident occurred in Kilkenny city, which, in time, would result in the investigation being temporarily sidetracked. Two English petty criminals, John Smith* and Trevor Williams*, were arrested while attempting to steal cash from a telephone box in a public house. The pair were equipped with a home-made key capable of opening most coin boxes.

★

At a time when mobile phone ownership was still in its infancy, and even land-line telephone ownership was limited, these public kiosks were in constant use. If not regularly emptied, the boxes could contain a substantial amount of cash, and were considered a 'soft target' by criminal gangs. Smith and Williams were regular visitors to these shores, and made a fairly good living out of stealing cash from the boxes. It was considered to be a very lucrative business.

Not satisfied with the return they were getting from the public phone kiosks, they had, in recent weeks, begun to concentrate on coin boxes in public houses and other establishments. The beauty of this type of crime lay in the fact that the owner only became aware of what had happened when the boxes were opened, sometimes weeks later, to be emptied, at which stage the thieves would be long gone. Unfortunately for them, the box they were caught emptying in Kilkenny that night was in a pub frequented by local off-duty Gardai, and their behaviour aroused the suspicion of two Gardai, out for a quiet drink after work.

Smith and Williams lived a very nomadic lifestyle. On the night of their arrest, they were driving a dark four-door Ford Sierra, with English number plates. They would usually either sleep in the car, or stay in remote bed and breakfasts around Ireland. Given the nature of their criminal activity, they needed to constantly travel the length and breadth of the country, never staying in the same area for any significant length of time. They had a number of acquaintances amongst the 'New Age' traveller community, scattered throughout Cork and Kerry, and often stayed amongst them.

Following their arrest, they were not immediately charged with stealing money from the machine. Charges could only be laid after details of the exact amount that should have been in the box was established by an engineer from the post office. They were released from custody, and informed that they would be summoned to court at a later date. They decided to lie low for a while, immediately leaving Kilkenny city and driving to Rosslare, where they took a ferry back to England. Over the coming months, they paid infrequent visits back to Ireland, varying the ferry ports they were travelling through and the areas in which they were operating, to avoid being arrested.

Details of the arrest in Kilkenny were forwarded to the original Jo Jo Investigation Team, and duly logged. During the course of any major investigation, intelligence of this nature would be routinely supplied. Given that there was both a Kilkenny connection and a reference to public telephone boxes, it was considered relevant. Indeed, all incidents in both Kilkenny and Kildare Garda Divisions over the relevant time period would have been collated and cross-referenced with information established during the investigation by the Incident Room Coordinator (IRC). There was no evidence to suggest that it held any relevance to the enquiry, and it was filed away accordingly.

★

Within a month of Jo Jo's disappearance, a second female went missing. On the night of 21 December, Marilyn Rynn, who was returning from a work night out, went missing from near her home in Blanchardstown, Dublin. Her naked body was found two weeks later; she had been raped and strangled. David Lawler – a neighbour of Marilyn's – would be arrested and convicted of her murder. Detectives also discovered a number of tenuous links between Lawler and Jo Jo, which qualified him as a POI to the investigation. Not only was Lawler a native of Baltinglass (a short distance from where Jo Jo had last been seen alive), he was also a regular customer in Bruxelles, the Dublin pub in which Jo Jo had spent the afternoon of her disappearance. Nicknamed 'Jesus', because of his long beard and unkempt hair, he would sit for hours in the bar watching the female customers, behaving in a not-dissimilar way to his cousin, the notorious rapist, Larry Murphy.

Eventually, Lawler was ruled out of any possible involvement in Jo Jo's disappearance, after it was established that he had used his bank card to withdraw cash from an ATM in the Blanchardstown area around midnight, on the night of 9 November. Further tests would also show activity on his personal home computer at around the same time. Lawler would once again resurface, however, as the TRACE investigations progressed in connection with another issue.

The remainder of 1995, and all of 1996, passed without Jo Jo's grieving family learning any more about her fate. Nineteen ninety-seven was still young when new information came to light, that moved the search area more than eighty kilometres south. It would also, for a time, push petty thieves Smith and Williams to the forefront as the chief suspects in Jo Jo's abduction.

In January 1997, Noel Dalton*, a Waterford-based taxi driver, contacted Gardai. He said that, shortly after 1 AM on Friday morning, 10 November 1995, he had finished working his shift with a local cab company. Having signed off, he had driven home to Kilmacow, a small village about three miles from the city, on the Dublin side of Waterford. Just before reaching his turn off on the main road, he observed a car pulled over onto the hard shoulder on the right-hand side. There was a male standing at the front driver's side of the car, who appeared to be urinating.

As Dalton was slowing down to make his turn, the rear passenger door of the parked car swung open, and a woman jumped out onto the roadway, and made as if to run away. A second figure, another man, jumped out of the same door, and ran after her. He grabbed the woman around the waist and, assisted by the man who had been urinating, roughly pushed her back into the car. The first man had then jumped into the driver's seat, and the car sped away in the direction of Waterford city.

He described the woman as being of thin build. As she started to run, he had noticed that she was barefoot. He added that she appeared to be very distressed. The timing of the sighting is very significant, given that, if one assumes that this female was indeed Jo Jo Dollard, the timeframe between the sighting of her at the telephone box in Moone, and Dalton's sighting of a woman running from a car outside Kilmacow, is compatible with the approximate length of time such a journey would take.

Dalton could not recall any individual details of the actual number plate, but was adamant, from the layout and format, that it was an English plate. He said that he believed, too, that it was a red Ford Sierra saloon car. As a man who, day-to-day, would spend a lot of time on the road, it is probable that he was correct in his recollection. The size and shape of a Sierra is also not dissimilar to a that of a Carina car, which a witness from the Moone area described seeing.

It is regrettable that this information came at such a late stage in the investigation. Had Gardai been aware of it earlier, there would have been a number of investigative leads from the area the car had been sighted that could have been followed up. It would certainly have influenced the location of all the various search areas that had, until then, been concentrated in Moone and its environs. It might also have meant that certain persons in that same area who had been considered as being of interest to the enquiry could have been eliminated earlier, saving considerable time and effort.

Mr Dalton gave a number of reasons, when asked why he had waited to give this important information to the Gardai. He claimed that he had called over to his local station within days of the news about Jo Jo breaking, looking for a particular Garda whom he knew, only to discover that he was on holiday. A busy Christmas had followed for Dalton, who then took an extended holiday himself. On his return, 'between one thing and another' he had not reported the incident.

Undoubtedly, the emphasis that was being placed on the various sightings in Moone, together with the reportedly intensive Garda activity in that area, must surely have caused him to seriously question the usefulness or significance of what he had seen and, equally, gave him some comfort for not reporting his sighting earlier. Whatever the reason for the delay, it was another lost opportunity. Any forensic evidence left at the scene outside Kilmacow had, by then, been completely obliterated.

The Jo Jo Incident Room was alerted to this development, cross-referencing it with all the other evidence that had been established. There was an obvious link between the car seen by Dalton, and the car that Smith and Williams had in their possession on the Friday night they were arrested in Kilkenny. Their whereabouts on the Thursday night were unknown. Gardai could not ignore the possibility that they may have been travelling on the road from Dublin to Kilkenny on the night of 9 November, and picked up Jo Jo. An all-out effort was put into locating them. A total embargo was put on discussion of this outside of the investigation unit. If this development appeared in the press, detectives believed that their two targets would go underground, and become very difficult to locate.

★

Senior Gardai were mindful of the last time two English petty thieves went on a rampage in Ireland. In 1976, John Shaw and Geoffrey Evans abducted, tortured and murdered two women in the space of four weeks: Elizabeth Plunkett in Brittas Bay in County Wicklow, and Mary Duffy in Ballynahinch in Connemara. By their own admission, they said when arrested that they had intended on kidnapping a new woman each week. Both were sentenced to life imprisonment. Evans died in custody in 2012, while Shaw is still serving out his sentence. The similarities in the backgrounds of these two pattern killers, and that of Smith and Williams, were frightening.

Over the next few weeks, the search for Smith and Williams intensified. In May 1997, the two of them were found sleeping rough in their car, in a wooded area outside of the village of Golden in South Tipperary. Their car had been 'flagged' on the Garda computer system and, when checked by a passing Garda patrol car, had shown up as being of interest to the Jo Jo investigation. Detectives from the team immediately travelled to Cashel town, where the car and its occupants had been brought for a full forensic search. Given their nomadic lifestyle, they were, naturally, unable to say where they had been on the night almost two years previous, but when reminded of their arrest in Kilkenny, began to piece their movements together.

When separately interviewed, both of them were able to tell Gardai where they had spent the night before their arrest. On the night of Jo Jo's disappearance, they had stayed in a bed and breakfast in the Blackpool area of Cork city. The landlady had been a Mrs Devlin*, described by both as a 'right tartar'. They had spent that day driving around Cork city, and had 'done' a number of telephone boxes. They had also learnt, that day, that William's mother was unwell, and so decided to return to England the following Saturday. At around 12.30 AM, with Mrs Devlin's permission, they made a reverse-charge call from her private phone to William's mother's home in Croydon, London, to check on her health. Early on Friday morning they left Cork, intending to take the ferry from Rosslare. Not wishing to miss any opportunity, they spent that day cruising the telephone boxes around Kilkenny city.

Detectives were immediately dispatched to the Devlin home. Mrs Devlin, who turned out to be a gentle and charming hostess, had no hesitation in recalling her two English guests and their late-night phone call home. She had actually taken down their car number in her 'Visitors Book' when they arrived, and showed it to Gardai. This ruled the two of them out of any involvement in Jo Jo's disappearance.

The publicity that surrounded Dalton's sighting outside of Kilmacow would open up another seemingly promising line of enquiry. Sergeant Dan Stapleton and Garda Jim Fitzmaurice were two local Gardai attached to Baltinglass Station, who had worked almost continuously on the Jo Jo case from the very beginning. They never gave up hope of locating the missing girl, and tenaciously followed up every lead that came in over the years, often on their days off.

In mid-1998, Stapleton and Fitzmaurice were contacted by a Dublin-based solicitor, who told them that a client of his (then serving a term of imprisonment) had important information concerning Jo Jo, which they wished to pass on. The information implicated a well-known Irish sex offender. They brought this information to Operation TRACE. Tony Hickey decided to second Dan and Jim to the team in a temporary capacity, so that whatever assistance and backup they needed would be available to them.

They met the informant, who told them that, on the night that Jo Jo disappeared, two cars had left Clondalkin in Dublin shortly after 10 PM, and travelled in convoy to Waterford. On board were a total of six persons: two males in the first car, and two males and two females in the second. All of them were wellknown to Gardai, particularly the front passenger of the lead car, Michael Henry*, who had just completed a lengthy prison sentence for a very serious sexual assault. The group had spent the day visiting a sick family member in Dublin. Both cars had slowed down as they drove along the narrow main street in Moone, just around pub-closing time. The last thing that any of them wanted was to be stopped for a road traffic infringement by an overzealous Garda.

As they drove past the telephone box, Henry had spotted Jo Jo, as she stood with the door open and her arm outstretched. He told his companion to pull in, and they then watched as she approached the car. He told her that they were travelling to Waterford, and offered her a lift. This was exactly what Jo Jo had been looking for all night. She readily accepted, and ran back to the phone box. Henry told his driver that they would 'have some fun' with the girl. After she returned to the car, she got into the back, and they drove off, closely followed by the other car.

There is no doubt, if this story is correct, that as Jo Jo ran back to the phone box to finish her call to Mary, she must have had some qualms about taking a lift from two male strangers in such a lonely area. However, by that stage, and after the long day she'd had, she would have been driven by a sense of desperation. In fact, she must have been delighted at the offer of a lift that would bring her so near to home after being on the road for so long. Ever the predator, Henry was also easily able to present himself as non-threatening, if not downright charming. Whatever the reason, if this story is to be believed, the teenager now made a decision that would, ultimately, cost her life.

The two cars had split up some time after they passed through Kilkenny city, and the car carrying Jo Jo had continued on towards Waterford. Those in the second car were described as having no doubt that Henry intended on having sex with the girl, whether or not she consented. So great was their physical fear of him, that they dared not interfere. They had driven away, leaving Jo Jo to her fate.

The direction of travel, the time of night, and the presence of two males and one lone female in the car, all appeared to tie in with the information that Noel Dalton had given to Gardai.

It was suggested that, later that same night, people living in a quiet cul de sac just outside of Waterford city were woken by the sound of a woman screaming. The occupants of all the homes in this small enclave were related to one another – either directly or by marriage. When some of them went to check on the source of the screaming, they found a distraught female running along the footpath. She was totally naked. Michael Henry came running out of his house, grabbed the girl and dragged her back inside. There was no further sound heard after that. This incident was allegedly witnessed by a number of persons, none of whom intervened.

After a great deal of good detective work by Dan and Jim, the informant was eventually 'turned', and told them that, around 9 AM on that Friday morning, they had actually helped Michael Henry and another man remove the body of a female, wrapped in a bed sheet, from his house, and placed it into the back of a van. The three of them had then driven to a remote mountainous area in Kerry, where they had buried the body in a wood. The informant readily agreed to point out the body dump site to them.

There was one big problem. The informant was, at the time of making this offer, serving a lengthy prison sentence for another matter. In addition, this person, when previously granted compassionate leave from that sentence to attend a family funeral, had gone on the run, and was therefore not eligible for any further time off in the sentence. Only after requests were made at the highest level in the Department of Justice, was it agreed to give the prisoner any further leave. The prisoner was collected from prison and driven to County Kerry, where a wooded area outside the small village of Castleisland was pointed out as the resting place of Jo Jo Dollard.

Given the highly sensitive nature of this information, it was decided to confine knowledge of the operation to a select few. The last thing that we wanted was to have to deal with media and onlookers, while a forensic search of the location was being carried out. A small team consisting of members of Operation TRACE, experts from the ballistics section and a cadaver search dog from the Garda canine unit, were sent to the scene. To avoid drawing any unwanted attention, we split up, and stayed overnight in a number of separate locations. We spent three days carrying out a forensic fingertip search of the wooded area, after an initial search made by the cadaver dog. It rained non-stop during that search period, and nothing was found that suggested that a body had ever been buried there. The search wound down as darkness fell on the third day.

Our informant, who, at that stage, was back in prison, was adamant that the information he had supplied was correct, and that we had not properly searched the wood. A larger search team was assembled, and arrangements were put in place for a further search of the same area. However, while visiting the prison to arrange a further release date for our informant, we obtained access to his prison record. To our amazement, we learnt that our informant had actually appeared in Carlow Court on the morning of the 10 November 1995, and had been remanded to prison. This meant, in turn, that his story about having assisted in the disposal of the body could not have been correct.

★

When this development was put to our source, they immediately altered their story. We were now told that the story about the removal of the body had been related to them by another person, with whom they were serving a prison sentence. It was, they added, this other person who had actually participated in the disposal of the body. In order to make the story more realistic and thereby to ensure that they were granted the weekend out of prison, our source claimed to have taken an active part in it.

In light of the information given to us concerning Michael Henry, we decided to arrest him and a number of other individuals, whose names had been indicated by sources as being present in the two cars in Moone on the 9 November 1993. A total of seven persons were arrested, most of whom came from the same family. All of them vehemently denied any involvement in Jo Jo's disappearance, and were released without charge. Law Officers were consulted in relation to the possibility of laying charges against Michael Henry, based on evidence from the informant, and backed up by the evidence supplied by Noel Dalton. The response did not surprise anyone involved in the investigation. Our informant dealt a fatal blow to their reliability as a witness, after claiming to have been involved in the removal of the body. Any credibility, regarding what appeared to have been a highly plausible account of events at Moone, was negated by that initial lie.

The validity of the story, as recounted by this informant, has since been thoroughly investigated. It has been denied outright during formal interviewing by Michael Henry. Others named as having been present have also denied it. It is conceded that the informant, who was then serving a lengthy sentence and had lost all privileges, had a lot to gain from currying favour with the Gardai. Unfortunately, nothing has arisen since that could lend any further credence to this story, or cause it to be revisited.

A second female came forward some months after Noel Dalton's information first appeared in the media. This woman maintained that she had been hitching a lift from Dublin to Carlow, around the time Jo Jo went missing. She was very much the worse for wear with drink, and had accepted a lift from two men driving a 'big' car. As she got into the car, she claimed to have noticed a second car pulling up behind. It had then followed the car she was travelling in. Both cars pulled into the deserted car park of a fast-food restaurant, situated between Castledermot and Carlow town.

The front-seat passenger had then climbed into the back, and sexually assaulted her. She managed, however, to open the rear door, and jump out. Both males then shouted a number of obscenities at her, and drove away. They were followed by the second car, and she was left stranded in the car park. The similarities between this incident and the story told about Jo Jo by our source, describing the two cars, are remarkable. It seems possible that this story was adapted by the informant, to try obtain a temporary release from their prison sentence. No one has ever been charged for this other incident.

★

There was one other matter that arose in relation to the review by Operation TRACE of the disappearance of young Jo Jo. In January 1999, just a few months after the establishment of our taskforce, a story appeared in a number of newspapers, suggesting that, in the months prior to her disappearance, Jo Jo had gone to England to have an abortion. The leaked story was attributed to a 'reliable Garda source', and created a sense of mistrust between ourselves, on the one hand, and the families of both Jo Jo and the other missing women.

It is, however, undoubtedly the case that it was indeed a Garda source that had spread this story. While it is unclear what the motive might have been in releasing this personal information, as it had absolutely no relevance to the investigation, it is clear that they were not driven by a desire to locate Jo Jo, or to assist in the investigation. This malicious act was, at the very least, not done by or on behalf of anyone at Operation TRACE.

Gardai were evidently found wanting in their day-to-day dealings with Jo Jo's family and, indeed, with the families of many of the other missing young women. The attitude popularly adopted by investigators at that time led to the practice of next of kin being, at best tolerated, but certainly never involved in, investigations. This insular attitude is something that we will revisit later. To each and every victim who suffered at the hands of Garda mistreatment, caused, certainly, by a lack of training, those dark days are hopefully long gone, never to be revisited.

Fiona Pender

Unlike the other two disappearances, Fiona Pender was last seen alive, not out walking, but in bed in the flat she shared with her partner at Church Street, in the centre of Tullamore town. She lived just a short walk away from the local Garda station. Her partner would later tell Gardai that when he left for work at 6 AM on the morning of Friday 23 August 1996, the heavily pregnant Fiona was complaining of heartburn. He further stated that he was first made aware that Fiona was missing by her mother, Josephine, on Saturday evening. At her parents' insistence, he called into Tullamore Garda station at around 10 PM that same night, to formally report her missing.

Fiona had spent the previous Thursday afternoon in the local Bridge Shopping Centre with her mother. They had purchased a number of items for her baby, due in less than eight weeks. After their outing, they went to the family home in Connolly Park, where Fiona spoke with her father. Sometime around 7 pm, they took a taxi back to Fiona's house in Church Street. Mother and daughter parted company outside the front door to her house, arranging to meet again the following day. They had a very close relationship – more like sisters than parent and child, as one neighbour later told us. Josephine had no idea that these would be the final moments spent with her daughter, and that her grandchild would be murdered while still in its mother's womb. Fiona's callous and savage killer would deny her parents of even a graveside at which to mourn the passing of a daughter and grandchild.

Fiona was just twenty-five years old. She had attended the local Sacred Heart secondary school, and left on completion of her Junior Certificate. She was apprenticed to a local hairdresser, and quickly found that she had an aptitude for the job. A bright, attractive and outgoing girl, Fiona had a wide circle of acquaintances in and around the town. For many years, she and many of her friends had been heavily involved in the local motorcycle club, and Fiona was considered one of their better motorcyclists. It was through her involvement in that club that she met and fell in love with John Thompson.

While Fiona could be considered an original 'townie', Thompson was of rural stock, and lived with his parents and sisters on their family farm in Grange, about eight miles from Tullamore. Where she was known to her peers as easy-going and friendly, Thompson was the exact opposite – a quiet, shy introvert. He was described by many as 'broody'. Thompson came to be involved in motorcycles through his love of all things mechanical. Fiona was introduced to him by her brother, Mark, who shared her enthusiasm for motorcycling.

★

Tragedy struck the Pender family when, in June of 1995, Mark was killed – knocked off his motorcycle in a traffic accident. The loss of her younger brother had a devastating impact on Fiona, who had always been very close to him. She felt the shock of his death deeply. Mark left behind a partner and a three-year-old son, both of whom remained close to the Pender family. For her part, Fiona would never again sit astride a motorcycle. As a mark of respect to him, both herself and her friends in the club buried the charred remains of Mark's motorcycle in the Sliabh Bloom Mountains. In an uncanny twist, little over a year later, it would be this very area that some suggested her body was buried in. Fiona's parents, who had also gone through the trauma of a number of miscarriages, would be struck with another devastating tragedy only a year later.

The loss of a greatly loved brother had, understandably, a very unsettling effect on Fiona. Everywhere she went, and everyone she met with in and around Tullamore, served as a constant reminder of her loss. She decided to move away from the town, and John, albeit reluctantly, agreed to go with her. Fiona's parents could understand her wish to get away from Tullamore, if only for a short while, but John Thompson's parents frowned upon his leaving the family farm. They depended totally on him for its upkeep. At around that stage, Fiona had an aunt living in London, who organised accommodation and employment for them. They moved in November of 1995, coincidentally just days after Jo Jo Dollard had gone missing.

The young couple secured work in the Croydon branch of the Hilton Hotel. Fiona fell in love with the fast pace of London life, but John became more and more homesick as the days progressed. Not for him the bright city lights; he was more at home in the fields and mountains surrounding his native Grange. By February of the following year, to save their increasingly fractious relationship, Fiona agreed to return to Tullamore.

Shortly after their return from England, the young couple discovered that they were to become parents. The news was greeted with great excitement by Fiona's parents, coming, as it did, just a few short months after the loss of their son. Arrangements were made for Fiona to move back into the family home for the first few weeks after the birth. In the meantime, the couple began looking for a house of their own. There was talk, in the early stages, of them moving into a vacant house on the Thompson land, but this came to nought. There were three sisters living in the Thompson home at that time, along with John's father Archie and his mother, who had been ill for a number of years.

The reaction of John's family to the impending birth is unknown. It is not known whether there were any celebrations at the news of this new Thompson heir in the privacy of their own home. Equally, following Fiona's disappearance, any sadness or upset they felt at her loss and the loss of their future grandchild and nephew was never publicly displayed.

★

The house at Church Street that John and Fiona moved into was subdivided into over ten separate bedsits. As Fiona's pregnancy advanced, the tiny room, for which they were paying an exorbitant rent, seemed to grow progressively smaller. Every sound in the cramped house carried from room to room. There was scant privacy available to the tenants, with every voice raised in anger carrying clearly throughout the house. Heated exchanges could regularly be heard coming from the youngsters' flat. It was certainly not an environment that one would consider bringing a newborn into. Fiona grew anxious for a place of her own. Acquaintances commented on the wedge which the pregnancy appeared to be driving between the couple, and said they were unsure about the level of commitment displayed by Thompson.

The difference between the socio-economic backgrounds of Fiona and John was marked. Her father had spent a lot of time unemployed, and it was a daily struggle to make ends meet. However, both her parents did all in their power to ensure that their three children received as high a standard of living and education as possible. They were regular attendees at the local Catholic Church.

John Thompson came from what was referred to in the area as 'Protestant English Planter' stock. As the only son, he was the automatic heir to the substantial farm, situated eight miles outside Tullamore. His three unmarried sisters worked the land with him. John also had a bachelor uncle, who farmed an adjoining, similarly sized estate. As things then stood, John Thompson would inherit his uncle's farm; a sizeable legacy awaited any child that John and Fiona had.

On the afternoon of Friday 23 August, Josephine called to her daughter's flat at Church Street. She observed that the curtains of the bedroom window were drawn and, thinking that Fiona might have been resting, she left without knocking. Later that night, her father noticed, as he walked past on his way home, that the blinds were still drawn, and the flat was completely dark. Neither parent thought, at that stage, that there was anything amiss.

By the following afternoon, with no contact received from Fiona, a sense of unease began to creep in, and Josephine and Sean decided to call back down to the flat. After receiving no answer, Josephine rang the Thompson home and asked to speak with John. When she asked him if he knew where Fiona was, he responded by saying that he'd believed her to be with her parents. He told Josephine that he had not been back to the flat since leaving it early on Friday morning, and had slept in his family home on Friday night. An increasingly concerned Josephine insisted that Thompson come back to Tullamore to help look for Fiona. On his arrival they found no sign of her in the flat. They spent the next few hours driving around the town, desperately searching.

★

By 10 PM that Saturday night, Josephine knew, by motherly instinct, that her daughter was in trouble. Accompanied by her husband, youngest son, and John Thompson, Josephine called to Tullamore Garda Station, where they made an official report about her disappearance. It had then been over forty hours since Fiona and John had spoken, prior to his leaving for work.

The Gardai reaction to the missing-person report again appears to have fallen far short of what one would expect. It would not be until Monday that Gardai would visit the Pender home, and establish that Fiona had not returned. It was, by that time, over seventy hours since she had last been seen.

The flat she shared with John Thompson was secured and preserved by Gardai. After a thorough examination, no trace of foul play was found. All her clothes, together with all the clothes she had been buying for her child, were neatly folded and in their proper place. The only items missing were a pair of white leggings, a pair of white runners and a navy T-shirt. It was assumed that Fiona was actually wearing these particular items of clothing when she went missing. Her case differed significantly from those of Annie and Jo Jo, in that

Gardai had a specific, enclosed area from which to begin their search. In Annie's case, she had last been seen going into a busy pub, while Jo Jo was on the open road. Technical examination of Fiona's flat was carried out, but no sign of a struggle or assault was found. The search area was gradually broadened to include the nearby canal, river and reservoir.

By lunch-time on Monday 27 August, appeals would be broadcast on local and national radio, for information in relation to her whereabouts. Given Fiona's popularity, Gardai were inundated with responses from members of the public. The majority of reported sightings referred to meetings people had had with her prior to the previous Friday. There were also a number of callers who claimed to have met her on the Friday itself, and over the weekend proper. All reports were fully checked out.

One report received from a member of the public caused a lot of concern within the investigation team. A male caller claimed that, early that Friday morning, he had been walking home from a local pub through Church Street. He stated that he had observed two men putting a bulky item into the rear of a four-wheel-drive vehicle. It looked, he would claim, like something wrapped up in a rug or a length of carpeting. To date, no one has come forward offering a reasonable explanation for this sighting.

Another witness claimed to have been driving along a narrow road in the Sliabh Bloom Mountains some distance from Tullamore, early on Friday morning, when he met a four-wheel-drive vehicle travelling at breakneck speed. He was unable to catch either the exact make or registration number. He was adamant, however, that there was only one occupant. His attention had been caught by a stick-on sign, emblazoned across the top of the windscreen, reading 'Keep Her Lit'. Again, no one has ever come forward with an explanation as to the origin of this vehicle, or of the erratic manner in which it was being driven.

★

On 24 April 1997, in a coordinated operation, the local Gardai, and detectives from the National Bureau of Criminal Investigation (NBCI), carried out a number of searches in the Tullamore area. A total of five persons – three females and two males (all of whom were related) – were arrested in connection with Fiona's disappearance. They were taken to Tullamore Garda Station, where they were questioned for a number of hours. However, no evidence to link them to her disappearance could be established, and they were later released from custody.

Fiona's heavily pregnant state struck a chord with the public, and her disappearance was the subject of much speculation. Even at that early stage there were rumblings of disquiet from the media concerning the standard of Garda investigation into this type of incident. It would be another two years before the formation of Operation TRACE.

The hospitals and health clinics, both in this and in neighbouring jurisdictions, received a lot of attention during the initial investigation. In her stage of pregnancy, she would require fairly constant medical attention. Given the sympathy that her condition attracted, the public displayed an unprecedented level of cooperation, seldom seen in murder cases of this nature. However, no trace of Fiona could be found.

Over the following years, Josephine Pender did her best to keep her daughter's disappearance in the public mind. Even the loss of her husband and life partner, Sean, in the year 2000, did not deflect her. In 2008, a grisly discovery was made.

On the weekend of 10 May of that year, a person walking in an area called Monickew, in the Sliabh Bloom Mountains, discovered a makeshift cross bearing the inscription 'Fiona Pender Buried here Thursday August 22 1996'. The actual area where the cross was discovered was some four miles from the town of Mountrath, and thirty miles from her hometown of Tullamore.

On receiving this report, Gardai sealed off a huge tract of the surrounding forest area. Despite their best efforts, news leaked out to the media, and a horde of people descended upon the area. An accredited forensic search expert was brought in from England, to oversee the resultant search and supervised 'dig'. Gardai were also assisted by trained military personnel. However, nothing was found that would suggest that Fiona's body had been buried there.

The motive behind the planting of the cross has never been fully established. The date is known to coincide with a huge personal trauma in the life of a male considered to be a person of interest to the investigation. Whether this prompted some soul-searching or feelings of guilt twelve years after the event is open to speculation. The writing on the cross is unique and will, in time, hopefully lead to the author of the message being identified, if it is indeed a clue, and not some twisted idea of a joke. Whether this will even be the same person who took Fiona's life remains to be seen.

★

On 9 July 2013, Tullamore Town Council unanimously voted to name a part of the canal bank walk, near the flat where Fiona was last seen alive, 'Fiona's

Way'. More than just keeping her in our memory, this should hopefully also serve as a reminder to the coward that took her young life, and how, in their silence, they continue to wound her friends and family.

It should never be forgotten that the same person who murdered Fiona also murdered her unborn child, due ten weeks later, on 22 October 1996. Fiona was going to christen the child Mark if it was a boy, in honour of her dead brother. There is one other death attributable to this same culprit. Fiona's death effectively led to that of her father, Sean, who, unable to live with the loss, took his own life on 31 March 2000. The culprit may as well have placed the noose around his neck. His hands, and the hands of those persons who are knowingly sheltering him, are stained by the blood of all three victims. How they can live with this knowledge, as each day passes, is something no sane person can comprehend.

Ciara Breen

There was a delay in the Garda response to Ciara Breen's disappearance from her family home at Bachelor's Walk, in the centre of Dundalk town. On this occasion, however, the delay would be in the actual making of the initial report. Her mother, Bernadette, had found her bed empty when checking her room at 1 AM, on Thursday 13 February 1997. However, she also found that the sitting-room window, giving direct access to the roadway outside the house, had been left partially opened. She suspected that the seventeen-year-old had slipped out the window to meet friends, some of whom she did not approve of. Breen spent the night sitting up, waiting for her return.

At 9 AM the next morning, Ciara had still not arrived home. Bernadette had to leave to keep a pre-arranged appointment at a clinic in Dublin. Prior to leaving Dundalk, she rang the former secondary school where Ciara was attending a FAS course to assist early school leavers, and left a message for her with her class tutor.

During the course of her appointment at the Blackrock Clinic, Bernadette was given the devastating news that she had developed cancer, and required immediate and intensive treatment. While still coming to terms with this news, she discussed Ciara's absence with her father, who had driven her to Dublin. They agreed that if, on their return, there was still no sign of her, they would contact a few of her friends and, if they still had no news about Ciara's where-abouts, would report her disappearance to the Gardai.

Ciara was just short of eighteen years. In the eyes of the law, she was still a child. When the report was received at Dundalk Garda Station, an investigation was immediately commenced. While any report of a missing child is an imme-diate cause for concern, there was another reason why this particular report was treated with such urgency.

At that time, a paedophile gang targeting and grooming impressionable local boys and girls for sex was said to be operating in the Dundalk area. A number of instances of adults plying minors with drink had come to light. A derelict for-mer piggery, situated on the outskirts of Dundalk town, was known as a favourite haunt for both youngsters and predators.

In one instance, following a proactive Garda investigation, a businessman from the North of Ireland was convicted of attempting to procure a local youth for sex. This conviction was later overturned on appeal. The group of vulnerable teenagers that the perverts were targeting included a number of Ciara's friends and acquaintances.

★

In addition, there was a rumour that a number of youngsters had been forced into prostitution by a local woman, to service growing demand in the area. Gardai did not suspect that Ciara or her immediate circle of friends were involved in any of these activities, but were afraid that they could be perceived as 'easy pickings'.

On the night of her disappearance, Bernadette and Ciara had spent an enjoyable 'girls' night out' together, going for a meal, then home to watch a film on television. Both were, naturally, nervous about Bernadette's appointment the following morning. For her daughter's sake, she attempted to play down the seriousness of her illness, but its shadow undoubtedly hung over them.

Apart from the problems with her mother's health, Ciara faced huge personal changes in the coming weeks and months. She would be eighteen soon, and was about to meet her birth father whom she had never known. Michael* had emigrated to America before his daughter was born, and had never even seen her. Through their extended families, the estranged couple had agreed to meet when he arrived home later that month. Ciara was both apprehensive and excited about this meeting. She was also awaiting a serious dental procedure involving the replacement of several bottom-row teeth, scheduled for before her father returned.

Although close, mother and daughter, like all other families, had their differences. Rearing a child by oneself in Dundalk in the 1990s was no easy task; the Troubles in Northern Ireland had a huge influence on day-to-day life in the border town. It was nicknamed 'El Paso', after the infamous American city bordering Mexico, renowned, in folklore, for its gunfights and murders, and was generally perceived as bordering on lawlessness. There had been a huge influx of immigrants from across the border. While, undoubtedly, the vast majority had moved south to try and make a better life for themselves away from the Troubles in the North, a large number had moved to avoid legal censure for their roles in various incidents connected with terrorist activities. With them, they brought a lifestyle and attitude that was completely alien to what the local youngsters knew.

In late 1995, Ciara had run away from home with another girl. Gardai had been notified at the time, and a full-scale search, with all the attendant publicity, had been mounted. The girls had camped in a derelict house just across the border, in nearby Jonesborough. What had prompted this impetuous act was unclear, but both girls returned home after four or five days. In many ways, this incident seems to have had a calming influence on Ciara, and she became much more settled after it. The fact that she had previously left home and returned unharmed may also have influenced Bernadette in her decision not to sound any immediate alarm bells, when she found Ciara's bed empty at 1 AM that Thursday morning.

★

What Bernadette could not have known was that, on that same Wednesday afternoon, after they had finished their FAS course, Ciara and a few of her friends had gone to a local chipper. All the local young people frequented the shop, and would happily spend hours there together, trying to make a bottle of Coke or a plate of chips last longer than seemed possible. All the news and gossip would be dispensed and discussed, friendships cemented and liaisons arranged. Gatherings like these are normally a harmless and essential part of teenage life.

As a moth is attracted to a naked flame, though, so too on the periphery of such groups could be found perverts whose only interest in the happy-go-lucky youngsters seems the total destruction of any vestige of innocence or happiness they had. The group that Ciara was with that day had attracted such a predator: a local man almost twice the age of any young person there.

Mature beyond her years in her relationship with her mother and in her concern for her mother's health, there was a certain naivety about Ciara in her dealings with the opposite sex that was worrying. This naivety would, ultimately, prove fatal.

Emblazoned across a wall in Barrack Street, near her home, was the message: '---- loves Ciara'. The older man whose name appeared in this message denied any involvement with the young girl, and it was generally accepted that Ciara had been the author. The man was not from the immediate area but was, at that time, staying with relatives nearby. He'd even been warned by Bernadette not to hang around outside her house. This was that same man who now sat in the chipper, watching every move the teenagers made.

As with Fiona Pender, Gardai investigating Ciara's disappearance had a definite area where she had last been seen alive. A forensic examination of her bedroom and the adjacent sitting room was carried out. No sign of foul play was established. In addition, the partially open sitting-room window showed no sign of having been forcibly opened. It had, in fact, been opened from the inside. The only latent finger-marks developed on it would be those that matched Ciara herself. There was a radiator just under this window, behind which Gardai located Ciara's front-door key. She had obviously dropped it as she climbed through the window.

The only clothes missing from her room were her blue jeans, a three-quarter-length leather jacket, and a distinctive white T-shirt which bore her own photograph on the front. The Mickey Mouse watch that she had received as a present while on holiday in Disneyland the year previous was also missing.

★

Despite intensive Garda investigations and a large number of planned searches, her whereabouts continued to remain a mystery. Established haunts that she had frequented during her first disappearance were carefully checked. Friends and associates of the young teenager were interviewed. The Police Service of Northern Ireland assisted in checks and searches on their side of the border.

It very quickly became clear that, unlike her last disappearance, Ciara's leaving was not voluntary. She had taken nothing of real or sentimental value, and none of her favourite clothing. When going to bed that last night, she had been aware of her mother's important medical appointment the following morning, one that could bring news of a serious illness. It was unlikely that she would be absent. She was also, of course, due to meet her father for the first time in the coming days.

When Operation TRACE started their examination of this investigation, we concentrated, at the outset, on statements taken from friends and acquaintances. We found that a number of her close friends referred to a conversation they had overheard between Ciara and the older man, Leo Flynn*, who had approached their group in the café that Wednesday afternoon.

Conversation was in full flow when the teenagers were joined by this man, who was regularly on the periphery of their group. He was well known to all the teenagers, and they were used to him shoving in, unwelcomed. Ciara, however, appeared to them to be smitten by him. Leo spoke briefly with her. Others in the group overheard him ask Ciara if he could see her later that day. They subsequently told Gardai that they'd heard Ciara tell him that she would sneak out of her house after her mother went to bed. According to her friends, Ciara often left home in this fashion, late at night.

We considered this allegedly planned assignation to be vitally important information, and discussed its potential significance with some of the original investigators. Based on their local knowledge, in their opinion, the youngsters who had given this information were not credible witnesses. They were consequently reluctant to give any credence to what they had said. Some of these friends, they added, had been involved in incidents of petty crime, and would, in their opinion, have no interest in assisting Gardai in any enquiries or investigations.

Nevertheless, on Tony Hickey's instructions, we revisited each of these witnesses. These visits took place over two years after the original interviews, when Operation TRACE was established. To our surprise, each witness remained adamant that their initial story was correct, and the account of the conversation between Ciara and this older man remained consistent throughout. There was no attempt by any of them to exaggerate or embellish the stories they had first given.

★

Consultations took place, following these interviews in early September 1999, between ourselves and the Law Officers. We were of the view, based upon the information we now had, that we had sufficient grounds to arrest Leo in connection with the murder of Ciara Breen. The real issue we all knew would arise would be proving that Ciara was actually dead. Sustaining a charge of murder without a body to show for it was a rare enough concept in this jurisdiction. Our investigation researched a number of court judgements, to identify a case that had been prosecuted without the benefit of a body. We found that the only recent conviction for murder without a body was that of IRA man Liam Towson, for the murder of Captain Robert Nairac. The Law Officers agreed that a precedent had been set with this case, and that we could use it in the Breen investigation.

Nairac, a British soldier attached to the Special Duties Unit of the infamous 14th Intelligence Company, carried out undercover and surveillance work on the various republican movements operating in Ulster throughout the 1970s. He was considered by many of his colleagues to be a bit of a 'loose cannon'. On 15 July

1977, he was abducted from The Three Steps public house in Dromintee, Armagh, by a group of eight men. He had spent the earlier part of the evening in their company, singing rebel songs, and openly telling everyone that he was a member of the Belfast Brigade of the IRA.

He was taken to Ravensdale Wood in County Louth, where he was subjected to a lengthy torture, but denied throughout that he was a member of the British Army. Such was the ferocity of the assault that he died. The only actual evidence of the fatal assault that was ever found was blood-staining on the grass and hedgerow. Legal history was made some months later when Towson was convicted of Nairac's murder. The following year a further two males, Gerard Fearon and Thomas Morgan, were also convicted in a Belfast court of his murder.

Robert Nairac was a committed Catholic, who was on his fourth tour of duty in Northern Ireland. The son of a well-to-do, London-based eye surgeon, he had studied at University College Dublin in the early seventies. He was a regular visitor to our shores, and spoke proudly of his Irish ancestry. He was posthumously awarded the George Cross in 1979 by the British government for his bravery.

London Member of Parliament Ken Livingstone years later suggested that he was in possession of information proving that Nairac had organised the Miami Band Massacre on 31 July 1975, when the popular Irish showband was ambushed at Buskhill, outside Newry in County Down, as they returned late from a gig in Banbridge, Northern Ireland. Five people, including three of the band members, were executed, when they stopped at what they believed to be a British Army checkpoint.

The other two who died, later identified as members of the Ulster Defence Regiment, were fatally injured, when a bomb they were placing on the band's bus exploded prematurely. Two other members of the regiment would later be convicted of the murders of the band members. On the night of the murders, they had all been wearing British Army uniforms. The regiment, consisting in the main of part-time volunteers, had been formed in Northern Ireland in 1970, to replace the disbanded Ulster Special Constabulary. By 1972, Catholic membership of the regiment, considered to be one of the biggest in the British Army, would account for only some 3 percent of the total.

The Historical Enquiries Team of the Police Service of Northern Ireland would subsequently carry out a cold-case investigation into the Miami Band murders and, in their 2010 report, linked a leading member of a paramilitary Protestant group, the Ulster Volunteer Force (UVF), to the weapons used in the crime.

Nairac would also be linked with the members of the Ulster Volunteer Force, who allegedly carried out the Dublin and Monaghan bombings on 17 May 1974. During that coordinated series of four separate car bombs, a total of thirty-three persons were killed, and over three hundred were injured. These explosions were carried out to show solidarity with the general strike, referred to as the Ulster Workers Council Strike, then taking place in Northern Ireland. The strikers were opposed to the peace initiatives that the Irish and British government, were attempting to put in place, with the signing of the Sunningdale Agreement.

This was a most unusual case for us to be using as grounds for making an arrest for the murder of a Dundalk teenager. However, the Law Officers agreed that a precedent had been set by the Nairac case, which we could use to our benefit.

Arrangements were put in place and, on the morning of 12 September 1999, Flynn was arrested by local detectives, assisted by members of Operation TRACE. He was taken to Dundalk Garda Station, and detained. Leo could now be held for a total of twelve hours, during which time he could be interviewed about Ciara's murder. The whole operation had been shrouded in secrecy. The majority of Gardai attached to the station only became aware of it after hearing about the arrest on local radio.

Immediately preceding the arrest, Ciara's mother, Bernadette, was visited by Detective Sergeant Maura Walsh, who broke the news. This, we were all aware, would be disturbing information for her. On the one hand, the hope was that, at last, there would be some closure in the case. By making this arrest, we were telling her that, based on the evidence we had established, we were of the opinion that her missing daughter was dead.

Strangely enough, when researching Flynn's background prior to his arrest, we discovered a connection between his family and one of the culprits involved in the infamous 'Railway Rapists', a series of multiple rapes and murders in and around the London area. We will be touching upon this odd detail later, in relation to the techniques of geographic profiling.

★

Throughout the course of his detention, Flynn continued to deny that he even knew the missing teenager. Even when confronted, while in custody, by one of those witnesses who had heard him arranging to meet Ciara the night she disappeared, he persisted in his denial. An off-the-record request to provide some solace to her grieving mother by helping to locate the body was greeted with derision. Lands associated with his extended family some miles from town were forensically searched while he was in custody. No trace of Ciara was found, and Flynn was released without charge later that same day.

We subsequently submitted a lengthy report to the Law Officers, containing all the various pieces of evidence that had been established in the case. Though we recommended that Flynn should be charged with the murder of Ciara Breen, it was decided that, given the complex nature of the case, we had not established sufficient evidence to warrant the laying of charges against him.

Now in his early fifties, Flynn remains, to this day, the only viable suspect in the murder of young Ciara. Her body has never been located but her mother continues to hope that, some day, her only child's body will be returned to her. There is only one person who can help her in her search, and he continues to live locally and to regularly meet both Bernadette and her missing daughter's friends, all of whom are now adults.

Fiona Sinnott

Fiona Sinnott was an independent soul who, after the break-up of her relationship with the father of her eleven-month-old child, had chosen to live alone in rented accommodation in the village of Broadway in south-west Wexford, about ten miles from her family home. Although she remained in touch with both parents and siblings, several days would often go by before there would be any contact between them. As a consequence, it would be a full ten days before they reported the nineteen-year old missing to Gardai.

During that time, her rented home at Ballyhitt, just outside Broadway, had undergone an extensive clean out. At one stage during this period, a local would even remark that on one day alone, he had observed over a dozen black refuse sacks lined up for collection outside the front of the house. Fiona, was not renowned for her housekeeping prowess, and it seems unlikely that this clean up was her doing. She was allegedly last been seen alive on 9 February 1998, almost a year to the day after the disappearance of Ciara Breen.

Gardai would find, during the course of their subsequent investigation, that a number of close associates of the main person of interest in the enquiry were reluctant to talk to them – such was their fear of him.

For some time prior to her move to Ballyhitt, Fiona had been in a physically abusive relationship with an older man. Gardai had attended at the various addresses they shared on a number of occasions, but after each assault the had refused to press charges, accepting his promises that it would not happen again, believing that, as he claimed, it had really been her fault and that basically, deep down, he only hurt her because he cared so much for her. Many continue to tolerate systematic mental and physical abuse over lengthy periods, trapped by this same thought process.

Following some brutal assaults, Fiona had actually needed treatment at the Casualty section in Wexford General Hospital. Her injuries ranged from bruising and other unexplained marks to what appeared to be bite marks. On one occasion, a neighbour had found her, distraught, lying on the side of the roadway in the middle of the night. Fiona said that her partner had thrown her out of the mobile home they shared, and had threatened her with a knife. When the

Gardai arrived, they found the drunken bully cowering inside the house. He refused to let Fiona back in, claiming that it was his home and that she was not welcome, and denied threatening her with a knife. She spent the rest of the night in a friend's house.

She told a number of her friends a harrowing story, involving vicious and prolonged sexual abuse that this man had subjected her to when she was heavily pregnant. I have personally read, with revulsion, the various reports concerning this particular assault, and can honestly say that if only half of it was true, then her assailant should have stood trial for it and never again been accepted back into normal society. Given her relatively young age and her late stage of pregnancy, the attack bordered on barbaric. Such was the influence he exerted upon her that, once again, Fiona chose not to report the matter to the authorities.

She was subject to a pattern of abuse that, on each occasion, was growing more and more vicious. The young girl began to realise that, as long as she stayed in the relationship, the assaults would only continue, and escalate in ferocity. She decided that the only way to break out of this cycle of violence was to leave it altogether, and set up a new life for herself and her baby daughter.

What amazes me also about this relationship was the fact that this man's behaviour was well known among his family and peers. How they could continue to tolerate and befriend him, knowing the level of abuse he was submitting this young girl to, seems incomprehensible.

On Sunday evening, 8 February 1998, Fiona, now living in rented accommodation in Ballyhitt, had gone to meet three female friends in her local pub, Butlers, situated in the village of Broadway. The friends sat together chatting and joking, discussing a night out they'd shared the previous Friday, in the Tuskar House Hotel in Rosslare. A group of them had travelled together in a mini-bus to the club. Fiona had, however, not travelled back with them.

Her baby daughter, Emma, was staying with the parents of her former partner for the weekend. Although the relationship with Emma's father had broken down, Fiona regularly permitted her daughter to spend time with her grandparents. At one stage during that Sunday evening, her former partner, Sean Carroll, had walked into Butlers. The couple had previously been together for a number of years. Fiona seemed surprised to see him, and did not greet him. Carroll spent the night drinking alone at the bar.

On several occasions throughout that night, Fiona's friends observed her wincing, as if in pain. When they asked her about this, she complained of pains in her upper chest area and in her arm, but did not elaborate on the cause or extent of this injury. Some of her friends attempted to speculate on the cause of her obvious discomfort, but she refused to discuss it.

At one stage during the night, Fiona had made a quick telephone call to her family home. She asked her brother, Seamus, if he wanted to join her for a drink. He declined, however, as he had just returned from work. It is possible that Seamus regrets that decision to this day, perhaps thinking that if he had joined her, she might still be alive. However, having read and analysed the various investigation reports into her disappearance, I am firmly of the opinion that when she decided to try to start a new life for herself and her daughter, Fiona had, in effect, sealed her own fate. It seems more a case of 'when' rather than 'if' there would be another physical assault on her person, an assault that would prove to be one too many.

Fiona left the pub alone, just after closing time, intending to walk the short distance to her house. She turned and waved goodnight to her friends, and they waved back in response. Little did they know that they would never see her alive again. Some still gathered in the pub stated that as she was leaving, they saw Sean Carroll walk out behind her. They were surprised at this, as there had only been limited conversation between the former couple throughout the night. Another witness claimed to have heard a brief but heated exchange coming from the porch doorway, through which Fiona had just left.

Butlers pub was about a quarter of a mile from Fiona's rented house, along a relatively quiet stretch of roadway. A passing motorist would later tell Gardai that he had observed a couple standing near the entrance to a local quarry on that road, shortly after closing time. They appeared to be arguing. Another person, living just off this roadway, would later come forward, and claim that they had heard the sound of a female screaming in or around the same time. The area where the female was heard screaming is known, locally, as the Millpond Cross. Again, this area lay on the route that Fiona would have taken home.

On Wednesday 18 February 1998, Fiona's father Patrick called to Kilmore Quay Garda station and reported, to local Garda Jim Sullivan, that his daughter was missing. Jim, on hearing that she had not been seen for some ten days, launched a full missing-persons investigation.

Fiona had, on a previous occasion, left home for two or three days at a time. She had gone to stay with a friend in the Cork area, in an attempt to resolve the problems in her abusive relationship. However, it was most unlike her not to have made some contact with her parents, or one of her two sisters or two brothers. The family were in the process of making arrangements for her sister Diane's twenty-first birthday, and Fiona, the youngest of the siblings, would have wanted to be part of that. She had even made arrangements to travel with other family members to Waterford to pick out a present for Diana over the next few days.

There was, however, another very important anniversary on its way, one that Fiona was not willingly going to miss. Saturday 28 February was her daughter Emma's first birthday, an occasion she had been greatly looking forward to; she had been making plans with her family and friends on how best to celebrate this big day.

When it was established that the last place she had been seen in public was Butlers pub, initial enquiries centred upon the people that had been there on the night. Gardai could confirm that she and her estranged partner, Sean Carroll, had left the pub together at around the same time. When contacted by Gardai and interviewed, Sean Carroll told them that he had walked Fiona home to her house in Ballyhitt after leaving Butlers Pub, and that when they arrived she had gone straight to bed. He said that she had complained of feeling unwell, complaining of pains in her arm and upper body area. He had, he said, spent the night asleep on the couch downstairs.

★

At around 9 AM on Monday morning, 9 February, prior to his leaving the house, Carroll said he had gone into Fiona's bedroom. She was lying awake in bed and she said that she was still in pain, and intended to go to see her own doctor later that morning. She told him, he claimed, that she had no money, and intended to hitch a lift to the surgery. He had given her about £3 (almost €5), and had then left the house.

As in the case of another missing Fiona – that is, Fiona Pender – we once again have a man claiming to have last seen their partner alive lying in her bed, complaining of feeling unwell. In another of those little coincidences that wide-ranging investigations often throw up, like John Thompson, Sean Carroll was a motorcycle fanatic, a trait that had initially attracted Fiona Sinnott. Carroll, who was some ten years older than Fiona, had previously been married.

Carroll said that when he left Fiona's house that morning, his mother had been waiting outside in her car. They drove back to their home in nearby Coddstown, where Emma was staying. Throughout the period between 9 and 18 February, Emma had continued to stay with his parents in their home. There is no documented attempt by the Carroll family to establish either Fiona's welfare, or when she intended to return to collect her daughter.

Again, as with the Thompson family, the family of Sean Carroll did not become actively involved in the various searches and media appeals for information concerning the fate of the mother of their granddaughter. For a number of years following her disappearance, the parents of Fiona Sinnott would be allowed only very limited involvement in the life of her child by the Carroll family. She would continue to live in Carroll's home.

Enquiries at her doctor's surgery in Bridgetown revealed that Fiona had not arrived there on the morning of 9 February, as had been suggested by Carroll's evidence. Neither had she attended, at any time subsequent to that date. Checks with other doctor surgeries and the County Hospital in Wexford were made; she had not visited any of them. Rolling road checkpoints were put in place to establish if Fiona had been seen trying to thumb a lift towards Bridgetown on that date. Investigators would draw a blank in this enquiry also.

In a subsequent forensic and technical examination of Fiona's house, Gardai found no evidence to suggest that foul play had occurred. What was considered most remarkable, however, was the complete absence of clothing and other personal items indicating that a teenage girl and her eleven-month-old daughter were actually living there. It was as if the house had lain vacant all the months that Fiona had lived in it. It had been stripped of all personal items. The owner claimed that, on previous visits, he'd noticed a great number of bits and pieces lying around.

★

Fiona's disappearance, and the Garda activity which followed, figured prominently in various news bulletins. This led to the Garda being approached by a local farmer, who had some disquieting news. Eamon Lawlor* said he had been checking on his cattle in the days before he learnt of Fiona's disappearance, and that he had found in the corner of the field, in a ditch (or 'gripe'), a number of dumped black refuse sacks. Believing this to be just another incident of illegal dumping that was, he stated, a regular occurrence, he had set fire to the black plastic bags, completely destroying their contents.

Before setting fire to the bags, Eamon had opened one of them to see if he could establish the identity of the person responsible for dumping them. Inside, he found various medicine containers and correspondence, all of which bore the name 'Fiona Sinnott'. He told Gardai, however, that the address on the correspondence was Georges Street in Wexford and not Ballyhitt, where he believed the missing girl lived. This was important information, given that Fiona had lived in Georges Street with her former partner, prior to moving to Ballyhitt. Unfortunately, any potential for forensic examination of both the bags and their contents was lost in the fire. This is a classic example of how a delay in reporting a disappearance can impact upon an investigation.

It would appear that, not satisfied with murdering the youngster and hiding her body, her assailant was also attempting to remove all traces of her existence. It is suspected amongst investigators that her callous murderer was attempting to set a scene suggesting that Fiona had wilfully abandoned her home and child, and gone off to start a new life for herself.

Gardai learned that, on her recent night out in the Tuskar Rock Hotel, Fiona had met an English truck driver, who had parked his forty-foot lorry overnight in a local car park, while en route to catch the first ferry sailing from nearby Rosslare the following morning. The couple had spent the night together in the cab of the lorry. At one stage a former male partner had approached the truck, banging on the locked door and angrily demanding that Fiona leave and come with him. She declined and he, not willing to risk a physical confrontation with the driver, had slinked away with his tail between his legs. Normally the bully was accompanied by two or three henchmen but, on this occasion, he had arrived at the dance alone. This loss of face may very well have played upon his mind, and influenced his subsequent actions.

One of the theories proffered to Gardai by a male acquaintance, a person of interest, as to the possible cause of her disappearance, was that she may have gone to England, either with or after the lorry driver she had spent the Friday night with. He went on to suggest that the driver could have collected her from her house and that she may have taken all her property with her at that time. The suggestion of a forty-foot lorry negotiating its way through the narrow roads around Ballyhitt and leaving unnoticed was greeted with a certain degree of scepticism. Nevertheless, the possibility had to be fully checked out.

★

An examination of the cargo manifest for the ferry threw up a number of possibilities as to the driver's identity. From comments he had made to others present in the hotel on the night in question, it was an easy task, based on the declared produce the various lorries were carrying, to identify the driver. Authorities in the United Kingdom were contacted and they, in turn, spoke with the driver. He agreed to return to Ireland and to meet with the investigating Gardai.

The driver, Andrew Murray*, readily admitted to spending that night with Fiona in his truck. The following morning he had, at her request, dropped her off in Kilrane village, which was on the main road to Rosslare Harbour. She had told him that it would be relatively easy for her to get a lift from there. He was able to prove his own whereabouts since then, as he had spent most of the intervening period driving on the Continent. Andrew also mentioned the palpable fear that Fiona had shown when the male had started banging on the truck door and shouting her name.

A story circulated locally, suggesting that the man who had killed Fiona had hidden her body in a nearby quarry and that, a day or two later, assisted by two of his closest friends, he had collected the body in a blue van. They had then, it was suggested, weighed her body down with chains, and dumped her in a nearby lake. This had led investigators to partially drain the local lake, an area popular for religious pilgrimages, named 'Our Lady's Island Lake'. This lake was just a short distance from where she had last been seen. Other lakes in the area were also searched by divers, both local and from the Garda Water Unit. Once again, as with the other missing women, no trace could be found.

The main suspect in the disappearance of Fiona Sinnott is a male who was well known to her. He was equally well known to the local Garda drug unit working out of Wexford town, through his suspected involvement in both personal use, and low-level dealing of cannabis, working with a number of associates. The gang were arrested in full in June 1998, and interviewed in connection with their drug-dealing activities. They were released, without any charges being laid against them. Any attempt by Gardai to raise the issue of Fiona's disappearance with them was met with a terse response of: 'Nothing to say'. In addition, they said that they had not been arrested on that charge.

Over the following years, a large number of planned searches were carried out within Wexford and neighbouring counties. Various rumours would, from time to time, surface within the local community, concerning the possible involvement of named local youths in the disposal of her body, together with suggested body dump sites. The one piece of information that would remain consistent throughout the years was the identity of the main suspect – the man who, it was claimed, had murdered the young teenager after she left the pub.

★

Information was later received suggesting that a local male was finding it increasingly difficult to live with the part he had played in the disposal of Fiona's body. He told another person that he had been pressured by the suspect, whom he physically feared, into assisting him to move Fiona's body. His conscience was now troubling him, and each public appeal for information concerning the whereabouts of the baby weighed more heavily on his mind. The person in whom he was confiding suggested that he should ring one of the confidential telephone numbers, and give the location of the body without identifying himself. He refused to do so, claiming that as there were only three of them, including the culprit, who knew the exact location, it would be tantamount to signing his own death warrant. In one of those deeply significant twists, the thirty-five-year-old-male would, unfortunately, die of a drug overdose in 2001 before sharing any further information. Whether the overdose was accidental or deliberate is unknown.

In another instance, a local person, on their deathbed, imparted information they claimed had been in their possession for a number of years. The informant stated that they had been told that Fiona's body was buried in a particular field, but that they had been so afraid of the persons involved in the murder that they had not come forward until now. The area was forensically searched, and no trace of the teenager was found. It did, however, bring some comfort to the troubled mind of the person who had, for many years, tried to live with this knowledge.

By 2005, Fiona, who had now been missing some seven years, could legally be classified as dead. Mark Kerrigan, who, for many years had served as an Inspector on Operation TRACE, was now the Detective Superintendent in the Wexford/Kilkenny area. Although we as a taskforce had been 'stood down' in 2000, I continued to act as National Coordinator, to ensure that any new information that came to light was passed on to the relevant investigation team and fully actioned. Operation TRACE had made a number of recommendations concerning actions that should be taken against certain POIs in Fiona's investigation. Following his appointment, Mark had discovered that they had never been implemented.

At Mark's request, an Incident Room Coordinator was seconded from the National Bureau of Criminal Investigation in June 2005 to join him in the Wexford area. In a very low-key operation, an office was set up in nearby Ballcullane Garda Station – the community was tight-knit, but the investigation still needed to be based locally. All the information upon which we had based our recommendations was revisited over a number of weeks. On 16 September 2005, in a carefully coordinated operation, Gardai arrested six people in connection with Fiona's disappearance. In a press conference that same morning, Gardai announced that they were now treating her case as a full murder investigation. At this stage, Fiona had been missing for over seven years. At that point, she could legally be pronounced dead.

The six prisoners – three males and three females – were held at New Ross and Enniscorthy Garda Stations. Some of those arrested had close family links to one another, and their ages ranged from thirty to sixty. They were detained throughout the course of that day, and questioned at length in connection with Fiona's murder. All six would later be released without charge. Files in relation to their suspected involvement in her death were submitted to the Law Officers, but no charges would be laid.

On the following day, a first cousin of Fiona's former partner would make an official complaint to Gardai. Robert Pask alleged that at sometime around 7 AM on 17 September 2005, Sean Carroll had called to his home and threatened him. Carroll, he claimed, had told him he was a 'dead man', adding that he himself would not do it, but that he knew 'someone who will' and that there were 'lads on the way over'. Pask added that he was in no doubt that his life was in danger, so much so that he did not stay at home, but instead got a friend to watch his house.

Sean Carroll denied having ever issued any such threat when arrested in connection with this matter on 30 September. The case was finally heard before Judge Donnchada O Buachalla at Wexford District Court on 6 July 2006. During the course of his evidence to the court, Pask said he had been aware that Carroll had been in Garda custody, in relation to 'another matter', on the day before the incident at his home. However, he also told the court that he now wished to withdraw the statement of complaint he had made to Gardai.

For his part, Sean Carroll would tell the court that the day before the threat had allegedly been made by him, he had been detained for twelve hours in New Ross Garda Station. During the course of that day, he claimed that Gardai had told him that Pask had raped his sister Sharon, with whom he had had a brief relationship.

Judge O'Buachalla, in passing a sentence of three months' imprisonment on Sean Carroll, said that he regarded the threat as being of the 'utmost seriousness'. Bail for appeal was set at €5,000. Carroll's appeal was finally heard at Wexford Circuit Court on 11 December 2007, the sentence was set aside and he was bound to keep the peace for a period of two years.

The searches for Fiona's body continued over the next few years. Local Gardai would regularly receive information from members of the public, suggesting that certain areas should be searched for her remains.

Earlier in 2007, a person out walking at Katt's Strand outside Wexford town had located a human skull. Initially, it was believed that this could have been part of Fiona's body washed up onto the beach. However, a subsequent examination by a forensic anthropologist would reveal that it was, in fact, the skull of a much older woman. It has to date not been identified.

Katt's Strand had, some years earlier, been the scene of another huge tragedy. In April 2005, local woman Sharon Grace had drowned both herself and her young daughters, Abby and Mikahla. Sharon had tried, desperately, to seek assistance for her ongoing psychiatric problems in the days preceding this horrific event.

★

Operation TRACE had included, amongst a number of operational recommendations it submitted, a suggestion for the maintenance of a dedicated DNA database, comprising specimens donated by families of long-term missing persons. In the event of an unidentifiable body being located anywhere inside or outside the State, a simple check would save a lot of grieving families from enduring further false dawns. Regrettably, this recommendation has never been acted upon.

★

In September of 2008, to mark the tenth anniversary of her disappearance, Fionna's family arranged a special ceremony in Our Ladies Island Cemetery, just a short distance from where she had last been seen alive. A special plaque to commemorate her life had been erected, at the request of the family, in the cemetery wall on the previous day, Saturday 12 September. Imagine the additional pain that had been caused to this grieving family when they discovered, on the Sunday of the planned ceremony, that the plaque had been stolen. It is almost certainly the case, from speaking with the locals, that this despicable act was carried out either by or at the request of her murderer.

Those who knew Fiona, and knew of her love for both Emma and her family, know that she could never have left voluntarily. No matter what steps her murderer took in erasing evidence of her life, they will never succeed in erasing her memory from the minds of her family and friends and, most importantly, from that of her daughter Emma, now fast approaching adulthood.

Deirdre Jacob

The summer of 1998 was an exciting time for County Kildare. Under the stewardship of Gaelic football superstar Mick O'Dwyer, the county's Gaelic footballers had qualified for their first-ever All Ireland final, beating Dublin, Laois and Meath on the way. That they were considered to be the underdogs in the upcoming final against Galway did not deter the football-mad 'lily white' supporters from enjoying every moment of the build-up to the game. For one Kildare family too, that summer would be unforgettable, but for all the wrong reasons. For Michael and Bernie Jacob, and their daughter Ciara, it was the start of a long search for their daughter, and sister, Deirdre, who disappeared without trace in July. Their search continues to this day.

With all the other missing females, there was a time-lapse between their final sighting, and the subsequent search launched by Gardai. In some instances, this delay was exacerbated by a delayed response of either a family member or the individual Garda to whom the report had been made. In the case of the disappearance of Newbridge girl Deirdre, however, there was no such delay. She had last been observed walking towards the front gateway to her home shortly after 3 PM on the afternoon of Wednesday 28 July 1998. When her mother Bernadette arrived home from work at around 6 PM, she was surprised not to find Deirdre there. Over the next hour, this surprise turned to concern. When she had not shown up by the time her husband Michael returned from work in nearby Lullymore at 7 PM, Bernadette knew that there was something seriously wrong. Both parents began to make frantic efforts to contact Deirdre's nearest friends and neighbours, none of whom had heard from her. They then called over to the Garda Station in Newbridge, to report their daughter missing.

Here, at least, their report was immediately acted upon. Teams of Gardai backed up by the public began a search of the immediate area at 11 PM that night, fearing that she may have fallen and injured herself. Early the following morning, more formal search teams were mobilised. Over the next few days, as the investigation intensified, the search-area parameters were broadened. The huge tract of bogland situated to the rear of the Jacob home was cordoned off, and a large number of persons were utilised in a grid-pattern search of that area. Garda sub-aqua units, augmented by a number of local diving clubs, concentrated their search along the banks and under the water of the nearby River Liffey. Indeed, at one stage there was even a partial diversion of the water flow to allow for further searches. All the searches failed to find any trace of Deirdre, or of property belonging to her. Furthermore, there was no sign of any area where a struggle or fight could have occurred.

★

Earliest enquiries concerned Deirdre's last known movements that Wednesday. She and her mother had spoken briefly before leaving for work at the Eastern Health Board offices in Naas that morning. She reminded Deirdre that the deposit on the flat she was to share in London while attending teacher training college was due to be sent over that day. Deirdre had already successfully completed the first year of the course, which was at Saint Mary's in Twickenham. She told her mother that she would visit the bank at lunchtime to pick up the deposit, which she would then post it. Mother and daughter arranged to meet back at their home around 6 PM.

Deirdre attended to various small household chores, leaving home sometime after 10 AM to make the pleasant, twenty-five-minute journey on foot into Newbridge town centre. She called first to visit her maternal grandmother, Bridget O'Grady, with whom she was very close. Bridget, then in her nineties, had for many years owned and operated a small sweet shop in the town. Deirdre also met with a few former school friends that morning; they had traded stories and gossip.

As with Annie McCarrick, who had visited her bank in Sandymount prior to her disappearance, and was caught on closed-circuit television, some of Deirdre's last known movements were captured on CCTV. Footage shows her purchasing a bank draft for £180 in the local branch of the Allied Irish Bank on the main street. She entered the premises at 2.20 PM. After leaving the bank, she then called to the post office and mailed the bank draft. She left there at 3.02 PM and set out on the journey homeward. Once more, the thoughtful youngster broke her journey to call into her grandmother's.

At least ten people, many of whom knew Deirdre well, later told investigating Gardai that they had observed her walking down the Barretstown Road, and then onwards towards Roseberry, heading home. As she passed the grounds of the Evangelical Church on the outskirts of town, a former school friend and her mother passed in their car. They exchanged greetings. A neighbour working on the roof of his house also recalled seeing Deirdre strolling along, and he shouted a greeting to her. Deirdre was observed, too, just before 3.30 PM, standing on the grass verge directly across from the entrance to her home, as if waiting to cross the road. This would be the last confirmed sighting of her by a person who actually knew her.

She cut an attractive figure, dressed in a navy Nike jumper with blue jeans and blue Nike runners. She also carried a distinctive black shoulder bag bearing the 'CAT' logo picked out in yellow.

★

The absolute normality of this scene makes her disappearance all the more bizarre. Deirdre was a bright, pleasant young girl from a stable and secure family environment, just on the cusp of a promising career as a teacher, something to which she had always aspired. If ever a case lacked a push/pull factor, then surely this was it. The last thing one would expect as they watched her ambling home was that, just minutes later, as she stood almost directly outside the entrance to her own home on a balmy summer afternoon, she would disappear, never to be seen again.

When her mother returned from work at 6 PM to find that Deirdre was not at home, she had, almost immediately, suspected that there was something wrong. Speaking years later on the Gerry Ryan radio show, she described her daughter as 'utterly dependable'. If she was going to be late, she would always let her mother know. Bernadette said that on not finding Deirdre in the house at 6 PM on that fateful evening, she panicked.

Her distraught family drew some solace from the sighting of a girl matching Deirdre's description, entering a café in the Tara Street area of Dublin a day or two after her disappearance. The sighting was immediately reported to Store Street Garda Station by two elderly females. Though never confirmed, the sighting had, naturally, to be considered and investigated.

Rumours spread, in the early days of the investigation, that some members of the travelling community had been driving around the area that afternoon in a white van, visiting relatives on a halting site a short distance from Deirdre's home. It would emerge, however, that the majority of the residents of this site were actually at a family wedding in Naas that same day. The fullest cooperation was afforded to the search teams by those persons still on the site. It was with their assistance that all potential hides or dump sites were fully searched without the necessity for a warrant.

As time went on, there would be other reports received from persons believing they had relevant information to offer the investigation. This included one alleged sighting that appeared to be hugely significant. A male, with a northern Irish accent, made a total of ten telephone calls to the Monaghan-based radio station Shannonside Northern Sound, claiming to have been driving in the Newbridge area on the date that Deirdre disappeared. He followed up these calls with a four-page letter, which he posted to the local *Leinster Leader* newspaper. In all this various contact, he claimed to have met Deirdre hitch-hiking while he was driving his lorry near the village of Clane, in County Kildare. He had stopped to ask her where she was travelling too, and claimed that she was trying to get to Carrickmacross in, located in County Monaghan. As this was actually on his route home, he offered her a lift. They had, he said, stopped briefly in Ardee, and he had then driven on to Carrickmacross, where he dropped off his passenger.

★

There was one particular reason why this information was taken as potentially genuine, both by the family and investigating Gardai. It was not generally known then to the public, but Deirdre had actually spent the weekend prior to her disappearance visiting Kingscourt in Cavan with friends. On both the Saturday and Sunday, they had gone into Carrickmacross for the day. It was this coincidence that lent even greater significance to the information.

The possibility that she might have struck up some sort of a friendship or relationship in the area around Carrickmacross was canvassed amongst local youths by Gardai, but no evidence was ever established to support this contention. The anonymous caller, however, persisted. The Jacob family spent many future weekends in and around Cavan and Monaghan, and across the border in Fermanagh, distributing Deirdre's photograph and carrying out their own enquiries at football games, parish socials and other public gatherings, in an increasingly desperate search for their daughter.

Despite repeated requests to come forward, reveal his identity and provide all the information in his possession, the caller refused to do so. In an attempt to identify him, Operation TRACE took the unprecedented step of releasing a recording of the caller to the media through the Garda Press Office. The caller spoke with a distinctive Monaghan/Fermanagh accent, and we felt that, by releasing the tape, it might either force him to come forward or trigger recognition with some family member or associate. We were amazed at the response we received following the broadcast of the tape, on 9 January 1999. We received in excess of one hundred telephone calls, all offering information in relation to the caller's identity. These included a number of persons living in a small village just across the border in Fermanagh. Some of these people identified the voice by name, and claimed that he lived in the immediate area. Earlier enquiries had revealed that some of the phone calls had been made from a public telephone box in that same village.

This posed a huge dilemma for us; we had no jurisdiction with which to follow up this claim. Extradition was out of the question. What is perceived by many of us at the coalface of law enforcement, is the huge anomaly that exists, whereby a person can only be extradited and brought to court for the purpose of being charged. Extradition of a suspect for the purpose of interview alone is not possible, no matter how the evidence stacks up. We could, of course, make a request to the Royal Ulster Constabulary (RUC), asking that they interview him on our behalf. In this case, we could only be present and ask questions if the person consented to allow us to do so. This was a less than satisfactory arrangement, that had seldom led to anything of evidental value being established.

The ever-resilient Hickey, through his personal contacts in the then RUC, quickly established that the male suspected of being our caller, Joe Robinson*, visited Monaghan town once a week, to shop in a local supermarket. Early on the morning of 21 January, we took up positions on the Irish side of the border. A spotter advised us that our target was en route, and we swooped down upon his Sierra car as soon as it crossed onto Irish soil.

★

The visibly shaken driver was taken to Monaghan Garda Station and, over the course of being interviewed about the abduction and murder of Deirdre Jacob, quickly admitted that he had been lying all along about being in the Naas/Newbridge area, and giving Deirdre a lift. The alibi he had provided us with immediately checked out. In addition, the RUC carried out a coordinated forensic search of his home, which he shared with his wife and young family. The only items of evidental value located in the search were a number of newspaper articles covering Deirdre's disappearance. To all involved, it was abundantly clear that any information he possessed concerning Deirdre's disappearance came from this material. He admitted, during the interview, that he had lost his young daughter in an unfortunate road accident for which he had been partially responsible, and said that his motive in making the false claim was driven by a wish to provide her family with some hope that she was still alive. Having suffered the devastating loss of a child himself, he said he was only too well aware of how they must have been feeling.

These revelations obviously came as a huge disappointment to us as investigators, but one cannot fathom the anguish that the Jacob family were, once again, forced to endure. The original information had carried them through six months of their loss, and was now, they discovered, total rubbish. Their incredible sensitivity of feeling was such that, on learning of this lie, Bernadette and Deirdre's sister Ciara still expressed their concern for the well-being of the caller.

In the case of Deirdre's disappearance, both the original investigation and the Operation TRACE examination proceeded incredibly closely. Daily updates were cross-referenced by both teams, investigative leads were followed to their conclusion and no line of enquiry was overlooked. In spite of all this, no trace of the missing girl could be established. It was as if the earth had opened and swallowed her whole. The theory most favoured amongst both teams of investigators was that she had been overpowered and dragged into a car or van, then taken to a separate location. This would indicate that her abductor had been highly organised and resourceful, and had pre-planned the snatch. In other words: the classic predator.

★

We did not, however, believe that Deirdre had been selected and targeted in advance. Rather, it seemed that her abductor was already hunting for a victim. A number of factors would have influenced whether or not the predator would strike on that day, and in that particular area. These would include finding a suitable victim presenting in a location in which it was safe to operate. To this hunter's mind, once satisfied that everything was in place, nothing could deflect him from going through with his plan. This theory places the unfortunate teenager in the wrong place at the wrong time. On this occasion, the wrong time had been the middle of a bright, warm summer afternoon, and the wrong place was just outside her family home.

Some eighteen months into the search for Deirdre, a sexual assault was made upon a female less than fifty kilometres from where she had last been seen alive, which bore all the hallmarks of an organised predator. His crimes quickly singled out Wicklow-native Larry Murphy as a person of interest to the investigation into Deirdre's disappearance. In the minds of both the media and the public, he would be tied to the disappearances of a number of the other females.

Murphy had pleaded guilty, in 2001, to abduction, sexual assault and attempted murder, and served out the majority of his sentence in Arbour Hill prison. Arbour Hill is unique, in that the majority of its one-hundred-plus prisoners are serving lengthy or life prison terms for serious crimes, which include murder and sex crimes. Although a high-security prison, day-to-day life inside is not as regimented as in the majority of detention facilities throughout the state. Rules governing fraternisation between prisoners are much more relaxed. Though visiting is strictly controlled, rules concerning physical contact between prisoners and their visitors, who undergo a rigorous search prior to entering the prison, are not so strictly enforced.

Amongst the many unofficial perks enjoyed by the prisoners, was the availability of kitchen facilities, in which many prisoners brewed their own vodka. Contained in plastic 7-UP bottles, at the time during which I visited the prison, it was openly on view in most cells you passed walking down the prison corridor. This illicit brew led to many an alcohol-fuelled night of talking among inmates who would normally not talk to one another. In the months leading up to my retirement, I learnt of one such conversation that had taken place in a cell, one night in early 2011. It is alleged to have taken place between Larry Murphy and another long-term prisoner. Deirdre's abduction and potential murder figured prominently as the main topic.

★

It is important that I stress that we have only ever heard one side of this alleged conversation. The issues outlined in subsequent paragraphs have not, to date, been formally put to Murphy, nor has he been afforded the opportunity to respond by denial or otherwise to them. Equally, I am not betraying any investigative possibilities, as these details have already been published in a national Sunday newspaper, and no attempt has been made, by or on behalf of any of the alleged participants, since their publication, to refute or dispute them. I have also met with and advised Deirdre's parents about the contents of this conversation. The details are set out here as they were dictated to myself and my colleague and personal friend from the Cold Case Unit, Noel Mooney, when we interviewed this other prisoner, who was, at that stage, incarcerated in the Midlands Prison. Noel would ultimately replace me, both as Sergeant in Charge of that unit and as National Coordinator of Operation TRACE upon my retirement. Not only is Noel a highly competent and professional investigator, he is also a fully certified psychiatrist – a formidable ally in any interview!

It must also be acknowledged that our informant was not what society would consider a reliable witness. The man had taken the life of another, in the course of a vicious assault, over a relatively minor debt. Any defence counsel would make great play on his motives in offering the information. I am, however, personally convinced that he genuinely recollected the specifics of the conversation that he had allegedly had with Murphy. He was serving out a life sentence. In my opinion, there could be no personal gain that he could hope to accrue from telling his story. Indeed, if and when word got out within the prison that he had spoken with us, it could have made life very difficult for him. 'Ratting' on another prisoner is rarely looked upon favourably by other inmates.

As with many men after taking a lot of drink, the conversation between the two allegedly turned into a bragging session, or, as Noel succinctly put it, a 'mine-is-bigger-than-yours phase of the night'. Each attempted to out-do the other with talk of crimes committed, for which they had never been caught. We were told that, during this conversation, Murphy had alluded to his involvement in the abduction of a young girl from outside Newbridge town some years previously.

According to our source, Murphy told him that he had been driving around in a non descript family saloon car, looking for a girl that he could snatch. He claimed to have casually tossed a number of children's toys across the backseat, saying that the presence of these innocuous items would reassure any female looking into the car. Neatly fitted into the back of the car was a child's safety seat, to serve the same purpose. Another ruse mentioned was the addition of a road map, laid across the front passenger seat, which could be picked up and held by the driver as he stopped beside an unsuspecting girl, and leaned across as if seeking directions. In addition, it was vital that the front passenger window be fully rolled down.

★

The source had claimed that, during their conversation, Murphy said he had pulled in beside a young girl on the roadside just outside of Newbridge, waved the map in her direction, and asked for instructions on getting to a particular place. When the youngster leaned in through the open passenger window to try to see where he was pointing to, he is alleged to have grabbed her by her hair, and roughly dragged her into the car, forcing her down into the 'well' of the front passenger seat. It was then suggested that he had driven away at speed. During this time, the victim had continued to struggle. We were told that he had taken a hammer from under the seat, and struck her head, knocking her unconscious. He had then, allegedly, driven a number of miles to an area where he had abused her, killed her and dumped her body.

We naturally questioned his motive in coming forward with this information, and what he hoped to gain by doing so. He told us that as a parent, who, in all probability, would never be there to protect his own daughter, he was terrified that Murphy might strike again. He told us that if, by supplying us with this information, he could save one girl's life, then whatever he had to endure in prison as a consequence of speaking with us would have been worth it.

Our contact with this man took place over a number of carefully pre-arranged and unsupervised visits to the prison where he was serving his sentence. From the outset, we emphasised that we were not there to make any arrangements or deals in connection with his detention. Telling us that he was aware of the reality of his situation, and that he would not even be eligible to attend a parole hearing for a number of years, he claimed that he was not looking for anything in return. When asked if he was prepared to go to court and give this evidence in a public forum, he said he would not hesitate to do so.

When asked if he was aware of how such an action might be viewed by his fellow prisoners, he said that he believed that there were very few of them who would have any sympathy for 'the likes of Murphy', and that, notwithstanding this, he was prepared to take his chances. Wearing a 'snitch jacket' (as he described it) for the rest of his life would be preferable to having the blood of someone else's daughter on his conscience. Knowing the violent nature of the crime for which this man was serving a life sentence, this was bizarre to hear. He added that he had 'done time' in solitary confinement, and would not be worried about having to go back into it again if it proved necessary for his own safety.

★

All information supplied by this prisoner to Noel and myself throughout our various prison visits was committed to writing in a lengthy statement, and was then signed and witnessed – without hesitation – by the prisoner. As an explanation for how an abduction could have taken place in such an open, public area on a bright summer afternoon, it must, at least, be considered a plausible scenario. Even allowing for other traffic being on the roadway at the same time, it could have happened so quickly that it would have gone unnoticed. It would have been over in a matter of seconds, with the victim so stunned, frightened and disorientated by the blitz nature of the snatch, that they would have taken precious moments to react, moments during which the car could have travelled a considerable distance.

A number of planned searches have already been carried out in the area in which our source claimed he was told the body had been concealed. In addition, all the information supplied is still the subject of rigorous and ongoing investigation. The majority of this evidence is already in the public domain via a number of press stories and, because of this, I do not hesitate to include it here. I will, however, reiterate what I stated at the outset, that what was related is just one side of an alleged conversation, and the other party mentioned in it must be afforded the opportunity to deny all or part of its content.

In addition, all cars, insofar as we could establish, that Murphy might have had access to at that time, were located and subjected to the most rigorous of forensic examinations, despite the considerable passage of time that had ensued. The various expert forensic scientists attached to the Forensic Science Laboratory in the Phoenix Park were consulted before this unusual line of investigation was taken. They had no hesitation in recommending that the tests be carried out, stating that, due to the advances in crime-scene technology, it could still be possible to locate certain trace evidence. The cars examined even included one which had been 'rescued' from a scrap yard in the west of Ireland, and was due to be crushed the very next day. Nothing of evidental value, however, was located. Our problem, in this instance, was that we could never comprehensively establish if the list of cars we had in our possession was either accurate or complete.

At least two tenuous links between Larry Murphy and Deirdre Jacob had been established through our investigations. At the time of her disappearance, he worked with a small building firm, based in the Wicklow area, that regularly did building and renovation work in and around the Newbridge area. Indeed, following his arrest, a number of persons had rung Operation TRACE to tell us that Murphy had, on that particular day, worked on their houses in the Newbridge/Naas area.

★

I myself have seen the firm's work diary for the week of Deirdre's disappearance. A number of Mohan's fellow employees were indeed on a job in Newbridge in and around that time, while others were employed on various jobs in different areas. However, the available records do not show exactly which employee was working on which particular job, or the day in question. It has never been established, either, where Murphy was supposed to be working, or was actually working, on 28 July 1998. The only person who could supply this information is the man himself!

As Deirdre strolled along the main street in Newbridge, setting out on her return journey home on the afternoon she disappeared, CCTV footage clearly shows workmen bringing building supplies into a pub that was then under reconstruction. Deirdre can actually be seen waiting as they carry planks of wood across the footpath and into the bar. It has been suggested that one of these workmen was none other than Larry Murphy. This suggestion is, however, totally without foundation. All those working there on that day were traced, interviewed and eliminated (TIE).

The second link established between Murphy and Deirdre Jacob came to light a number of years later. In December 1999, Deirdre's grandmother, Bridget Grady, then aged ninety-four, died. Sometime later, family members cleaned out her sweet shop, a chore that none of them had been able to face for some time after her death. While going through the paperwork that had accumulated in drawers and tin boxes, they came across a leaflet advertising the availability of a carpenter, for general building work. It bore Larry Murphy's name, and was one that he himself regularly handed out when canvassing areas for work. How it ever came to be amongst Deirdre's grandmother's possessions has never been established. Equally, we do not know if it was handed in at a time when Deirdre herself was present in the shop. Once again, there is only really one person who knows. The suggestion that Murphy ever carried out work in the shop is, however, without foundation.

While Murphy remains a person of interest in the Deirdre Jacob investigation, it is important that the ongoing investigation not go down the road of putting, in terms of potential suspects, all its eggs into one basket. It would be positively dangerous to do so; an open mind must be maintained at all times. Nowhere are the risks of adopting such an approach more evident than in the case of the Grangegorman murders, which we will discuss later.

Before closing discussion of this particular investigation, I should pay tribute to a colleague, Sergeant Seamus Rothwell of Newbridge Garda Station, who, for sixteen years, has acted as liaison officer with Bernadette and Michael Jacob, Deirdre's parents. I am aware that Seamus has always been available to the family and has always put their interests first. He is just what a true Family Liaison Officer (FLO) should be.

The Establishment
of Operation TRACE

Although there had, over the years, been a number of other high-profile disappearances, very little consideration had ever been given by investigating Gardai to the possibility of a connection or pattern linking one or more of them. This attitude in media reports and in the minds of the public changed dramatically with the disappearance of Deirdre Jacob. What up to this point had been no more than a feeling of disquiet expressed in occasional pieces by some investigative journalists, now blossomed, almost overnight, into widespread fear and panic, following what appeared to be the kidnapping of a young girl from outside her home in an idyllic, rural area.

Garda Commissioner Pat Byrne, dubbed 'P.R. Byrne' by the media, who frequently commented on his unflappable handling of each new problem, had quickly realised, following Deirdre's disappearance, the extent of the disquiet felt by the general public. The belief was being openly expressed that Gardai were not adequately trained to properly investigate matters of this nature. Satisfaction ratings with the police service, generally hovering around 70 to 80 percent, now dipped to a dangerously low level. Pat Byrne was also well aware that these same concerns were not going to go away. Commissioner Byrne knew that, in order to allay the genuinely held fears of so many people, a different approach to the investigation was urgently required.

The investigation of missing-persons reports was a particular field of police work that usually drew very little comment or interest. Unless directly affected by a disappearance, public interest in following up on individual cases was often, at best, cursory. The problem for the media, when reporting on individual incidents, was the very real possibility that, having hyped up the circumstances surrounding the disappearance of a particular person, they could be left with a lot of egg on their chin were that person to turn up voluntarily. In policing circles, missing persons were considered to be very much a 'local' issue, best dealt with by the nearest Garda station personnel and with little, if any, input from the more specialised national units.

It had now, however, reached a stage at which Garda failure to locate Deirdre and the other missing girls – disappearances which many now believed to be linked – was viewed as symptomatic of the low level of professionalism possessed by the Garda force as a whole. How, people asked, was it possible for such incidents to go unresolved, in a country of our size? Pat Byrne was only too well aware of these allegations of incompetence, and knew that they had to be addressed.

This placed the Garda Commissioner in a very unenviable position. Up to this point, he had staunchly defended the professionalism and thoroughness of the police work into these investigations, dismissing any murmurings of dissent from either the families or the media. Were he now to take any action that could be viewed as critical of demonstrating any concern about investigative procedure, he would, in effect, be admitting that he had gotten it wrong.

★

The investigation into Deirdre's disappearance was being personally headed up by Detective Chief Superintendent Sean Camon, the most senior investigative detective in the State. His team included some of the most experienced detectives attached to the elite National Bureau of Criminal Investigation (NBCI), based at Harcourt Square, in Dublin. Both Chief Camon and his team had previously been directly involved in the Fiona Pender investigation. Fiona was, in fact, the daughter of Sean's sister. Any suggestion that the Commissioner was casting doubt on the professionalism of NBCI could seriously undermine their role as the experts in crime investigations.

Another consequence would be the suggestion that Gardai were now questioning their own ability to properly investigate serious crimes. Almost a year to the day before Deirdre's disappearance, detectives investigating the murders of Sylvia Shiels and Mary Callinan (known as the Grangegorman murders) had charged a local drug addict, Dean Lyons, in connection with the crimes. Along with two other members of that Investigation Team, I had voiced our concern about the alleged culprit's guilt prior to his being charged. These concerns were dismissed out of hand by some senior Gardai. Within weeks of Dean appearing in court, another person (who had been arrested for an unconnected double murder) had made certain admissions concerning the Grangegorman murders.

A rift had quickly formed within Garda circles, between those of us who believed that it was wrong to charge Dean, and those who stoutly defended it. Commissioner Pat Byrne had allowed himself to be swayed by the force of argument and seniority of those claiming that Dean was the right man, and had actually congratulated the team for their work in his arrest of Lyons. This support had disastrous consequences when, within months, the Director of Public Prosecutions would strike out the charge against Dean, and order that he be freed from custody.

I have written extensively about that particular investigation elsewhere.

Were Byrne now, by any act or deed, to suggest that he had problems with the investigations into the cases of the six missing women, a number of which were still ongoing, it would certainly be seen as a serious indictment of his leadership throughout his tenure as Commissioner. At the same time, he could not be seen to ignore the open disquiet that was now being voiced at all levels, including, even, by several senior politicians. To this end, a compromise of some form had to be found, and quickly.

On the one hand, the existing investigations had to be supported. However, the popularly held notion that any one person or group of persons had been involved in one or more abductions could not be ignored. At that point, the concept of a cold-case review of ongoing investigations was unheard of. It would be another ten years before a permanent cold-case unit would be established. I was eventually appointed as Detective Sergeant in charge of that unit, when it was set up by Commissioner Fachtna Murphy.

★

It was decided that, in order to address the overall problem, a specialist investigative taskforce would be established to re-examine the investigation files into these six missing persons cases. The six cases had, as we have already seen, occurred between 1993 and 1998. Again, it was these same cases being highlighted by the media, with the suggestion that they were all the work of one single predator, or of a predator working as part of a team. We saw one example of this type of crime just a few years earlier, when the two aforementioned English vagrants, Shaw and Evans, abducted, tortured, raped and murdered two women, one in Wicklow and one in Galway.

Any taskforce that was set up, it was decided, should be case-specific and would not, under any circumstances, address any other cases. This rule was quickly overturned once the work of the taskforce began. In addition, TRACE was to have a single remit and goal. In time, we would find that the issue of the single remit was too confining, and prevented the unit from participating in a more hands-on manner in the investigations. The ramifications of this limitation were brought home to me most forcefully when, in response to a number of recommendations concerning his investigation that I made to the SIO of a particular case, I was reprimanded in writing, and informed that my brief was one of research only and, furthermore, that I did not have any investigative input or any role in the actual investigation! The role of each taskforce would be confined to establishing any commonalities existing between the various cases showing definitive links or, indeed, a common perpetrator.

The process for selecting members for the taskforce required addressing. As word got out about the Commissioner's intentions, speculation grew about the size and make-up of the proposed unit. It was assumed in certain quarters that it would be based at the National Bureau of Criminal Investigation, and that the personnel would be drawn from amongst the vastly experienced detectives attached to that unit. In several instances, some of those same detectives would have actually worked on one or more of the nominated enquiries.

Personnel from the NBCI were regularly dispersed countrywide, to assist local units in the investigation of serious crimes. Their range of expertise included serious sexual and violent assault, abduction, robbery and murder. As a consequence, they were considered the obvious choice for such a high-profile and prestigious operation. Unofficially, within NBCI, the task of choosing the members for the specialist team had already begun.

★

Ever his own man, Pat Byrne had certain ideas about whom he wanted on his taskforce. Given the uniqueness of the operation that he was putting in place, he decided to adopt a totally new approach to the setting up of the investigation team. He announced that he would appoint a senior officer with a background in crime investigation to head up the unit. This member, far from being just a figurehead, would actively participate in the investigation. He would, in addition, be given carte blanche to select his team members from anywhere within the nationwide Garda force. The only criteria would be that each member chosen must have already proven themselves in the field of criminal investigation. Tony Hickey, then Assistant Commissioner, Eastern Region, was the man chosen by Byrne.

Hickey, in many ways, was the obvious choice for this role. He was a career detective, with over thirty years' experience in the investigation of serious crimes. He had been centrally involved in the arrest of Shaw and Evans, for the murders of Elizabeth Plunkett and Mary Duffy, in the summer of 1976. He had also been the arresting member when Malcolm McArthur, wanted for the double murders of Bridie Gargan and Donald Dunne in July 1982, was found hiding out in the home of the Attorney General, one of the highest ranking legal officers in the State. Hickey was widely respected for his investigative abilities and his management skills, both within and outside the force.

In 1996, he successfully led the complex investigation into the circumstances surrounding the murder of Veronica Guerin. Guerin, an investigative journalist with a national newspaper, had, through her investigations into the drug lords of the Dublin underworld, made several very dangerous enemies in those quarters. She was callously gunned down on 26 June 1996, as she travelled back to Dublin from a court appearance at Naas District Court. Her assassins, who travelled on a high-speed motorbike, had come level with her car as it paused at traffic lights, at the Tallaght/Naas Road intersection. A fusillade of shots was fired into her car, fatally wounding her. At the time she was shot, Veronica was on her mobile phone speaking with a friend of hers, who happened to be a Garda detective. It was not even the first time that Veronica had been shot. In January 1995, a masked gunman had shot her in the leg as she stood at the front door of her home. A few months before that incident, shots had also been fired through the window of her home.

Her murder sent shockwaves through Irish society. Only three weeks earlier, Detective Garda Gerry McCabe had been shot dead, during the attempted armed robbery of a cash-in-transit van, at Adare, in County Limerick. A second Garda, Detective Ben O'Sullivan, had been seriously wounded. Their patrol car was rammed by a Pajero jeep, and a masked gunman had fired fifteen shots at them from an AK47 assault rifle, as they sat in their patrol car. Detective McCabe was struck three times, and died at the scene, while Ben O'Sullivan survived eleven gunshot wounds. Though the involvement of the Provisional IRA was originally denied, it was eventually admitted that it had been an 'unauthorised' action by four of their members: Pearse McCauley, Jeremiah Sheehy, Michael O'Neill and Kevin Walsh.

★

Sinn Féin members of Parliament, both north and south of the border, would, in time, actively canvas for the early release of these men from prison, under the Good Friday agreement. Sinn Féin leader Gerry Adams called, on 1 August 2000, for their release, claiming that had the Irish government wanted to exclude them from the Good Friday agreement, they should have written it into the agreement! One Sinn Féin TD was so concerned about the welfare of these same thugs that he actually collected one of them in his private car following te man's eventual release from prison!

The casual targeting of a journalist and members of An Garda Síochána was considered, at the time, to be symptomatic of the general attitude of major crim-inals, who appeared, to the public, to be operating with total impunity. The criminal gangs preyed on the needs of vulnerable addicts, where even the small-est debt or failure to pay invited disproportionate retaliation, often including their extended families when the addicts themselves could not pay up.

The gang bosses who, for the most part, hailed from a background of petty crime, displayed trappings of wealth hitherto unknown in this country. Their lieutenants strutted through local communities, engendering feelings of fear and envy. With their four-wheel-drive vehicles, their saunas and their holiday villas abroad, they were looked up to by the local youths. In their new up-scale houses, the religious imagery so favoured by their parents' generation had been replaced by the snarling image of a heavily armed Al Pacino, in a still from the film *Scarface*. To fund this lifestyle, they strictly enforced their regimes, often even amongst their own circle of friends and relatives.

At the time of Veronica's murder on 26 June 1996, Tony Hickey was the Detective Chief Superintendent in charge of the National Bureau of Criminal Investigation. He was tasked, by Pat Byrne, with investigating her death, and took up the investigation with his usual gusto. An Incident Room was set up at Lucan Garda Station, staffed by some of the best investigators that An Garda Síochána had to offer. One of the first pieces of equipment to be installed in this room was a blown-up image of a happy, smiling Veronica. Hickey maintained that having such a photograph was important, as it focused the minds of all the investigators on the human face of their work. This was a belief that he carried with him onto Operation TRACE; the noticeboard in our new operations room had blown-up photographs of all of the missing women.

So successful did the Veronica team (officially called the Guerin Enquiry) become that, eventually, an armed guard had to be placed on the station prem-ises, while admission to the investigation unit offices was electronically con-trolled. This was because of threats from within the criminal fraternity to burn it to the ground and, by doing so, to ensure that the fire took with it all the evidence it had amassed. Operation TRACE became the most wide-ranging and successful investigation into organised crime ever launched in this country, delivering a body blow to organised crime through arrests and drug and gun seizures. Death threats would be made against Hickey himself. With his typical knack for understatement, he greeted the threats with the laconic, 'We must be winning so'. This unflinching approach to the solving of crime, despite the personal cost, was the hallmark of his career. He refused to allow himself to be intimidated or bullied, no matter what the reputation of his target.

Two males, Brian Meehan and Paul Ward, close associates of drug baron John Gilligan, were convicted of Veronica's murder. Gilligan, nicknamed variously 'Little' John or 'Factory' John, had begun life as a small-time and singularly unsuccessful criminal, who concentrated on burglaries in lock-up factories in Finglas. At the time of Veronica's murder, his gang were being targeted by the Gardai in a covert operation, codenamed 'Pineapple'. That he graduated from minor crime to becoming one of the most powerful drug dealers this country has ever produced is testimony to the judicial system's failure. The fall of his empire would see a drop of almost 15 percent in all drug-related crime in Ireland, for that year alone.

Paul Ward's conviction was overturned by the Court of Criminal Appeal in 2002. The evidence upon which he had been convicted had been given by a former associate of his, one Charlie Bowden. Bowden had been another of Gilligan's most trusted lieutenants. The court ruled that his testimony was unsafe. He had been 'turned' by the Hickey team and, after serving a sentence of six years for firearm and drug offences, had, on his release in 2001, become the first person in this country to enter the witness-protection programme. He gave vital evidence before the courts against his former colleagues. Brian Meehan's conviction for the murder was upheld by the appeal court as late as 2006. He is now serving a life sentence, with a concurrent lengthy sentence for drug offences.

Two other high-ranking members of Gilligan's gang also gave evidence that brought his empire crashing down. One of them was Russell Warren, who was regularly referred to by Gilligan as being his 'bagman'. He received a sentence of four years, for money-laundering offences. It was estimated that Warren, personally, had laundered approximately €3 million of Gilligan's illicit haul of cash from the drugs trade – almost 20 percent of his empire's total profit.

John Dunne was convicted for his part in arranging the importation of much of these drugs through Cork port. That port was seen as a much safer venue for bringing illicit goods into the State, more so than the assiduously policed Dublin and Drogheda ports. Like his former gang-member friends Bowden and Warren, Dunne also gave evidence against Gilligan. All three now live under false identities, outside of Ireland. It is believed that there are still contracts for their murder.

The actual trigger man on the Guerin murder was identified as Patrick 'Gene' Holland. Holland, a former US Marine, had built up a reputation in the criminal underworld as a hit man for hire. By the time of Veronica's murder, he was in his late fifties. Age had not mellowed him, however, and he was still considered to be one of the country's most prolific and dangerous criminals, with a history of involvement in serious and subversive crime, stretching back into the sixties and seventies. He had, when it was fashionable to do so, been a member of the IRA, and of the Irish National Liberation Army (INLA). Gardai were satisfied that Holland had been the pillion passenger on the motorbike, who had pumped the bullets into Veronica from a .357 Magnum revolver as she sat in her car.

Holland had also murdered Dublin man Michael Brady, shot dead in 1995. In this case, the shooter had, once again, been a pillion passenger on a motorbike. Brady had been sitting in his car, waiting for the entrance gates to his apartment off Benburb Street to open. This particular murder had been carried out as a 'favour' for another notorious drug dealer, Marlo Hyland. Some ten years earlier, Brady had been convicted of the manslaughter of his wife, who was Hyland's sister. Other murders known to have been committed by Holland included that of Paddy Shanahan, a builder who was shot leaving a Crumlin gym in 1994, and Johnny Reddin, at the Blue Lion Pub in Parnell Street, in 1996. Holland was also suspected of involvement in the murder of Wicklow publican Tom Nevin, that same year. It would be Nevin's wife, though, who would later serve time for her involvement in her husband's death.

Marlo himself was shot dead in December 2006 by another former IRA hit man involved in ordinary crime, aided by some former associates, who identified his hide-out in a safe house in Finglas, Dublin. Anthony Campbell, an apprentice plumber who happened to be in the house doing repair work, was also taken out by the cold-blooded assassin during the 'hit', ensuring that no witness to the incident survived. Hyland's gangland associates suspected him of having ratted them out to the Gardai following the seizure of over €2 million worth of cannabis resin at Brown's Barn on the Naas Road on 31 July 2006. At that stage the gang was being targeted as part of a covert ongoing Garda operation, 'Operation Oak', which ultimately led to over forty arrests, and almost thirty charges being laid. Two of Marlo's closest lieutenants, John Mangan and Willie Hynes, were arrested in the Brown's Barn sting.

Holland was never convicted of the murders of either Veronica Guerin or Michael Brady, or any of the other crimes that criminal intelligence linked him too. He was, however, sentenced to a total of twenty years in prison for drug offences. This sentence would be reduced, on appeal, to twelve years. Holland always denied his involvement in Guerin's murder, and on his release from prison in 2006, he engaged the services of Giovanni Di Stefano, the self-appointed Italian solicitor, known in criminal circles as 'The Devil's Advocate'. Di Stefano later claimed that he had subjected Holland to a barrage of psychological tests that definitively showed that his client had not been involved in the murder. Di Stefano was later convicted by the English courts of a number of deception-related crimes, and received a lengthy prison sentence.

While all his public posturing and play-acting was going on, Holland, who had moved to London, would revert to type and, in 2007, was arrested, with a number of English criminals, in the process of carrying out a kidnapping. He would be sentenced to eight years in 2008. On this occasion, there would be no early release or appeal for Holland, who died on 19 June 2009, in Parkhurst Prison – a passing, I believe, mourned by few right-thinking persons.

The arrest of Gene Holland, on 9 April 1997, also brought to prominence a young detective who would play a vital role in the Operation TRACE taskforce. Marion Cusack was on secondment to the Guerin investigation from the Garda National Drugs Unit. She had been selected for her knowledge of the illicit street-drugs trade in Dublin's city centre. Though considerably junior in service to her peers on the team, she gained recognition and admiration for her investigative abilities. Marion gave evidence during the Holland trial that she was satisfied that he had murdered Veronica, evidence which she refused to withdraw or dilute.

Following his arrest in connection with Veronica's murder, and prior to his being interviewed, Holland was found to have had a transmitting device built into his shoe. It is suspected that he planned, during the course of his detention, to engineer a situation that could be used to discredit the thoroughness and professionalism of the Hickey investigation.

John Gilligan had left the country on the day before Guerin's murder. He had, in fact, come before the courts at that stage, charged with serious physical assault against Veronica. She had called over to Jessbrook, the equestrian centre that he had built on a ninety-acre plot of land at Mucklon, County Kildare, to interview him regarding the various allegations of drug dealing on 13 September 1995. Gilligan had reacted in the only way he knew – by beating her to a pulp.

While in England he lay low, but, in early 1997, he was arrested as he attempted to fly out of London carrying almost €500,000 in cash. He was remanded in custody, and Garda authorities sought his extradition to face charges in connection with Veronica's murder, as well as with various drug offences. With all the illicit money he had at his disposal, he fought this request tooth and nail through the English courts. Justice would eventually prevail, however, and on 3 February 2000, just a few short weeks into the new millennium, Gilligan was brought back to Dublin to stand trial. Iconic press photographs taken at that time, as he was led down the staircase from the aeroplane, show a diminutive man, totally overshadowed by two burly detectives on either side – hardly the most impressive first public appearance of our 'Public Enemy Number One'!

Gilligan was not convicted of Veronica's murder. However, he did receive a total of twenty-eight years in prison, for his involvement in the importation and distribution of over twenty tonnes of cannabis resin. This sentence was reduced, on appeal, to twenty years. During his sentencing, the trial judge commented that, 'Never in the history of this country has one person caused so much harm to so many people'. Far from learning from this lengthy sentence, Gilligan received a further sentence while in custody, for threatening to kill two prison officers and their families.

The jewel in his illegally obtained property portfolio, Jessbrook Equestrian Centre, was confiscated by order of the Special Criminal Court. Gilligan fought this order ferociously. The ensuing legal battle lasted until November of 2012, some sixteen years after the murder of Veronica Guerin. The order for seizure and sale of the lands was eventually upheld by the Supreme Court. The land and buildings had, at one time, been valued as being worth in the region of €6 million. They would be sold for less than a quarter of that.

During the course of his comprehensive investigation, Hickey even discovered that we had a corrupt copper in our midst! His all-encompassing enquiry led detectives to the front door of Garda John O'Neill's home. Over the course of one day alone, it was found that he had received over thirty calls from the phones of some of the targeted criminals. O'Neill, who was attached to Tallaght Garda Station, had, some years earlier, been awarded the prestigious Garda Scott Medal for valour in the execution of his duty – the highest award that could be obtained. Perceived by many of his colleagues as a good policeman who would go far, his arrest came as a total shock.

Neighbours in the affluent estate in Tallaght where O'Neill had resided later commented on the lavish lifestyle that he had seemed to enjoy. Following his arrest, they said that they now knew exactly where this wealth had originated from. In time, he pleaded guilty before the Circuit Court to accepting bribes from a total of seven separate criminals, including Meehan and Ward. By his own admission, he had, between November 1995 and October 1996, received more than £16,000 in bribes. This is equivalent to about €20,000.

On 3 April 1998, Judge Cyril Kelly sentenced O'Neill to a total of four and a half years in prison. When passing the sentence, Judge Kelly branded O'Neill as 'morally corrupt', adding emphasis to the 'huge disfavour' he had done both to his family and to his colleagues in An Garda Síochána. Members of the investigation team would later say that they had gotten almost as much satisfaction out of nailing this 'bent copper' as they had from bringing the gang behind Veronica's murder to justice.

The Hickey investigation into Veronica's murder highlighted, for the first time, the real extent of the drug trade in this country. The sheer amount of money that this business generated had often been speculated upon in the national press. Here, though, was actual proof of just how lucrative a business it really was. Criminals with histories of violence were becoming millionaires through crime, suffering and death. Our legislators could no longer ignore the problem, which had been highlighted for years by Gardai and media alike.

The fallout from the investigation led to the establishment of the Criminal Assets Bureau, and to various legislative clampdowns on money laundering. These two new laws would be brought into force within weeks of the murders of Veronica and Jerry. The Criminal Assets Bureau Act (1996), the legislative framework setting up the Criminal Assets Bureau (CAB), and the Proceeds of Crime Act (1996) were quickly passed into law. The gang bosses were now being asked to account for their enviable lifestyles. Assets were being seized, and money trails followed. This had a knock-on effect across the whole community; they all began to feel the heat.

★

The Guerin investigation led to over two hundred arrests of gangland figures being made, forty of whom would be convicted by the courts of various serious crimes. A considerable blow was struck when the investigation team disrupted a major supply chain for illegal firearms. There were countless searches carried

out on warrant, and these searches alone led to huge amounts of stolen or illic-
itly obtained property being recovered. Supply lines were disrupted or closed
altogether, bank accounts scrutinised and assets frozen. The criminal fraternity
began to turn against Gilligan and the remnants of his sordid empire.

Gilligan was released from prison on 15 October 2013. Between time served
in England and time on remand here in Ireland, he had spent almost fifteen
years behind bars. However, his former underworld associates, still smarting
from the storm he had brought down upon them, were not in a conciliatory
mood. Oblivious to all this, Gilligan started to push his weight around again. In
December of 2013, there was a failed attempt on his life. Gilligan, in subsequent
television interviews, rubbished the attempt, and in so doing infuriated those
behind it even further. Anyone with a modicum of intelligence, it seems, would
have lain low for a while. Not so John Gilligan, who had long ruled over huge
swathes of the underworld, through fear and intimidation.

On 1 March 2014, two gunmen chased him into his brother's house, at
Greenfort Crescent in Clondalkin. It was the same house where he had had his
much-publicised 'Welcome Home' party on his release. He was found cowering
in the bathroom, and was shot a number of times. He was then rushed to
Blanchardstown Hospital, where doctors managed to save his life. Media
reports at the time suggested that he had been wearing a bulletproof jacket
when he was shot. Gilligan would never have worn such an item, believing, as
he did, that he was virtually bulletproof, and that there was no one around who
would dare take him on.

On 15 March, Stephen Dougie Moran was shot dead as he walked from his
armoured jeep into his fortified home, at Earlsfort View in Lucan. Moran, a
man who had built up a considerable reputation for himself as an 'enforcer', had
been acting as chauffeur and bodyguard to Gilligan. Just two days later, and only
a month short of the fourteenth anniversary of his extradition from England,
Gilligan left the country by ferry, heading to a relation's home in Birmingham.
Once again, his movements were caught on camera by the media. If his last photograph had been less than flattering, then these new shots, portraying a
diminutive, wheelchair-bound figure, face contorted in pain and fear, huddled
in an overcoat and clutching a Dunnes Stores bag, were even more so. As a former colleague commented, 'How the mighty have fallen!'

If his work on the Guerin enquiry made Tony Hickey the only real candidate
to lead this elite unit, then, undoubtedly, several prominent members of the
Guerin investigation team were automatic choices for appointment to the new
team.

Gerry O'Connell had been one of the Detective Inspectors working on the Veronica team, and had played a leading role in ensuring its successful outcome. Gerry and Tony Hickey had worked together on a number of major investigations and, indeed at one stage, all three of us had served together in the old city centre 'D' district, during the seventies. He was known to be a methodical, thorough and dedicated investigator of the 'old school'. His inclusion would ensure that well-established investigative methods would form part of the team's approach to the enquiry.

Following the conclusion of the Veronica investigation, Gerry had been promoted to the rank of Superintendent. This promotion was due, in no small part, to his sterling work during that investigation. Of course, having been promoted because of his detective abilities, he was immediately rewarded for his expertise in investigative work, by being transferred back into uniform and forced to languish in a small rural town. This system of promotion within the Detective Branch has been in place since the mid-eighties, following successful lobbying for change by the Garda Representative Association (GRA) and the Association of Garda Sergeants and Inspectors (AGSI), to the detriment of its own members! Gerry was one of the lucky ones, in that he was rescued from his virtual exile by Tony Hickey, and brought in as the Superintendent in charge of the new unit. He would return this loyalty as a consistently hands-on leader. Marion Cusack was also seen to have earned her investigative stripes, and was brought into the task force.

Given the hierarchical rank structures in An Garda Síochána, Hickey needed a member of the rank of Inspector, to serve as second in command to Gerry O'Connell and, more importantly, to be sufficiently competent to take over in the event of Gerry's non-availability. This particular appointment was much sought after among members of the same rank, as it carried with it the potential of almost guaranteed promotion if the person proved themselves within Operation TRACE. The lobbying that ensued was considerable. However, Hickey had, in fact, already selected his man.

Mark Kerrigan had spent many years as a detective in the original Central Detective Unit (CDU), and had played an active role in most of the major investigations throughout the seventies, eighties and nineties. A tenacious and hard-working detective, who would confront any problems the unit might meet head on, Tony saw him as the perfect foil to the more pedantic Gerry. At this time, Mark, who again had been promoted from detective branch because of his abilities, was serving as a uniform Inspector in a rural town. Needless to say, Mark had jumped at the opportunity when it was offered.

The selection of two members of Sergeant rank was the next hurdle to be crossed. Hickey asked for Maura Walshe, a detective sergeant then serving in NBCI. Maura had worked for many years with that unit, and was considered to be one of their best investigators. She had played a central role in a large number of serious investigations during her service there.

Maura was so highly rated as a detective, that it was a regular occurrence, when famous Detective Inspector Ned 'The Buffalo' Ryan, leader of the original 'Flying Squad' in CDU, was putting together a team, for him to call for 'ten men and Maura', who was, as a consequence, as good as ten men! Intelligent and thorough, she was, no doubt, one of the better detectives in the job. Given the attitude at the time to women in An Garda Síochána, this was no mean achievement. Year after year, Maura represented An Garda Síochána with distinction as a marksman at the World Police Games.

Of course, this was where the politics of the job really came into its own. Some of her bosses, still smarting from being passed over for inclusion on the new investigation team, initially refused to let her go, saying that she was required for ongoing investigations. Tony, however, put his foot down, and within days Maura became part of the team.

His choice of second sergeant for the unit took many people by surprise. Pat Treacy had served, for many years, in the old CDU, and had eventually become the Incident Room Coordinator (IRC) in the Tallaght/Rathfarnham area. He had also been centrally involved in a large number of murders and other serious investigations in the Southern Region of the capital. One of the cases in which he had had a significant input was the investigation of the murder of Esther McCann and Jessica, a child she was in the process of adopting, in September of 1992. Due, in no small part, to Pat's detective work, her husband Frank McCann was later convicted of their murders, a grim figure whom we will meet again in this book. Pat had been promoted and transferred to uniform duties in Mountjoy Garda Station. Nicknamed 'Dick Treacy' after the comic-book detective hero, he was widely respected within the job, both for his professionalism and his investigative capabilities.

To summarise, the team now consisted of one Superintendent, one inspector, two Sergeants and one Garda. To fill his allocated quota, Tony Hickey now required one more member of Garda rank.

At that time, I was attached to the District Detective Unit (DDU), at the Bridewell Garda Station, in Dublin's north-inner-city area. DDU units are responsible for the investigation of all local crime in their area of operation. Normally, the unit consists of a detective sergeant and four to six detective

Gardai. This figure can, if required for any major investigation, be augmented by the temporary allocation of uniform personnel, colloquially referred to, while so employed, as 'buckshees'. If the situation warrants it, detectives can also be drafted in from neighbouring stations, and from NBCI.

I was employed full-time on the unit as an IRC, in the investigation of serious crime. The eighties and nineties had seen a huge increase in the number of murders in both the Bridewell District and in the city-centre area generally. Although officially attached to the Bridewell Station, I was often transferred to other stations to coordinate their major investigations. Over the years, I had built up a reputation for my work in this field.

Originally referred to as the 'bookman', the role of the IRC in a serious investigation is a pivotal one. He is required to analyse all information and evidence established during major investigations, to ensure that it is properly disseminated and acted upon, and to make sure that any further evidence thereby established is properly categorised and followed through to a conclusion. The IRC feeds information and investigative duties to the members 'on the ground', and ensures that all investigative steps are followed through. It is seen as one of the most important roles in the investigation of serious crime.

Oftentimes, the competence or otherwise of the IRC can be the difference between a successful outcome to an investigation, or a serious crime remaining unsolved. Overlooking or misinterpreting a particular statement or item of evidence can cause considerable delay, and can sometimes have fatal consequences for an enquiry. Many investigators actually shy away from taking on the role.

Once a culprit is charged with a crime, the IRC must, within forty days, prepare a full report, containing all the evidence established throughout an investigation for the attention of the Director of Public Prosecutions. It must also contain recommendations about the continuance or laying of charges against identified suspects. In major cases, this evidence can run to several volumes. I myself have completed cases that have involved over two thousand statements alone!

The previous year, 1997, I had been the IRC on the investigation into the deaths of both Sylvia Shiels and Mary Callinan (the 'Grangegorman Murders'). That particular investigation went on for a period of some six months, with almost three thousand witnesses interviewed and over two hundred males identified as persons of interest (POIs). A POI, to elaborate, is someone whose actions and alibis do not stand up to rigorous scrutiny and, as a consequence, require further investigation. They are not, it must be stressed, considered to be suspects. This is an important line to be drawn in legal terms, because once a person becomes a suspect, certain protocols and parameters must be introduced. Each person of interest has to be traced, implicated or eliminated (TIE) over the course of an investigation.

As was discussed earlier, in the investigation into the murders of Sylvia and Mary, a homeless drug addict, Dean Lyons, had surfaced as a POI and, while being interviewed by Gardai, had admitted the murders, and had subsequently been charged with Mary's murder. Based on our intimate knowledge of the investigation, myself and two of my colleagues openly questioned the reliability and truthfulness of Dean's admissions before he was even charged. In our opinion, Dean had not committed those crimes. Subsequent judicial review found that he was attempting to curry favour with Gardai, as well as being very suggestible and possessing quite a low IQ. Our stance brought us into open conflict with some of the most senior figures in the Gardai, and even led to our being cautioned about our behaviour by one senior officer.

★

Within a month of Dean Lyons' appearance in court, a male, arrested in connection with a separate double murder in the west of Ireland, had made unsolicited admissions to the murders of Sylvia and Mary. Following an investigation, the charge against Dean was dropped, and the enquiry would praise the stand we had taken, though, it must be said, it was never widely appreciated.

I did, however, receive numerous private messages of support from both within and outside An Garda Síochána, including from the brother of one of the victims. Tony Hickey was the most senior officer to come out from within the Garda and lend us his support. From the start, he too had expressed grave reservations about the laying of charges against Dean. Having the support of someone of that experience and repute meant a great deal to me during some of those dark hours I endured because of the position I had taken.

In early September 1998, I was visited in the Incident Room at Bridewell Station by a colleague, Bernard Masterson. Bernard had been one of the central figures in the Veronica Guerin Incident Room team. I also knew him on a personal level. In the time-honoured tradition of all 'bookmen', Bernard asked me what case I was currently working on. He told me, then, that he had been asked by Tony Hickey to see me.

Bernard said that Tony was, as I was no doubt aware, in the process of putting together a taskforce to examine the cases of a number of missing females.

He added that Tony had told him to tell me that he intended to put my name forward as a member of his new team, and wanted confirmation that I would be available. Without hesitation, I told Bernard that I would be honoured to be a part of it. To be chosen from amongst all my colleagues nationwide was indeed an honour. In time, I received a similar accolade when chosen from amongst the entire Garda force, to become the Sergeant in charge of the newly formed elite Cold Case Unit.

I was warned that I could not discuss Tony's invitation with either colleagues or family members until such time as my selection, and that of the other team members, was formally ratified by Pat Byrne. Only after his approval could membership of the team be formally ratified.

The waiting over the next few days seemed interminable. I honestly believed that this dream of an appointment would be snatched from under my nose. I had no illusions that, along with many new friends, I had also made a number of powerful enemies within the job, arising from the Grangegorman-case fiasco.

Finally, on 8 September 1998, word was passed down through official channels that I, along with the other five Gardai I have named, were to attend the inaugural meeting of the new taskforce the following week, at Naas Garda Station. It had been decided that we would work out of that station. Naas was considered the ideal location for a number of reasons; it fell within Tony Hickey's area of operation, was only a short distance from the Forensic Science Laboratory based at Garda Headquarters in Dublin, was close to Newbridge, where the ongoing investigation into Deirdre Jacobs' disappearance centred, and, equally, to Baltinglass, where a small Garda team was still carrying out enquiries connected with the disappearance of Jo Jo Dollard. Whether deliberately or not, it was also situated within the 'Vanishing Triangle'.

In a subsequent media briefing, Pat Byrne, flanked by Tony Hickey, introduced Operation TRACE to the public for the first time. He cautioned against undue expectations, stressing that, in none of the cases under consideration, was there a definitive crime scene, and there were no bodies. When asked if the Gardai were working on the theory that a serial killer was operating, he described it as an 'aspect that was being considered'. Tony Hickey further suggested that it was a theory that would be 'foolish to ignore'.

Our first meeting as a unit, which was chaired by Tony, was spent establishing the extent of the new team's knowledge of the six disappearances. My knowledge had been, for the most part, confined to what I had read in the media over the years. Most of the team were in the same position, a situation that Hickey said allowed us to approach the task with a more open mind. Our role in the re-examination of these cases was then made clear.

Formal introductions or renewed acquaintances were made. I had worked, for instance, with Jerry in the early seventies, and I would have crossed paths with Maura in several investigations over the years. Marianne was well known to me as we had both, at one stage, been based in the city's North Central Division.

All of us were cognisant of the huge responsibility being placed on our shoulders. Tony emphasised that this was the first time in the history of the State that a planned manhunt for a potential serial killer had been mounted. Notwithstanding the collective experience and expertise that we all, as a group, possessed, we were each of us then entering totally uncharted waters. The enormity of the task, together with the honour of having been selected to play a part in it, weighed heavily on each and every one of us. Even the physical make-up of the unit was unique: rank structures, we were told, would only apply in formal correspondence. Each of us would be expected to contribute fully in all our enquiries, from the most vital to the smallest tasks.

★

It was an unlikely grouping, which now consisted of one Assistant Commissioner, one Superintendent, one Inspector, two Sergeants and two Detective Gardai. Three of our number had been taken off uniform duties to work on the enquiry. Maura's background was in serious-crime investigation, Marianne worked exclusively in drugs, and I had been part of what was referred to as the 'Crime Ordinary' scene. However, we were all considered to have vast and quantifiable experience in our particular fields.

Tony explained that he had deliberately limited the unit to just six, because he feared that, given both the uniqueness of the task and the narrow focus required, some minute detail that could prove or disprove a line of enquiry could be lost in a larger type of investigation. 'Not merely are we looking for the proverbial needle in a haystack', he added, 'we are, in fact, looking for that same needle in six different haystacks!' Tony commented, furthermore, that our dilemma was such that we had no idea how many needles existed, or how we would recognise one. 'We are faced with another huge dilemma, in that we don't even know if the self-same needles exist, or what they should look like if we actually come across them.'

We were instructed to read up on all six of the cases, so that we would all possess an informed view of each of them. Each of us would then take an individual case, and proceed as if the actual disappearance that was allocated to us had only just then been reported to Gardai. We would also be ready to 'step in' should a member who was dealing with a separate case not be immediately available. For the first time in an ongoing Garda investigation, we would also be provided with a stand-alone computer system, and we were to ensure that all details and minutiae of the case we were given were entered onto our own, unique, database.

This system, as devised by Tony Hickey, was far in advance of its time: the year was 2008. I visited a police college in Chilliwack, in Vancouver, Canada, some ten years later, to hear the Royal Canadian Mounted Police suggesting a somewhat similar approach to the review of cold cases which, it was suspected, could have a common link. They were basing their advice on experiences following the investigation into the activities of Robert 'Willie' Picton, a pig farmer arrested in 2002, and charged with the abduction and murder of a number of females. Grotesquely, he fed the corpses of his dismembered victims to his pigs. In interviews with the police, he would claim to have murdered forty-nine women, though he was only ever charged with twenty-seven of the murders.

One item repeatedly stressed by Hickey at our inaugural TRACE meeting, was the necessity to keep anything we uncovered 'in house'. Given the nature of the hunt we were about to undertake, he stressed that nothing be leaked either within the force or to the public. He stated that over the next few months, our taskforce would be subject to massive interest from the media, and intense scrutiny. It was important that nothing be leaked, either inadvertently or otherwise. He made reference to the old admonition, 'if you want to spread a story, tell a secret to a policeman'. Any queries that we received from colleagues and friends concerning what progress, if any, we were making, were to be met by a noncommittal answer.

★

Gerry O'Connell was appointed our liaison officer for all queries, from both within and outside the job. In this instance, he was to refrain from adopting the time-honoured quotes attributed to Garda investigations of either 'No comment' or 'We are following a number of lines of enquiry'. At that time, the media were viewed by certain Garda management figures as 'the enemy': to be told nothing, and to be kept in the dark until it came time to go to court with the prisoner. Revealing any information about the progress of a case was never an option. Of course, all that actually happened was that you had media reports laced with comments attributed to 'a senior Garda said' or 'a source close to the investigation has revealed'. The possibility of using the media to the advantage of an investigation was seldom canvassed.

Back in the late seventies, following the abduction of German industrialist Tiede Herrema, Gardai had surrounded the house in Monasterevin in County Kildare, in which he was being held captive. There followed a protracted stand-off, with the culprits demanding the release of certain subversive prisoners in return for their hostage. The Garda Press office did neither themselves nor the strong police work involved any favours, when their daily response to media questions about ongoing negotiations was a vague comment that 'meals were supplied' to the participants. In another case involving the larceny of a famous racehorse, media personnel from all over the world began to turn up for the daily briefings wearing a trilby hat similar to that favoured by the Senior Investigating Officer. It was reckoned that he was the only person in the room who did not realise they were 'taking the mickey'.

Tony stated that we should remember that our investigations could turn on the smallest nugget of information provided from a family member, from an associate or friend of one of the missing girls or, alternately, from a member of the public. As a consequence, we were, at all times, to be approachable and available. To this end, our public profile was very important. Media enquiries were to be handled properly, with every query or piece of information received by the unit from all sources to be responded to and documented for cross-referencing and analysis.

One further, very important matter raised during our first meeting, concerned the issue of 'inter-police rivalry'. Tony told us to expect a certain level of resistance from within the force to our work, even from Garda members who had had an input, no matter how small, into the original investigations. We would probably find that it was those with minimal to no input who would be the most vociferous in their opposition. It was important that we, as a unit, did not create the impression that our sole ethos was to cast doubts or criticism on work they had already completed. We were to make it clear that we were just a separate facet of the ongoing investigation, rather than, as some already feared, a watchdog or fault-finder, there to point the finger for a 'slipshod' investigation.

★

Tony added that, while we had all been selected for our expertise and/or experience, if he found any of us implying, by our actions or statements, that we considered ourselves to be superior to our colleagues, we would, very quickly, find ourselves returned to our stations. An attitude like that would only alienate people from whom we might later be looking for assistance. More significantly, it would strengthen the hand of those opposed to our formation. It was important, he said, that we be aware at all times of just how deep this opposition actually was.

In the event that we encountered opposition from within the force to any enquiry or request we made to our fellow Gardai, we were to avoid confrontation and withdraw immediately. Any such incident was to be reported directly to him through Gerry, and he would ensure that it was dealt with at the highest level. This would include situations where particular members were not making themselves available to meet with us, or were found to be failing to cooperate fully with our investigations. Under no circumstances were we, either individually or collectively as a unit, to enter into any arguments or 'stand-off' situations.

A date was set for the holding of a general conference, to be attended by representatives from all of the teams involved in the original investigations. In each instance, the local Superintendent, supported by his Senior Investigation Officer (SIO), and his Incident Room Coordinator (IRC), was expected to attend. Each team would provide a briefing on the background and status of each investigation. Individual case conferences would be arranged later. The attendance of the SIO and IRC was ordered by the Commissioner's office.

Each team was directed to bring with them the originals of all documentation, records, exhibits and other relevant items that had come into their possession throughout the course of the investigations. Individual members of our taskforce would, in turn, take possession of the evidence relating to the case they were tasked with reviewing. This managed hand-over was necessary to ensure that there would be continuity in the possession and retention of all the amassed evidence. Where, for one reason or another, original documentation could not be made available to us, a certified copy was to be provided.

As I sat through our first briefing, it began to dawn on me that not every Garda we would be coming into contact with in our enquiries might share the same enthusiasm, at this stage, in relation to the investigation, and that all our diplomatic skills would be called upon on a regular basis. On a personal level, I could, to a certain extent, empathise with the feelings of the original investigators. I had just spent the previous twelve months having my work on the Grangegorman murders scrutinised, both from within and from outside the force. Indeed, at that very stage, the third investigation into that investigation was actually in progress! This, ludicrously, consisted of an investigation into the investigation that had been held into the original investigation. I fully knew, on the other hand, the importance of giving my entire cooperation to any review.

A further important aspect of our work (one that, at that time, often did not get the attention it deserved), was the necessity of ensuring that liaison was maintained with the families of the missing girls, and that they be kept briefed on all developments. In police procedure today, this is considered one of the most important roles in any investigation into the sudden loss or death of a loved one. We now have, as of the last ten years or so, qualified Family Liaison Officers (FLOs), attached to each major investigation, whose role it is to ensure that the families and other secondary victims are kept up to date on developments in an investigation, insofar as is humanly possible.

Prior to the eighties and nineties, such an approach was virtually unheard of. At best, some member of an investigation team would be told to talk to a family occasionally, without actually telling them anything. Years later, in my capacity as Sergeant in charge of the Garda Cold Case Unit, I would find that when talking to the families and friends of victims whose unsolved homicides we were reopening, one of the most common complaints was the manner in which they had been treated by the original investigators; at no stage had anyone let them know what was happening. Regularly, when they attempted to contact the only member of the team who was actually known to them, they would find that he had been moved to a different enquiry, transferred out of station or retired. When the investigation into their loved one's death was downgraded or put away unsolved, the family were often either never informed or were the last to be told.

One grieving mother actually told me that, after the murder of her son, the only way they were kept informed of the progress, or lack thereof, of the Garda investigation was through occasional contact with her husband by one of the lead detectives on the case. Though known personally to both herself and other family members, this same detective would not deal with any of the rest of them at any level. Following the subsequent death of her husband, even this totally inadequate conduit ceased. When, as a Cold Case Unit, we arrived on her doorstep, it was the first contact she had had from Gardai in over ten years!

Each team member of our taskforce was appointed to maintain liaison with an agreed spokesperson for a particular family. In addition, contact details for all the family spokespersons were to be maintained by each of us in the event of the non-availability of the contact Garda. This, itself, was a ground-breaking move, and one which, I think, reflected the more humane side of Hickey. Little did I know then that some thirteen years later, as my retirement approached, it would fall to me, as the only surviving member of the original team, and in my capacity as National Coordinator for the taskforce, to pass on these same contact details to my successors on the team. One of my last formal duties, on the day I retired, would be to ring Annie McCarrick's mother in New York, to pass on the name of my successor, who would be her new contact in the Gardai.

I would also witness, first-hand, the extent to which relationships between the Gardai and the family of one of the missing girls had deteriorated. When Tony Hickey and I had a 'surprise' visit to one of the families, we were told, in no uncertain terms, to leave the house before violence was visited upon us. We beat a hasty retreat!

As our first historic meeting drew to a close, Tony Hickey presented us with two separate tasks that he wanted us to have completed by our next meeting, set for the following week.

The first of these was the perennial problem faced, at that time, by all new investigations. Whilst it might sound great now that we were being trained in Information Technology, and that, for the first time in the history of the Gardai, were being issued with our own computerised system, in reality, we didn't even have desks to put the computers on! We begged, borrowed and stole every item of office furniture that we could lay our hands on, but were still a long way short of being properly set up. As with everything in our job, all applications for additional equipment had to be made through certain channels, and had to follow a set paper trail. However, the reality was that having the right contact could often circumvent all of that. Gerry O'Connell would prove invaluable in this regard. Drawing on all the contacts he had nurtured during Veronica's enquiry, we were able to obtain almost everything we needed.

There was one particular item of furniture that even Gerry, despite all his contacts, was unable to source. Tony had insisted that we should obtain six lockable, fireproof filing cabinets, each of which would be dedicated to an individual investigation. It eventually took a direct order from him to secure the promise of them being allocated to our operation. Privately, none of us held out any hope that we would actually receive even one. Two or three days later I was alone in the office when, to my surprise, a van arrived from the Garda Depot, containing not six but nine state-of-the-art fireproof cabinets.

I was handed a set of keys and, as the cabinets were being manoeuvred into position in the office, I opened one of them. I was shocked to find that the cabinet was actually full to overflowing with files and papers. With a sense of dread, I quickly checked all the others and found that they, too, were full of paperwork. When I brought it to the attention of the Garda who had delivered them, he told me that he had been ordered to deliver nine cabinets to our unit in Naas Garda Station. No one, he emphasised, told him that the cabinets were meant to be empty. 'I was', he added, 'only following orders'. When I suggested that it did not require an extraordinary degree of intelligence to work out that full cabinets were unlikely to be of any benefit to anyone, he asked me if I was attempting to insinuate that he was not fit for the job of Stores Delivery. With Tony Hickey's admonition ringing in my ears about not displaying any sense of triumphalism, I decided not to respond to that question. When I told him that the cabinets were no good to us full and that he should bring them back to the Depot stores, he very politely told me that his job was to deliver cabinets and not to collect them.

His attitude reminded me of a conversation I had with a friend and colleague a number of years earlier. This member, a good detective, had fallen foul of a particular senior officer and had been transferred to the Stores Section in the Garda Depot for a number of months in order to afford him sufficient opportunity to reconsider his position and to purge his contempt! Given his background and expertise in crime investigation, he was, on his arrival in the Stores, appointed to the task of separating the official-issue wellington boots that were to be issued to every Garda in the State, by size. When this chore was completed he was then moved on to the next level, where, armed with an indelible marker, he was to write 'R' or 'L' on each individual boot, thereby designating, for all time, the particular foot upon which they would be worn. He told me that, in order to ease the burden of his sentence, he began to mislabel the boots by both size and foot type. Not once, he said, in the three months he spent in the Stores, was his 'silent protest' ever twigged, and he regularly mused on the number of Gardai around the country who must, as a result of his sabotage, have spent a fortune with the local chiropodist trying to establish exactly what was wrong with their feet!

With this in mind, I began glancing through the contents of the lockers. File after file bore logos stamped across them, such as 'Top Secret', 'Confidental', 'For Commissioner C Branch', 'Do not photocopy', 'Do not remove contents without Permission', and so on. Becoming more and more concerned, I started to open all the drawers – the same designations appeared on all the files. I asked the driver where he had collected the cabinets, and he told me that he had found them in some offices beside the Stores in Garda Headquarters. The keys, he said, had been lying in a desk drawer nearby. Knowing the general layout of the Garda Depot, I quickly realised that the complex of offices he was referring to were those that housed that most secret and sensitive section of the Gardai, referred to in conversation, and even then, only in hushed, reverential, terms, by its designated name of 'C3'.

C3 is the section that deals with the gathering and dissemination of all intelligence reports within An Garda Síochána. Here, reports on movements, associates, property and crimes of subversive and other serious criminals are indexed and stored. Details of police informants, secret operations and various crime 'stings' were also included. C3 would be considered as the equivalent of the Garda Secret Service. Access to their office complex is carefully controlled and monitored. It is completely out of bounds to most officers, and to all rank-and-file Gardai. Years later, while involved in a very sensitive investigation, I and a senior colleague were granted permission to enter these hallowed offices, and to read a particular file. Throughout the entirety of our visit we were escorted, and at all times were in the view of another Garda. Note-taking and photocopying were strictly forbidden. On another occasion, during the course of a conversation with a colleague with whom I had worked for many years prior to his transfer to C3, I asked him what exactly he did in that section. His response was a terse, 'Sorry, but I am not at liberty to discuss my work with anyone outside of my section'.

★

Our Stores Delivery Garda had, in one fell swoop, infiltrated the security headquarters of the Gardai, and removed a vast quantity of its most secret files and reports, collected through years of dedicated police work. Not since Michael

Collins infiltrated the Intelligence Archives of the British Army, carefully stored in the bowels of Dublin Castle, had there been such a major breach of security in this country!

I told him what these cabinets actually contained, and advised that he get them back to headquarters immediately. As I spoke, I could see the blood drain from his face. 'No way', he said, 'am I touching that stuff'. He added that he could be ambushed and killed on his way back to Dublin carrying that 'sort of shit'. When I reminded him that it hadn't happened when he was driving down from Dublin, he responded, 'Yeah, but I didn't know what I had then, did I'. This, he said, was 'a job for the Special Branch'. Saying this, he ran out of the office, jumped into his van and drove out the gate of Naas Garda Station as though every hardened criminal in the country was on his tail!

This still left me with the rather thorny question of what to do with this treasure trove of intelligence. I rang Gerry O'Connell, who, in turn, rang Hickey. I don't to this day know whom he contacted or what he said, but within the hour the office was full of some very worried-looking detectives. Detectives attached to C3 are referred to in the job as 'Spooks'. On this particular day, however, it was difficult to say which of us appeared the most 'spooked'. The filing cabinets were carefully placed into an unmarked van parked against the back door of the station, and then escorted back to their home in the Depot.

Two senior officers then began to question me about which of the files I had read. On the one hand, I couldn't very well say that I never looked at them: I had, after all, reported the matter. At the same time, I knew that if I said I had read any of the files, I was going to face an inquisition. Taking the line of least resistance, I said that, on opening the cabinets and observing that the file covers all bore the 'C3' logo, I had immediately closed the cabinets and placed them under my protection. This response was greeted with silence. Eventually deciding that it was best all around to run with this story, they left the station after admonishing me not to say anything about this sorry breach of security to anyone. I, of course, agreed with this warning. Needless to say, the story was in every Garda Station in Dublin city before they arrived back at their base.

At our inaugural meeting, Tony also set us the task of selecting a suitable name for our new unit. The name should, he said, be all-encompassing, setting out both our role and the wide diversity of our cases. Mark Kerrigan took on this task with gusto. He asked us all for our suggestions, each of which he greeted with derision. It soon became very clear to us that he already had a name in mind.

★

Mark told us that, in his opinion, in our new role we were expected to ensure that all the established evidence in the various cases was in our possession, and that we would then have to review all this evidence, gather it all together and finally explore, through this same evidence, the possibility that a serial killer might be in operation in our jurisdiction. We all agreed with this summary. He continued that, in simple terms, this meant that we would have to Trace, Review and Collate all the Evidence. The initials, he said, formed the acronym TRACE, a name that perfectly captured the essence of what we were all about. We adopted it without any further discussion.

By week three, Hickey considered us ready to take on the task for which we had been established. That week passed in a flurry of meetings with the individual investigation teams and the structured intake of the various files, documents, exhibits and all other paraphernalia that any major investigation attracts. Box after box of paperwor, piled high in the office, was carefully separated by investigation. A formal conference, intended as a 'getting to know you' session, was arranged for week four, to be held between ourselves and all the various investigation teams.

On the evening of this meeting, six officers, accompanied by their lead investigators and Incident Room coordinators, sat down with us at Naas Garda Station. It was a meeting that was unique in Irish policing. Seldom had so many senior and experienced investigators from so many different parts of the country been drawn together to discuss such a large number of ongoing operations. It was obvious from the demeanour of one or two of those in attendance that their presence was not entirely voluntary. It was clear that it would be vitally important for us to sell the whole concept properly.

Tony Hickey opened the conference by outlining, in detail, the reasoning behind the establishment of Operation TRACE, and the role it was expected to perform in the various cases that had been chosen. He stressed that it was not intended as a fault-finding or blame-apportioning exercise. He asked for the cooperation of each and every individual involved. He emphasised the necessity that we be provided with every snippet of information available to the teams. He further requested that we receive every cooperation and assistance in dealing with local issues and sources. Ever the pragmatist, Tony told those gathered there that they should not oppose our involvement in their investigations but rather that they should welcome, support and encourage it. We were to be considered, he added, to be no more than just another facet of their investigation. In finishing, he again requested complete openness and transparency between the teams and ourselves.

He then went around the table, inviting a spokesperson from each individual missing-person investigation to present a full background report, and bring us up to date on current developments and ongoing enquiries. I was impressed, while sitting there listening and taking notes, to hear just how actively the investigations were still being pursued. The investigation, for instance, into Annie's disappearance, was heading for its sixth year, yet listening to the lines of enquiry that were still open and being actively pursued was both surprising and reassuring.

Hickey's request for openness and transparency was almost immediately responded to by one particular Superintendent present at the meeting, a man not known for his diplomacy and tact. There was, he addressed us all in a loud voice, an alleged political dimension to his particular investigation. As a consequence, he said, it could not be openly discussed at our conference. However, if the Assistant Commissioner so requested, then the Superintendent was prepared to sit down with him after the conference and brief him on that particular aspect of the investigation, insofar as he could. There was an almost audible intake of breath from all those present, went completely unnoticed by the Superintendent.

Whether this comment was genuinely based on his naivety, a calculated 'throwing down of the gauntlet' on behalf of certain other interests, or merely an attempt to establish early on the parameters of the information that he was prepared to share, we will probably never know. Whatever the reasoning behind his comments, it became the moment, as Mark later commented, when 'the canary in the coal mine died'. Suffice to say, Hickey, in a loud voice tinged with both anger and sarcasm, proceeded to tear this unfortunate, to coin an American phrase, a 'new asshole'.

In my twenty-five years' service in the police force, I had never witnessed such a public execution as that visited upon the hapless Superintendent. He was told that this was exactly that type of attitude that could skewer both his and our whole investigation. The dressing-down ended when Hickey expressed the fervent hope that in our research into his investigation, for the sake of his career and pension, we not find any evidence of the prevalence of this mind set. We were, he insisted, all experienced investigators, who could – and were – to be trusted implicitly with the source, nature and content of all information. He then adjourned the meeting for ten minutes, to allow all present to refocus their thoughts.

Whatever his intention had been in throwing down this gauntlet, it had backfired completely. All present were left in no doubt that, in Tony Hickey, they had met a formidable leader who would not allow himself to be bullied or his investigation to be compromised. Looking around the conference table, I could see the wry smiles on the faces of a number of those detectives who, in the past, had worked with Hickey, and had experienced his 'zero tolerance' policy for incompetence or pig-headedness. Needless to say, our meeting progressed without further incident, and ended with a commitment from all present for full cooperation and assistance.

★

Amongst the detectives present at the meeting that day was a good friend of mine, Martin Donnellan, an experienced and highly professional detective, whose reputation was known to us all and with whom I had worked in the past. He was flanked by two of the most competent and thorough investigators in Dublin city, Tom Rock and Val Smith. They were there to present the details on Annie McCarrick's disappearance and to update us on their progress.

At that stage a Detective Inspector, Donnellan, would, in time, go on to be promoted to Assistant Commissioner and eventually follow Hickey's footsteps and take over in NBCI. Martin would also show his commitment to the job when, on reaching the compulsory retirement age of sixty, he applied to the courts to be permitted to work on, although, by so doing, he would effectively he be working for half wages. His application was refused, notwithstanding the fact that those same members of the judiciary, to whom Martin had addressed his selfless appeal, are themselves permitted to serve into their seventies!

Adding Extra Cases

As our investigation gathered momentum, the studying, inputting and cross-referencing of all the information which had been supplied to us continued apace. It was a mammoth undertaking. We had received in excess of two thousand nine hundred statements, from the six separate investigations. There were over six hundred memos of interviews, each of which contained a short synopsis (not in statement form) of information which had been proffered, but had not, at that stage, been deemed relevant. Between the various investigations, there were four thousand separate questionnaire forms, each of which contained details of persons who had been visited in their homes and places of work if the locations were considered relevant to the ongoing enquiry. In addition, there were all those new lines of enquiry that had been generated following the publicity that had accompanied our formation.

To help in our research, we were allotted a dedicated database. This database contained reports into all sexually motivated crimes that had occurred in the State over the previous decade. A team of analysts had been set up, and was working flat-out in the Garda Computer section to ensure that all this information was available to us. We christened our database OVID: Offender, Victim and Incident Database. It was, as I have said, unique to the Irish police force, the culmination of weeks of hard work by our Computer section, assisted by our Research Unit.

Details of all sex crimes were included, ranging from larceny of underwear from clotheslines, through to voyeurism, frotteurism, and so on, and graduating onward to the far more serious offences of sexual sadism, rape and aggravated sexual assault. The theory behind this all-encompassing sweep of sexual deviancy was really quite simple. If a serial killer did actually exist then it was likely that there had been a progression in his level of offending or dabbling in sex offences. Research regularly shows that even the most violent and depraved sexual predator will begin his eventual career path of abduction, rape and murder at the most basic level, and will accumulate a history of minor sexual offences.

It is difficult, in this age of iPads, iPhones and personalised laptops, to comprehend just how new the use of computerised research was to policing. My personal usage – or even familiarity – with computers was minimal. Some other members of my new unit were similarly challenged, and senior personnel from the Garda Computer Section were sent to Naas Garda Station to instruct us in basic computer skills. In my own case, this necessitated lessons in switching on and logging in!

★

That same year, 1998, would see every single member of An Garda Síochána receive compulsory instruction in the use of computer software, prior to the introduction within the 'Job' of the much-heralded and long-awaited PULSE computer system (Police Using Leading Systems Expertly). This system would only go live in late 1999, after every single member in the force had received basic instruction in its usage. By the time of my retirement in 2011, it was of course common practice to issue personal computers for use during major investigations.

The OVID database differed significantly from our normal record-storage methods, in that it allowed us direct access to all intimate details of the crimes themselves, details that would not normally be available in the average crime statistics. Contact details of the original investigators were also included, to allow their opinions about a particular incident, suspect or offender to be canvassed.

While the computer system was the ideal repository for the storage of all relevant details, we would find, as our research developed, that it was limited in scope when it came to the actual analysis, collation and comparison of the information it contained. The successful outcome of the investigation of the majority of serious crimes is oftentimes dependent on either the results of the post-mortem examination of the hapless victim, or an analysis of the crime scene itself. In each of the cases targeted by TRACE, neither of these options was available to us. Indeed, we even lacked the proofs that an actual crime had been committed in any of them.

What we required was a system that could compare all salient details connected with the background and deviant tendencies of the aggressor, with any relationships, either real, claimed or suspected, between the victim and predator. We would also be reliant upon the adoption of other investigative tools and sciences that are not normally utilised in day-to-day investigations. These would include Geographic Profiling of home addresses, last known movements, regular haunts and so on.; Victimology, for the purpose of establishing if any linkages existed between the missing women, e.g. mutual friends and lovers, joint membership of social outlets, shared interest and hobbies; Modus Operandi (MO), that is, strong and persuasive similarities between the separate incidents; Signature Aspect, that is symbolic or ritualistic aspects of the cases; and a host of other facts and issues upon which we could base our comparisons. A brief explanation of these sciences, together with examples of their use, is set out hereunder.

Victimology, also known as 'Victim Profiling', is the analysis and study of every facet of the background, lifestyle, social habits, personality traits and relationships of the person against whom the offence has been committed. Through gaining an understanding of the victim, the investigator may also come to certain important conclusions about the perpetrator.

Details for consideration when creating a victim profile should include the last known activities and movements of the victim; their personal lifestyle, marital and employment status and details; friends and enemies; general background; and contact with the criminal justice system. It is vitally important that the Garda member tasked with establishing these details makes it clear that the information is required for the investigation, and no other purpose.

Awareness of a person's lifestyle may have contributed to their being chosen as a victim and can often provide certain indicators to the lifestyle of the offender himself. In the interaction between them the level of risk to both is an important facet. The chances that a particular person has of becoming a victim must be balanced against the risks that another person is prepared to take in order to carry out a crime against that same person. The old adage of a person being 'in the wrong place at the wrong time' does not apply in circumstances where either the person themselves, or indeed a particular type of person, has been selected and targeted by a predator.

The lifestyle of a low-risk victim will not readily place them in a situation where the offender believes that the chances of his getting away with the crime are at their highest. On the other hand, to the sexual predator, females employed in the sex business are in the high-risk category. In plying their trade they are placing themselves in situations that make them increasingly vulnerable.

It is important, however, in applying or using this science, that the investigator does not begin to apportion blame to the victim, suggesting that his or her lifestyle, dress, behaviour and so on, may have, in some way, directly led to their placing themselves in jeopardy. It would not be a quantum leap to envisage a situation in which an investigator's approach, potentially, be damaged if a totally non-judgemental approach is not adopted by all those concerned. For instance, if the investigating Garda were to decide that a particular sex worker had, because of her involvement in that trade, left herself open and vulnerable to abuse, he or she then may, as a consequence, not be sufficiently robust and professional in their subsequent investigations. A good investigator will go to great lengths to avoid falling into the trap of either blaming the victim, apportioning part of the blame or even assigning guilt to them.

In any investigation, a number of issues should be considered in the approach taken by the police in assessing the victim. These would include deciding whether or not they were a random victim of opportunity, or one that had been carefully selected. A normally cautious victim will provide a much more difficult target and, furthermore, dictate the approach and method of attack that will be taken. This will have a bearing on any assessment of the risks to himself that the perpetrator had taken prior to carrying out his crime, and, as a consequence, reveal a lot about his own physicality and background. Understanding how or why a particular person came to be selected as a victim, the initial approach or confrontation between victim and perpetrator, and how the attack was carried out, can, in turn, tell the investigator quite a lot about the offender.

Given that the selection of both the time and venue of a crime is, ultimately, the prerogative of the assailant, it is undoubtedly the case that these are elements that can provide certain clues as to the origin of the offender. This is the theory behind Geographic Profiling.

In order for a crime to occur, both settings and opportunity are required.[1] To ensure the successful outcome of any attempted crime, three elements are considered to be necessary.[2] They are:

(a)   Motivated Offenders
(b)   Suitable Targets
(c)   Absence of Guardians

Geographic Profiling is the methodology used in the analysis of the locations of the various scenes connected with a particular crime, or series of crimes, up to and including actual body dump sites. Analysis will concentrate on four major locations. These are:

(1) Area of first encounter with victim
(2) Area in which initial assault is carried out
(3) Crime scene
(4) Body dump site

It is a rule of thumb that a predator will, insofar as it is possible for him to do so, operate within a carefully designated 'Comfort Zone'. It has long been established, through empirical research, that an offender will only travel as far as is necessary in order to commit his crimes. The reasons for this are obvious; the more time he spends travelling on the open road, the greater the chance that he will, for one reason or another, come to the notice of a law enforcement agency. The simplest traffic stop can unravel the most thorough planning and preparation. This is particularly important where the offender is in the process of transporting the fruits of his crime, be they property or victims.

Sexual predators and serial killers, during the process of selecting and taking their victims, will use one of four identifiable search criteria, coupled with one of three attack methods.[3] These include:

Search:
(a) Hunter, operating within own space
(b) Poacher, travelling outside his own area
(c) Troller, that is, a random encounter
(d) Trapper, where the victims come to him

Attack:
(1) Attack on encounter
(2) Stalker, follow and watch
(3) Ambusher, attacks in area in which he has most control

The profiler will, in his analysis of the crime scenes, consider and take into account issues such as the day, date and time of offence; the movements of the victim prior to the incident; local geographic features; access to the crime scene (including streets, thoroughfares and availability of public transport) and, where it is suspected that a series of crimes are linked, distances between the various scenes. When selecting a particular area to carry out his crimes, the predator will, at the outset, ensure that he is familiar with his 'hunting ground' – that the area contains sufficient suitable victims, that his risk of being apprehended or disturbed is minimal, and that there are sufficient escape routes available to him should this become necessary. When satisfied that all these elements are in place, he has then found his comfort zone. As each of these matters is indicative of the choices made by the predator and are of certain significance to him or her, they, in turn, possess the potential to provide important information to the investigator.

One of the greatest living exponents of the science of Geographic Profiling is Doctor David Canter, founder of the International Academy of Investigative Psychology. In 1985, the London Metropolitan Police were investigating a series of over twenty serious assaults and rapes of females spread throughout London city and suburbs. The level of violence in each case had risen as the assaults continued: the process culminated in the murder of three further victims. Seemingly unconnected, Dr Canter established, however, that all the assaults had occurred within a short distance of a railway station. Working backwards through the crimes, he identified an area he believed the culprit resided in, and which had been his original comfort zone. He also suggested that the culprit either worked for or was very familiar with the local railway system. When arrested, the culprit would be found to live within the area identified by Dr Canter and that, furthermore, he fitted a total of thirteen of the seventeen characteristics that David had included in his offender profile.[4] This case was mentioned earlier in the book, in relation to the investigation into the disappearance of Ciara Breen.

Modus Operandi (MO),[5] consists of techniques, habits and peculiarities which the criminal will perform in order to:

(A) Complete his crime
(B) Effect escape
(C) Avoid capture

An MO is actually the distinct pattern that a criminal displays in the commission of his various crimes. MO is a learned behaviour, and is the method or manner of working that the career criminal is most likely to adhere to throughout his criminal career. The actual style can alter as his career progresses, either through his experiences or through his interaction with the forces of law and order. As a source of learning, instruction and education, few institutions can match the efficiency of the prison system. At its most basic level, the criminal quickly learns that forcing the front door gives him a better chance of avoiding detection in a house that does not have a burglar alarm than one that has all the deterrents in place. However, there will be certain habitual and established methods that the offender will follow.

★

In the commission of a crime, the presence of some particular act or object not required for the actual success of the offence is known as the Signature Aspect of the offender. Often referred to as the offender's 'calling card', it is a symbolic gesture or deed and is considered deeply significant to the offender. If he or she is denied the opportunity to perform a certain ritual or inflict a particular type of injury, the satisfaction derived from the crime will be diminished. These acts or peculiarities are considered to be indicators of the offendor's definitive personality. The signature differs, therefore, from the MO insofar as they are part of the culprit's emotional requirements or desires, as opposed to a component considered necessary to successfully carry through his crime. They are stable, and will, even with slight variations, have a common theme.

Examples of signature aspects would be the use of excessive force, abusive language, making his victim dress in a certain way or pose in a provocative manner, binding his victim in a certain way or forcing them to repeat certain phrases or expressions during the course of the physical assault. These acts will only be of relevance to the offender but are, at the same time, deeply significant to him.

The significance and importance that is afforded to the study of Signature Aspect displayed at crime scenes by both police and the judicial system is best reflected in the case of the American David Vasquez. Vasquez was convinced by his legal team that, in order to avoid the death sentence, he should plead guilty to the murder of a female in Arlington, Virginia, in 1984. Some three years later, another female was found murdered in the same neighbourhood, just a short distance from the first victim. Vasquez was then serving a life sentence. The investigators at the second scene, some of whom had been involved in the first investigation, became so concerned about what they found that, at their request, both murders were analysed by the National Centre for the Analysis of Violent Crime (NCAVC).

The NCAVC is a section within the Critical Incident Response Group (CIRG) of the Federal Bureau of Investigation (FBI) which provides behavioural-based operational support to police agencies worldwide. It consists of four separate and distinct units:

(1)   Behavioural Analysis Unit (BAU), Counterterrorism
(2)   Behavioural Analysis Unit, Adult Crime
(3)   Behavioural Analysis Unit, Child Crime
(4)   Behavioural Analysis Unit, Violent Criminal Apprehension (VICAP)

★

In 2008, I delivered a paper to agents at the BAU Adult Crime Section Headquarters on a Staged Crime Scene Investigation, becoming, in the process, one of the few serving Gardai to have ever done so. Staging is normally carried out at crime scenes to deflect suspicion from the person considered the most probable suspect. This particular case referred to an unresolved homicide that had occurred in Dublin city in the early eighties, and which I had subsequently been involved in reviewing.

The services provided by the BAU included crime and linkage analysis, investigative suggestions and tactics, interview and media strategies, expert trial testimony, and Geographic Profiling.

In the Vasquez case, in both the 1984 and 1987 crimes, the victims had been sexually assaulted and had died of ligature strangulation. Both bodies had been left nude, face-down and openly displayed. In addition, they had both been bound with what appeared to be venetian-blind cord tied around the wrists, over the victim's left shoulder and around the neck.

The signature aspects in both these crimes were so similar that it prompted a full-scale review, together with a number of other unresolved homicides. This eventually led to a linkage being made between three further murders, and a total of ten rapes of women who had survived. A local male, Timothy Wilson Spencer, was subsequently identified through DNA evidence as the murderer of at least three of the victims. He became the first person to be convicted on DNA evidence in the United States of America, preceded only by the conviction of Colin Pitchfork on the same type of evidence in England. He was executed in 1994.

DNA evidence was not available in the case for which David Vasquez had been sentenced. However, the circumstantial evidence surrounding the signature aspects was so convincing that it led to the pardon and freeing of Vasquez, who received the princely sum of less than $100 per day from the State for every day he spent in custody for a crime he did not commit.

The similarities between Vasquez and the young heroin addict Dean Lyons are significant. Dean, as I mentioned earlier, was charged in 1997 with the murder of Mary Callinan, one of the Grangegorman murder victims, a charge that would later be struck down by the courts. In both instances, the suspects had a borderline IQ of seventy, and the evidence against them consisted solely of their verbal admissions.

The failure by investigators to pick up on or even recognise the existence of certain behaviours or actions at crime scenes, in particular, where a series of crime scenes are being investigated, is referred to as 'Linkage Blindness'. When entering a crime scene, normally when the body is still '*in situ*', investigators should be constantly looking for behavioural clues that the perpetrator has left behind.

★

To demonstrate the difference between MO and Offender Signature, it is useful to study the career of the Whitechapel Murderer – the official name given by police at the time to a series of murders in the early nineteenth century. The culprit is more commonly known, of course, as 'Jack the Ripper'. In a three-month period in late 1888, a total of five sex workers were found ruthlessly murdered in the East End of London. A reporter with a local newspaper had claimed, at the time, to have received a letter from the culprit in which he had given himself the name 'Jack the Ripper'. Although this letter was accompanied by a body part, its provenance is likely dubious.

The MO used by the culprit in the selection of his victims was that they were all in their thirties and forties, worked the streets at night and had huge alcohol-abuse issues. As a consequence, their lifestyles contributed significantly to their vulnerability. They were all taken in the early hours of the morning, and then only on weekends. The signature aspects in each of their murders were remarkably similar. The five victims all had their throats slashed and had also been eviscerated. All these wounds were inflicted by a right-handed person. Their bodies were carefully displayed for discovery.

A further six murders were committed in the same area over the next two years. They were immediately linked to the other crimes. However, the wounds inflicted in these instances bore no resemblance to those found on the victims of the earlier killings. The complete variation in the signature aspect of the later crimes is enough to convince expert investigators who, in recent years, have attempted to analyse all the various murders, that they are not attributable to the same killer.

The importance of a database, with full search-and-comparison facilities, capable of providing information that could assist the fledgling TRACE task-force in their review of the six cases of missing persons, was becoming more and more apparent as our work progressed. Lacking, as we did, identifiable crime scenes or body dump sites, pathologist and forensic reports, or even definite last movements in all our cases, we would not be able to depend on the more traditional policing techniques and were, for the most part, reliant on witness recall. We revisited each and every reported sighting of the missing females, and assessed their reliability, accuracy and content.

A person's ability to recall exact sequences can be affected by a wide number of variables, which can include preconceived ideas about what they should be looking at, as opposed to what they are actually seeing. In many instances, witnessing an act of violence being perpetrated can lead to a partial shutdown of a witness's sensory perception, as a defensive mechanism to protect them from the reality of the traumatising assault occurring before their eyes. As a consequence, they will often have no difficulty in later recalling the raised hand, but not the actual blow being struck; the colour of the blood, but not of the assailant's hair; on the fact that the vehicle used in the crime turned left, but not the registration plate, colour or model.

In assessing the reliability or otherwise of a witness, a number of factors must be considered. These include deliberate attempts to mislead, hostility, gap-filling, reliance on assumptions, unintended bias, genuinely held beliefs, mistaken or false memories, suggestibility and introduced facts or memories. It is very important to be, at all times, cognisant of the fact that a witness, while sounding both genuine and believable, is still only human.

There are two cases that have been dealt with by the courts in recent years that best reflect this issue. In one murder investigation, although the assailant pleaded guilty to the abduction, rape and murder of his victim on a particular, verifiable, date and time, Gardai could not convince a neighbour of the victim that he could not have seen her leaving her house on the morning after her body was recovered. In the second case, the failure of Gardai to properly address a suggestion from a witness that he had observed the alleged culprit some distance from the crime scene at the relevant time, led to the charge of murder being struck down. Gardai believed the witness to be mistaken, but had not taken sufficient steps to address the issue.

The good investigator will always endeavour to substantiate any facts presented by a witness with some additional independent, verifiable fact. For instance, the witness who claims to have met Johnny so-and-so in a particular area at a definite time should be asked who else they had met either prior to or subsequent to their sighting, how they fixed the actual time, what the lighting conditions, weather and visibility were like, and where they were coming from or going to themselves. To accept a statement unchallenged merely because it appears to contain the information that fits in with the belief of the investigator, is as fraught with danger as is dismissing a statement because its contents do not gel with the 'facts' as perceived.

To address the problem with the limitations presented by the OVID programme, I was tasked with examining the various systems available and currently in use in other jurisdictions, for the identification and analysis of patterns and linkages between separate crimes. I very quickly found that there were a number of such systems available 'on the market' to law-enforcement agencies. These included the FBI model 'Violent Criminal Apprehension Programme' (ViCAP), the 'Washington State Homicide Investigation Tracking System' (HITS), the New Jersey 'Homicide Evaluation and Assessment Tracking' (HEAT) and the Royal Canadian Mounted Police 'Violent Crime Linkage Analysis System' (ViCLAS).

For our needs, it soon became apparent that the ViCLAS system was the most suitable. The other systems that I have mentioned above were, in our opinion, reliant on a lot of information being provided both from crime scenes and from post-mortem examinations – luxuries we did not possess.

★

ViCLAS was designed by four frontline Canadian Police officers: Inspector Ron Mackay, Sergeants Greg Johnston, Sharon Oliver and Gerald Seguir. It was intended as a replacement for the existing Major Crimes File (MCF), which bragged of having over 827 serious crimes on file, but was actually found to have never had a 'hit' between crimes. The new system, ViCLAS, was intended specifically as a central repository for the capturing, collation and comparison of all salient details of a crime or a missing-person report. It had been introduced into Canada, a multi-jurisdictional country, following the investigations into abductions and murders committed by serial killers.

A classic example of the type of cases it was intended to address were the various investigations into the crimes of Clifford Robert Olsen. We will be returning to this particular predator later, as he actually surfaces in the TRACE operation as a result of certain admissions he made. Olsen was convicted of the abduction and murder of eleven teenagers over a two-year period in 1980/81. A prison psychiatrist would later tell a parole hearing that Olsen had admitted between eighty and two hundred such crimes to him. He had flown below the police radar throughout his killing spree, but through the use of ViCLAS for all missing persons and other serious-crime reports it was hoped that this would never happen again.

All the various Canadian police forces must, by statute, complete a ViCLAS report on any major unsolved crime after thirty days. The law also specifies that, within a further sixty days, they must act upon any information that was provided to them through the use of ViCLAS.

The actual ViCLAS report consists of some two hundred and sixty-two questions, set out over almost ninety pages of a report booklet. On the face of it, this sounds like a mammoth task, but having completed a number of them personally throughout my service, I can say that, to the trained investigator, they are very user-friendly. Each of the questions they contain was drawn up to cover all aspects of an investigation by qualified psychiatrists, psychologists, forensic scientists, trace-evidence experts, investigators and interviewers. It is designed to completely eliminate all 'open-ended' questions – the 'ifs' and 'buts' that are the bane of every investigator. As a means of standardising data collection, analysis and retrieval, it has been found in all those jurisdictions worldwide in which it is in use to be completely without parallel. Indeed, so high would our praise of the system be that within the space of five years, the Gardai would have their own specialist ViCLAS unit up and running.

When I contacted the Royal Canadian Mounted Police in January of 1999 to enquire about obtaining a licence to use ViCLAS as a once-off investigative tool in the TRACE investigation, I learned that it was actually being used across the forty-odd police forces in England, Scotland, Wales and Northern Ireland, as well as several other European countries. The British ViCLAS facility was then located in the Police Staff Training College at Bramshill House, Hook, in Hampshire, where a dedicated team of trained analysts was involved in inputting and analysing the details of all major crimes committed in the British Isles, including all those so-called 'subversive' crimes in Northern Ireland.

★

The college proper was based in and around one of the most important Jacobean mansions in England, set in some two hundred and sixty acres of grounds about fifty miles south-west of London. In 2013, the British government put the entire complex up for sale. It is currently on the market for some £25 million. At that stage, the running costs of the college were reckoned to be in the region of £5 million per year.

Following introductions from the Canadian authorities, I had a number of telephone conversations with the Chief Crime Analyst, and also with the college authorities. Over the course of these calls, an invitation was issued to us to visit the faculty and input all the details of the various TRACE cases into the ViCLAS system. Not alone would the analytical work we required be carried out on our missing-persons investigations, but the salient details would also be cross-referenced for comparison with all serious crimes in that jurisdiction. This facility, including transport and accommodation, was offered to us free of charge.

Needless to say, while we as investigators jumped at the idea of being permitted the use of such an investigative tool, permission to travel, and to reveal the intimate details of a number of ongoing Garda enquiries, could only be given at the highest level, both within the job and from our political masters. There were, indeed, some of our own superiors who viewed this offer with suspicion, even in 1999! One got the distinct impression from some of the feedback we were getting that the same people doubting this, viewed our revealing these 'state secrets' as something akin to treason! Sanity, however, prevailed, and in March of 1999 Gerry O'Connell and I flew into London Heathrow, where we were met and transported, complete with copies of all our investigation files, to Bramshill.

Our first day on the campus was spent orientating ourselves with the various police-training facilities that were available. In addition, to the local 'Bobbies', a large number of the students were police officers from both current and former British colonies, spread throughout the world. There were representatives there from every police force whose administrative laws were based on the old Common Law process. The variety of police uniforms on view throughout the complex, as students went about their educational and practical training, was truly staggering.

What came as a shock to us, however, was the fact that, without exception, all the analysts involved in the inputting and analysis, far from being case-hardened detectives, turned out to be bright young twenty-somethings. Considering the graphic details of the cases that they were dealing with on a day-to-day basis, I was astonished at the young men and women's professionalism, detachment and extensive knowledge of deviant behaviour.

We would spend a total of eight days on the campus. The first day was spent in demonstrating how the appropriate case reports were to be completed, and a full day was then given to inputting each individual case. On the last day, a briefing conference was held, attended by Gerry and myself, and a number of the key analysts. It was suggested to us during the course of this meeting that consideration should be given by our team to the inclusion of a number of additional cases, as this would, in turn, provide a wider field of research for the ViCLAS analysis. They felt that confining the research to just six cases was not giving sufficiently wide scope upon which to base their research, and suggested that we include a number of other cases. They, in turn, would provide us with two cases from Northern Ireland that would broaden the geographic search parameters even further.

We were conscious, throughout, of the instructions we had already received, which strictly forbade us from taking on any additional cases. But when we told Tony Hickey that the analysts required the extra cases, he instructed us to get them together. We could, he maintained, justify this decision if a problem later arose.

We returned to Bramshill less than a month later. We brought with us, on this second occasion, sufficient data for inclusion on the ViCLAS system of the disappearances of Phyllis Murphy (last seen at Newbridge on 22/12/1979), Antoinette Smyth (last seen in Dublin's city centre on 3/4/1988), Patricia Doherty (last seen in Tallaght, Dublin, on 23/12/1991 and Marie Kilmartin (last seen in Portlaoise on 16/12/1993). While all of these disappearances fell within the area of the 'Vanishing Triangle', they differed significantly from our original cases in that, in each instance, the bodies of the missing females had been located.

We also brought with us details on two other cases, one of which referred to the rape of a young sex worker on 30 December 1994. Although two persons had been charged and convicted of this crime, the details were considered to be of interest, as the assaults had occurred a short distance from the areas where the bodies of Antoinette and Patricia had been located.

We were also in possession of all known facts surrounding the murder of young Dublin girl Layla Brennan. Although her murder had occurred on 1 March 1999, her body was only recovered some four or five days later, when we were still in Bramshill with the details of our first six victims. Significantly, she had been found in the Killakee area of the Dublin Mountains, the same general area as some of the other cases.

We were not to know then that some eleven months later we would be returning to Bramshill again, with the details of yet another serious case involving the abduction and multiple sexual assaults upon a young woman from Carlow town. In this instance, her death was only prevented by the timely intervention of two passers-by. Wicklow man Larry Murphy was arrested, and subsequently convicted of these crimes.

The analysts suggested, also, two other cases occurring in Northern Ireland, outside our jurisdiction. One of these cases concerned the abduction and murder of a German tourist, who had just arrived at Larne ferry port on 6 April 1988. The body of Inga Hauser had been discovered in woods in Ballycastle some two weeks later.

★

The second case that they felt might be of significance to our research concerned the disappearance of teenager Arlene Arkinson. A native of Castlederg, she had attended a discotheque in Bundoran with some friends on the night of 13 August 1994, and was never seen alive again by her family. The person in whose company she had last been seen alive was a native of southern Ireland, with a long history of extreme violence towards women of all ages.

Given that all of the cases whose details we brought with us to Bramshill are ongoing investigations, it would be completely unprofessional for me to set out, in any great detail, the outcome of the various analyses and comparisons that were conducted on our behalf by the ViCLAS analysts. The results and accompanying recommendations we received will, going forward, form part of both investigative and interview strategies.

While a number of these cases may be viewed as completely 'stand-alone' in nature, there are issues connected with common signature aspects, modus operandi and victimology that will, in certain instances, form the nucleus of further investigations and enquiries. Undoubtedly, certain similarities did present themselves, and they will all need to be addressed. While nothing was established to definitively suggest that a serial killer was responsible for a number of the disappearances and murders, Tony Hickey kept emphasising to us that denying the possibility was not an option.

Having seen first-hand the potential for investigative opportunities that were presented through the use of the ViCLAS system, Tony would, by the end of 2003, set up our own ViCLAS computerised search and storage facility within An Garda Síochána, staffed with trained analysts. I later spent a number of years working closely with Ronan Mahon, one of our chief ViCLAS analysists – an education indeed!

Salient details of the additional cases taken on by Operation TRACE at the request of the British ViCLAS analysts are set out here.

Phyllis Murphy

Philomena 'Phyllis' Murphy was last seen alive by her friends as she walked towards the bus stop at Ballymany, on the outskirts of Newbridge town, on the evening of 22 December 1979. She was laden down with Christmas presents, and planned to take the 7 PM bus to her family home at Rowanville, Kildare, where she intended to distribute the gifts to her siblings and widowed father.

Phyllis was looking forward to seeing the family reaction to the new 'afro'-style haircut she had received that same afternoon. She was not to know that they would only ever see her new hairstyle in sketches created by a local artist to help assist in the search for her.

Her naked body would be located by a Garda search team almost one month later, on 18 January 1980, at Ballinagee – a desolate, wooded area in the Wicklow Mountains, some forty-five kilometres from Newbridge.

Because Phyllis was at that time living away from home, an official missing-person report was not made until 8 PM on 23 December 1979. Her father reported her missing at Kildare Garda Station after learning, from her friend Barbara Luker, that Phyllis had been due to meet her coming off the 9.30 PM bus in Kildare town the previous day, but had not shown up. The third-youngest of ten children, Phyllis had only just moved out of the family home into lodgings in Newbridge the previous year.

An appeal for assistance from the public to help in the search for the missing girl was broadcast on RTÉ radio, on Christmas Eve morning, 1979. The family would spend the Christmas period scouring the highways and byways between Newbridge and Kildare town, in a desperate attempt to find some trace of their daughter and sister. Christmas would never again be the same for this close, loving family.

Phyllis had left her rented accommodation on the outskirts of Newbridge town, sometime around 5.50 PM on 22 December, with a blue denim shopping bag full of Christmas presents. She had spent the previous hour carefully wrapping each present, and writing the family members' name on their gift. She was also carrying a navy weekend case, in which she had packed a change of clothing.

She intended to socialise with her friend Barbara after finishing the family visit. Certainly, nothing in her demeanour or preparations suggested any change in these plans.

After leaving her lodgings, she had called into her brother's home, which was nearby, and stayed for a few minutes. She had then called to the Luker family home nearby, to confirm her meeting with Barbara later. She left to take the five-minute walk to the bus stop, situated outside the very popular and busy Keadeen Hotel, on what was then the main Newbridge-to-Kildare road. A number of persons, who were subsequently identified as having been in the vicinity of the bus stop at the relevant times, were later interviewed. They would all, from their testimonies, suggest that Phyllis had never arrived at the stop. Both bus passengers and driver would confirm that she had never boarded the bus.

Late on the evening of 23 December, a father and son were out walking through a wooded area some two kilometres from Kildare town, known as Colgan's Cut. Situated on the edge of the rolling plains of the Curragh, it was an area of wild gorse and scrub that was regularly used as both a location for lovers' meetings, and as an unofficial dumping site. For the latter reason, the father and son were not surprised when they found a pair of tan-coloured ladies' boots, and a new child's cardigan, still on the shop hanger. They would also find a piece of Christmas wrapping paper, which bore the poignant, handwritten legend, 'To Daddy Love Phyllis'. It was later confirmed that when Phyllis had left the Martin home, these same boots had been inside her weekend case. Someone had obviously opened her case, and, more importantly, torn open her carefully wrapped Christmas presents at Colgan's Cut between 22 and 23 December. Not realising the significance of this find, they did not report it to Gardai until 28 December.

Gardai involved in the investigation of her disappearance had immediately cordoned off Colgan's Cut. In follow-up searches a pair of brown mittens and a belt for a tweed coat were found. Inside the gloves, later identified as Phyllis's, was the sum of sixty pence (roughly seventy-five cent). This was the exact bus fare from Newbridge to Kildare. Her friends said that she had a habit of keeping her bus fare in her glove in order to avoid having to fumble for change when getting onto the bus.

Another significant find was made on 28 December. It was, however, some eighteen kilometres east of Colgan's Cut, at a spot on the main road between

Brannockstown and Ballymore Eustace. A man out fox-hunting located a navy blue weekend case together with a shopping bag full of Christmas presents. The bags were hidden behind a stone wall which bordered the roadside. Their position suggested that they may have been just dropped across the wall, as opposed to having been thrown over it. The man who made the discovery immediately brought them to the nearby family home of Garda John McManus, and handed them over to him.

John saw that the topmost present bore the handwritten note 'From Phyllis'. Realising their significance, he had immediately brought the items to Naas Garda Station. By coincidence, John would, only weeks later, also be the Garda member who located Phyllis's naked body during a planned search. Some nineteen years on, as the local Detective Sergeant, he would be part of the Operation TRACE team that would finally arrest the culprit for the murder of Phyllis.

The finding of her property so far from Colgan's Cut, and, indeed, from Newbridge, meant that Gardai now had to broaden their search parameters further. In the first week of January 1980, parties of Gardai were drafted in from neighbouring divisions to assist in searches, and a staged search was initiated in the hills and valleys between Turlough Hill Power Station and Hollywood village, the general area where the last bag had been located. Working on the tried-and-tested theory that a person dumping a body will carry it for the minimum possible period, it was decided at the outset to concentrate the search area with a radius of some two to three hundred yards from the nearest vehicle access roadways. Despite the cold and damp conditions, this task was attended to diligently and conscientiously by all who took part.

By the morning of 18 January, the search team had reached the densely-forested townland of Ballinagee near the Wicklow Gap. This forest was in close proximity to the Turlough Hill electricity-generating station. Personnel were allocated to both sides of the narrow main road, and the search commenced. John McManus was part of the sweep that was searching the forest below the level of the roadway. His position in the team put him about twenty feet from the roadside, and some ten feet below it. Sometime around 11.50 AM, he discovered Phyllis's naked body, partially covered by pine branches. She lay on her back, with her right arm crossed over her abdomen, and her left arm fully extended. Her legs were crossed, with the left leg lying across the right.

Years later, John would tell me that he had actually walked past the body, before fully comprehending what he had just seen. He retraced his steps as he did so, saying a silent prayer for Phyllis. Only then did he alert his colleagues to his grisly find.

Visual identification of the body would later be made by Phyllis's brother Michael John. To ensure that no doubt could be cast on this identification, a dental and fingerprint comparison was also carried out. This attention to detail would prove invaluable when, some twenty years later, we in Operation TRACE revisited the case.

Searches continued for further forensic evidence in the Wicklow Mountains after the discovery of the body. Some ten days later, a fire scene was located in a drain in the townland of Lockstown Upper at Valleymount, Wicklow, approximately seven kilometres further on from the body dump site. Various partially burned items were identified as having been either part of the clothing worn by Phyllis, or of the Christmas presents she had purchased.

Despite all the searches that were carried out, a number of personal items belonging to Phyllis that she was known to have had with her when she disappeared were never recovered. These included a silver charm bracelet with two charms, a silver dress ring with a large blue stone, tan-coloured high-heeled shoes and a small plastic 'clutch' bag which contained her make-up, cash and other personal property.

The taking of personal items as 'souvenirs' or 'trophies' is a well-established trait of the true predator. They assist him in continuing to act out the fantasy that he enjoyed as he engaged in the assault and murder of his hapless victim, and will also further act, for him, as a psychological reminder of his deed.

It is interesting, from a crime-scene-profiling perspective, to examine the relative distances between the various scenes connected with this brutal crime. The distance from the bus stop at Ballymany to Colgan's Cut, where the wrapping paper of her father's Christmas present was discarded, is five and a half kilometres. From Colgan's Cut to Brannockstown, where the bag containing the rest of the presents intended for her brothers and sisters was found, is eighteen kilometres. From there to the fire scene at Lockstown is some fifteen kilometres, and from there to Ballingagee, where her naked body was located, is a further six kilometres. This makes the total journey from snatch-point to body dump site forty-five kilometres. As part of the evidence for the subsequent trial in this case, this journey was undertaken by a car travelling at moderate speed – the sort of speed that a driver transporting a load like that in the boot of his car would take, in order to avoid attracting any unwanted interest. The journey would take forty-five to fifty minutes, depending on traffic, and other factors.

Some years later, the presents that Phyllis had so carefully selected and wrapped for her family members were handed over to them by Gardai, on 10 March 1987. They would serve as an emotional reminder of her sweet, kind and caring personality; she was a girl who lived, first and foremost, for her family – a gentle soul who was, if anything, too trusting and innocent in the ways of the world.

The post-mortem on the body of Phyllis Murphy was performed on the night of 18 January, by the State Pathologist in the mortuary at Naas General Hospital. Professor Harbison had been anxious to ensure that as little delay as possible occurred between the removal of the body from its makeshift grave to the completion of his examination in the morgue, to avoid the possibility of the loss of any trace evidence. He worked all through the night. It was his dedication and attention to detail that would, ultimately, ensure that the perpetrator of this crime stood trial.

At the outset he had taken a number of swabs from various body orifices. These included a total of seven from the vagina. Semen would subsequently be detected on these swabs. From both its condition and concentration, it was estimated that Phyllis had been murdered within twelve hours of intercourse having occurred. Some twenty years on, these same vaginal swabs would help convict her murderer. We should not leave this subject without first commenting on the fact that all the evidence offered by both male and female friends suggested that Phyllis had, by choice, retained her virginity. How sad it is to think that the animal that snatched her off the roadside as she was going to deliver Christmas presents to her family, would take even that choice away from her.

During the post-mortem examination, bruising was found on the inside of her thighs and knees. This, together with internal bruising to the vaginal wall, was taken as a clear indication of forced sexual intercourse. The pathologist also found a total of seven lacerations and bruises to the head and neck, and further bruises to her chest and limbs. Professor Harbison would suggest that the bruising on the arms were 'grip marks', while that on the inside of the knees was consistent with a forcible parting of the legs. The existence of any bruising of this nature is important when attempting to rebut any suggestion by the defence that a sex act had been consensual in cases of alleged rape. The actual cause of death was established as manual strangulation. The injuries to the neck area indicated that there had been violent compression for as much as one minute.

★

Professor Harbison commented on the degree of preservation of the body, both internally and externally, considering that it may have lain naked in the open for upwards of twenty-eight days. He reconciled the remarkably good condition of the body with the fact that the temperature had been consistently below freezing (given the time of year), and had lain in the shade of the forest at a high altitude. The body had, in effect, been refrigerated. The actual altitude at Ballinagee Woods is some eight hundred and fifty feet above sea level, placing it above the 'freezing line'. The temperatures during the times Phyllis was missing fluctuated between minus four and plus seven degrees Centigrade.

The similarities between this case and the murder of Marlyn Rynn, which occurred almost on the same day some sixteen years later, and about which I will be making further comment later, are truly remarkable. In both instances, their naked bodies were left exposed in wooded areas where, between predator activity and climatic conditions, any trace evidence left on the body would have been completely destroyed. However, the opposite was actually the case for Phyllis, and those same climatic conditions had contributed to the preservation of the evidence.

As the investigation progressed, a large number of males would, for one reason or another, come to be considered as persons of interest (POIs). This would occur because of their previous criminal records, because of some suspicious activities on their part, as a consequence of their alibis not checking out, or through being nominated as such by a third party. Those persons who could not be immediately eliminated were, in most instances, asked to voluntarily supply a blood sample for comparison with the swabs taken during the post-mortem examination. It is important to recall that, at this juncture, when these trace-evidence swabs and blood samples were taken in 1980, there was no such thing as DNA comparison. With the technology then available, all that could be done with them was to group the blood sample, and then to compare this grouping with the semen sample. It was generally considered a more useful tool in the elimination of suspects, rather than in their identification.

A separate Garda team was involved in, what is for most investigators, one of the most mundane tasks in any investigation: 'house to house' enquiries. Each member involved in this line of enquiry is allocated a particular area or set of streets. He must then visit every single household in his patch, and ensure that the whereabouts and alibi of every single person living or visiting there on the night of the particular crime are checked and accounted for. An individual questionnaire form containing all personal details must be completed in respect of each person in the house. These forms are then analysed and cross-referenced by the IRC in the Incident Room.

★

This line of enquiry, though tedious, regularly turns up people who actually had very relevant information in their possession, but were genuinely not aware of its significance. The drawback is that a household with a number of teenagers or young adults can be a nightmare, as you will seldom find everyone home together. An interminable number of 'call backs' can often be the outcome. The effectiveness or otherwise of this facet of investigation is completely dependent on the professionalism of the Garda making the enquiry. In Phyllis's case, the filling of one such form by a thoroughly dedicated and professional policeman would provide the first major breakthrough.

The questionnaire forms are normally a generic set of questions, adapted to reflect the requirements of that particular investigation. In the form used during the investigation into Phyllis's murder, the first four questions establish the identity of the person being interviewed. Question 5 asked if the deceased was known to the person being interviewed. The remaining questions were more case-specific. Question 6 and 7 asked if the person had seen Phyllis herself, or any suspicious activity, at either the Keadeen Hotel in Colgan's Cut or Brannockstown, any time after 6 PM on 22 December 1979. Question 8 was used to establish the whereabouts of the person themselves during the relevant times. In Question 9, the Garda member is asked to express his opinion about the person he is interviewing.

On 7 January 1980, Sergeant Kevin Derrane of Kildare Garda Station called to the home of a local man named John Crerar, at Woodside Park in Kildare town. Crerar, a retired army sergeant, would be just one of a large number of persons Kevin would call to that day, and for whom he would complete a questionnaire form. During the completion of the questionnaire form, in answer to Question 5, Crerar told Kevin that Phyllis was not known to him. When asked his whereabouts over the relevant time, Question 8, he said he had been in a local pub with several others whom he named, and that he had left the pub briefly at 6.45 PM to bring a friend home. He had then returned to the pub, where he had stayed for a further twenty minutes. He said he had then driven home, arriving there at 7.30 PM, and, after eating his dinner, had gone to work at the local Black and Decker factory as a uniformed security man. He had started work at 8 PM, and had not left the factory until 9 PM on Sunday morning. He had been accompanied throughout his tour of duty, he said, by another security officer.

This, in effect, gave him a watertight alibi for that Saturday evening, and all through the night. However, there was something about his demeanour and attitude that rang alarm bells in Kevin Derrane's mind. His police instincts told him that there was something contrived, or at least not quite right, about John Crerar and his story. As he signed off on Crerar's questionnaire form that night prior to handing it in to the Incident Room, he had, prophetically, written along the top: 'Would recommend that his story be checked'.

In July of 1999, some nineteen years later, while preparing the court file against Crerar, we would visit Kevin, who was since long since retired. He became quite emotional when we showed him the questionnaire form. He told us that hardly a day passed when he did not think about Phyllis, and her brutal murder. Something about Crerar had, he told us, convinced him that he had been involved in her murder. He had always hoped and prayed to see him, finally, being brought to justice.

Around the same time that Kevin Derrane was carrying out his interview with Crerar, allegations surfaced which suggested that he might have been involved in the sexual assault of two pre-teen female relatives. One persistent rumour that did the rounds was that one of the young females had been babysitting for him one night, and had awoken to find him in her bed. He only left when she threatened to scream and wake his own children, who were asleep in an adjoining bed. This information, coupled with Kevin's comment, led the investigation team to decide to have a closer look at Mr Crerar.

On 16 January 1980, Crerar had called by appointment to Kildare Station, where he met with D/Sgt Joe Higgins and D/Garda John Canny. He was again asked to account for his movements on the day of the murder. He told them he had spent the morning of 22 December Christmas shopping with his wife, and that sometime after 3 PM he had called briefly to the Black and Decker factory, and left in a portable TV. His work colleagues there gave him a tip for a horse, and, after leaving, he went into Kildare town to McWey's pub. He had shared his tip with a number of friends who were in the pub. Crerar said he had stayed on in the pub drinking, and that at some time during the evening had been joined by Paddy Bracken*, who was due to work the night shift in the factory with him that night. Between 6.45 PM and 7 PM he had left the pub for ten minutes to give a lift to a friend, who was carrying a full turkey and ham home. He claimed that he himself had left the pub at 7.30 PM and had driven home, had his dinner and then driven directly to work, arriving there at 8.10 PM.

He added by adding two further pieces of information. He said that he had left work at around 10.30 PM and had gone to O'Leary's pub to collect a turkey he had won previously. He was back in work by 11.15 PM. He also told the investigators that when he was driving home from McWey's pub earlier that night, he had driven on the route that had taken him past Colgan's Cut. The reason he had done so was, he claimed, to avoid the possibility of driving into any Garda checkpoint on the main road. As he was driving his new car on the Melitta Road, a spot very near to Colgan's Cut, he had heard a noise coming from the engine of his car. He stopped and lifted the bonnet lid, discovering that the battery had come loose from its moorings. He tightened them before continuing on his journey. He said that he had not seen anyone on the road.

In hindsight, this was a very astute way of relating the information, in case anyone had seen him or his Datsun 120Y car, purchased some two days earlier, in the area of Colgan's Cut, where some of Phyllis's property had been found just the next day.

The allegations concerning the sexual assaults were also put to him. He admitted the incident with the young girl who had been babysitting for him. He had been very drunk, but had desisted when she objected. There had also, he admitted, been some 'messing around' with another young girl who, he claimed, used to charge him fifty pence to kiss her. Neither of these allegations had ever been proven, nor had Crerar been charged in relation to them.

★

His wife Betty confirmed that that they had returned to the house after finishing their shopping at around 3.30 PM, on the day of Phyllis's disappearance. John, she said had eaten a sandwich, and then left to go to the bookies. His usual Saturday routine was to go to the pub for a drink, and to watch the horse-racing on television. He had returned home at 7.30 PM and, after eating his dinner, had then left for work.

A total of seven persons recalled seeing John Crerar in McWey's pub at various times throughout the afternoon of 22 December. One patron, Peter Maher*, confirmed that Crerar had given him a lift home from the pub sometime around 6.30 PM with his turkey and ham for the Christmas dinner. After dropping him off at his house at 6.40 PM, Crerar had, according to Maher, driven away as if heading home. The owner of O'Leary's bar, Brian O'Leary, said that Crerar had called to his pub shortly before 11 PM and collected a turkey for himself. He had left just after 11 PM.

However, by far the most compelling alibi evidence came from his fellow security officers at the Black and Decker factory, where he worked as a static security guard. Crerar had served in the army for thirteen years, and had then retired to take up this employment. Security personnel at the factory were all ex-army, and most of them would have served together in the local barracks. We would, during the course of our review of the evidence in this case, discover the close bonds that these former colleagues had towards one another. James O'Donnell*, the security man on the day shift, said that he was relieved at 8 PM by Paddy Bracken and that as O'Donnell was driving away some minutes later, he had seen John Crerar arrive at the factory.

Paddy Bracken told Gardai that he had been drinking with John Crerar in McWey's pub that Saturday afternoon, until around 6.50 PM. When he was leaving the pub, Crerar was still there. Patrick said that he started work at the Black and Decker factory at 8 PM, and that John Crerar had arrived at about 8.10 PM. They had been together for the rest of the night, except for a period between 11 and 11.30 PM, when Crearar had briefly left to collect his turkey.

All the various witness statements, including that of Bracken, effectively meant that John Crerar's whereabouts were confirmed at all times that afternoon, except for a period of one hour, between 7 and 8 PM. The evidence of both Crerar himself and of his wife Betty, however, placed him at home at 7.30 PM. This would have to be viewed as a fairly comprehensive alibi. Despite this, he was still viewed by members of the investigation team who came into contact with him as a person of interest. At that stage, all were in agreement with Kevin Derrane's initial assessment that he was a gentleman whose story needed to be 'checked out'.

On 6 March 1980, John Crerar returned, again by appointment, to Kildare Garda Station. He was one of eight persons whom Gardai had asked to call to the station on that day. A local doctor was in attendance, and each of these men were asked, in turn, if they were willing to voluntarily provide the doctor with both hair and blood samples. They were told that there was no compulsion on them to give them. Crerar agreed, as did the seven others, to give the relevant samples. During those few weeks, similar samples were taken from a total of forty-nine other persons of interest.

All the samples were handed over to Doctor Tim Creedon, who was then attached to the State Forensic Science Laboratory, throughout the course of the investigation. He mounted each blood sample on individual stain cards, and then discarded the container. The stain card bearing the sample donated by John Crerar was labelled '4/80 J Crerar 6/3/80'.

In his examination of the post-mortem swabs taken from Phyllis's body, each of which were contained in separate sterile glass tubes, Dr Creedon found that he could only detect the victim's blood grouping. He suggested, however, that given the standard of such tests at that time, he could not rule out the possibility that he had simply been unable to detect the blood grouping of the semen. This latter statement was very important, as it left open the possibility that there might, indeed, be further evidence available from the post-mortem swabs. This possibility would be revisited many years later, at a time when John Crerar must have quite confidently felt he had gotten away with murder.

Despite the fairly comprehensive investigation that had been centred around John Crerar, no further evidence that would have pushed the case against him across the line was established. Indeed, it was privately felt amongst the team that, barring some miracle or an actual admission from him – a situation considered highly unlikely – he would never stand trial for the murder. As the months turned into years, this hope never fully faded. However, as the new millennium approached, just such a development would arise.

Two local Garda officers would, over the ensuing years, ensure that the potentially important evidence found on the post-mortem swabs, together with the stain cards containing the blood samples from the various POIs, were not lost or misfiled. This was, unfortunately, a regular occurrence in historical cases, and something that I would often come across later, in my role as sergeant in charge of the Cold Case Unit.

Sergeant Christy Sheridan, the Exhibits Officer in the original case, had collected all the exhibits from the Forensic Science Laboratory on 22 July 1981. He retained them, along with all the original investigation documentation, in a locked press in his office at the old Naas Garda Station. Naas was, and still is, the Divisional Headquarters of the area, an area that included Newbridge and Kildare Garda Stations. On 20 December 1988, nine years to the day after Phyllis had last been seen alive, Christy contacted Garda Finbar McPaul of Kildare Garda Station. The new Garda station in Naas was now ready for occupation, and he feared that the exhibits from Phyllis's case which he had so carefully preserved over the years might be lost in the move to the new premises.

Finbar was the District Clerk in Kildare Garda Station, and had been attached to that station during the initial investigation of Phyllis's murder. As with all the other local Gardai who had worked on the case, it was one that he believed might one day be solved, bringing some for the well-liked local family who remained traumatised by their loss. He secured a wooden press for his office, and locked the exhibits into it. There was only one key, a key that Finbar, in all the coming years, would zealously guard.

Throughout the nineteen-eighties and nineties, the science of the forensic categorisation and comparison of blood and other bodily samples (including semen) would be turned on its head by advances in DNA profiling. DNA technology or, to give it its full title, Deoxyribonucleic Acid, had been around for a number of years. Its origins can be traced back as far as the Swiss physician Miescher, who first discovered the nuclei on discarded wound dressings as long ago as the 1880s. The DNA molecule carries all the genetic information of the donor, and, except in the case of identical twins, is unique to that person. All living things require the genetic information stored in their DNA to allow them to function and reproduce. To facilitate proper analysis, the science required that large samples of both blood and trace evidence from a crime scene or victim be available before any definitive comparison could be made, that would be able to stand alone as uncontested evidence in the courts. New advances in the science meant that samples as tiny as blood specks, and even degraded samples, could now be analysed.

One person who had followed these developments closely was Brendan McArdle, a Detective Sergeant attached to the Ballistics Section at the Garda Technical Bureau. Ballistics Officers, nowadays referred to by their American title of CSIs (Crime Scene Investigators), specialise in crime-scene examination, and are utilised in the search and examination for trace evidence at the scenes of serious crime. This is meticulous work, requiring total dedication and expertise. Brendan had, in his nineteen years in that section, been involved in the technical examination of most of the major crimes that had been committed in the State in the intervening years. A thoroughly competent and professional expert, he was considered unequalled in his profession. In time, he would go on to head the Ballistics Section. Although a native of County Louth, he lived in the Naas area, and was well acquainted with the Phyllis Murphy investigation.

Through various conversations he had had with serving and retired Gardai who had worked on the murder, he became aware that the post-mortem swabs and the donated blood samples from the forty-nine POIs were all safely and securely stored, and, more importantly, readily available. From the reading of Doctor Harbison's report, Brendan was also aware that trace evidence of semen had been located on the vaginal swabs. What he could not know was how good this trace evidence would now be, given the time that had elapsed. Would the fact that the swabs had not been stored under laboratory conditions mean that they would no longer be of any use? Would the standards used in the 1980s in the collection of such minuscule evidence withstand the rigours of time?

Brendan discussed these issues with Dr Maureen Smyth, of the State Forensic Science Laboratory. Maureen was, and still is, Ireland's foremost expert in DNA profiling and analysis. In her, Brendan found a kindred spirit. Instead of dismissing his suggestion out of hand, as so many others would have done, she agreed to examine the swabs, and establish whether any evidence still remained on them.

★

On 17 July 1997, Brendan collected Christy Sheridan, now retired, at his home. They travelled to Kildare Garda Station, where they met with Finbar McPaul. In their presence Finbar opened the press containing the Murphy report and exhibits. This was the first time in almost nine years that the press had been opened. Christy identified the swabs and stain cards to Brendan, thus completing the 'chain of evidence', which was so important if this case were to ever go to trial.

A few days later, Brendan handed over the exhibits to Maureen. Over the next few months, she would work on them in any spare time she had. On 13 February 1998, having completed all her tests and analysis, Maureen called Brendan up to her laboratory. Barely able to contain her excitement, she told him that not only was the seminal staining still available on the swabs, but, more importantly, it was, in her expert opinion, suitable for further comparative analysis. The only drawback was that our own Forensic Science Laboratory was not fully equipped, at that time, to deal with the actual analysis and comparison of historical samples. This task was normally performed for Gardai under contract, by a private firm called Cellmark Diagnostic Limited, who had their offices and laboratories in Oxfordshire, England. They performed similar work for a number of the British police forces. Up to the development of our own laboratory early in the new millennium, they continued to carry out this work on behalf of the Gardai.

The normal practice at the time, was that exhibits containing staining for analysis, together with samples donated by POIs, would be hand-delivered. When analysis and comparison were completed, the samples would eventually be collected by a Garda officer at the Cellmark premises in England. One of their experts, dependent on the outcome of their examinations, would later attend court in this jurisdiction, and present his or her findings. Although vigorously challenged in our courts by defence barristers, their evidence had withstood the rigours of cross-examination, and brought about some very notable convictions.

The actual work involved in the analyses and comparison of donated materials and crime-scene traces is both pain-staking and time-consuming. It is, as a consequence, enormously expensive. Payments were due on a test-by-test basis, as opposed to case by case. This meant that, to complete the testing for Phyllis's murder properly, the Gardai would have to submit all forty-nine blood samples that they had for testing, and then to pay for forty-nine separate tests. This would take up a huge chunk of the annual budget provided for DNA tests. Maureen also told Brendan that, in addition to the original forty-nine blood samples, there had been, over the intervening years, a further twelve persons who had been considered as POIs in the Murphy investigation, and from whom samples had been taken. To ensure that the investigation complied with the required standards, the additional samples would also have to be submitted for testing. This meant that there were now a total of sixty-one separate samples to be analysed and compared.

Although the news about the high quality of the seminal staining was something that Brendan had been waiting to hear about for months, the hard part would now begin. The problem was that he had to convince his superiors to invest huge sums of money in a system of testing and analysis that many of them were still very unsure of. The concept of there being something invisible to the naked eye that could link crime scene to suspect was proving a difficult sell in certain quarters of the Gardai. Throw in words like 'double helix', 'chromosomes', 'polymers' and 'deoxyribose' and, almost invariably, you would lose your audience. Nurtured on a regime of physical trace evidence, fingerprint technology and admissions by culprits, they were reticent to place too much faith in this new system. Add to this the overall cost of sixty-one separate tests, being able to convince those who controlled the purse strings that it would be a worthwhile investment to spend so much on testing samples that had sat in a drawer for some twenty years, was proving to be a difficult task. The one positive that Brendan had going for him was that he had Maureen Smyth's complete support.

After much lobbying and arm-twisting, the Garda authorities finally agreed to allow Brendan to submit the swabs taken during the post-mortem examination to Cellmark, to have DNA profiles created. Using a new process, the scientists were able to separate the spermatozoa and vaginal cells, and thereby isolate the semen donor's DNA. A full profile was created, which, in the opinion of the

Cellmark analysts, was capable of being compared with any profile created using the stain cards bearing the blood samples donated by the various POIs.

The next phase was to bring the bloodstained cards to the laboratory, to have the process completed. Here, however, was where the real problem kicked in. Brendan was told that he could now bring his samples to England to have them profiled and compared with the profile created from the post-mortem samples. However, some mandarin in the Department of Finance, for reasons best known to themselves, would only permit him to submit a total of twenty-three of the stain cards! They could not be persuaded otherwise, so, rather than run the risk of having the consent randomly withdrawn altogether, Brendan, without reference to the donors names, selected that number from among all the cards. On 18 September he travelled to Oxfordshire, where he handed over the cards to Matthew Greenhalgh, the manager of the laboratory. This date would prove to be significant for another reason, in that it was also the date of the establishment of Operation TRACE.

By mid-December, Brendan would learn that the testing had been completed on the twenty-three samples, and none of them matched the profile obtained from Phyllis. This news also had the effect of convincing those who had opposed the original testing that they had been right all along, and they would not agree to let him submit the remaining cards for analysis.

At that stage, Brendan approached Tony Hickey. They had served together on a number of previous investigations, and had formed a good working relationship. He outlined the developments in the case, in detail, to Tony, who was familiar with the original investigation. He had been a young Detective Sergeant attached to the 'murder squad' at that stage. Brendan asked Tony for his support in his capacity as the area Assistant Commissioner, in one final attempt to have the testing on the outstanding samples completed. Hickey was a very progressive policeman and, in him, Brendan found an ardent believer in the possibilities that DNA presented as an investigative tool. Tony knew that if he could bring the Phyllis Murphy case on board as another one of the cases targeted by Operation TRACE, he could obtain a budget to have the testing completed.

He was, however, acutely aware that were we to take on the case, and it was subsequently established that the profile did not match any of the other blood samples, he would not only have spent a sizeable portion of his budget, but he would also be playing into the hands of those who had opposed the setting up of TRACE from the outset. They would not hesitate to point out that, already, we were going outside the parameters that had been set for us. Furthermore, we were wasting scarce resources chasing non-existent shadows. Nevertheless, he told Brendan that he would get back to him in a few days.

Unlike some other senior officers in An Garda Síochána, Hickey was a great believer in obtaining the opinions of those who worked for him, prior to making any decision that would directly affect them. Our weekly TRACE conference was scheduled for the next day, and Tony very quickly brought us up to speed on his conversation with Brendan McArdle. He told us that it was the case that, in his opinion, we should be more actively involved, but then proceeded to outline the various pitfalls that he could envisage, should we fail to make any progress in the case. He canvassed each of us in turn for our opinion, and we all agreed that we should take on the case. I was appointed Incident Room Coordinator, and tasked with ensuring that all the documentation and exhibits were in place, and contained sufficient evidence to support a request for a prosecution, should we come up trumps in the tests. Tony conveyed the news to Brendan, and arrangements were then put in place with Cellmark.

Early into the new year – 1999 – and just days after the nineteenth anniversary of the finding of Phyllis's body at Ballingagee, Brendan McArdle travelled back to England. In his briefcase he carried a total of thirty-eight stain cards, one of which bore the name 'J. Crerar', the number '4/80' and the date '6/3/80'. Upon his shoulders, though, he carried an equally important burden. Not only did he hope for some closure for the Murphy family, and the opportunity to bring a rapist and murderer, who for almost twenty years had gotten away with his crimes, to justice, but he also carried the burden of the very real possibility that the science of DNA analysis would finally receive proper recognition and funding in the Gardai. To a lesser extent, he carried the reputation of TRACE itself.

★

The various samples were worked on throughout that spring, and into the early summer. Professor Greenhalgh was assisted in this task by two of the foremost scientists attached to Cellmark, Andrew John McDonald and Harkiran Kaur Amrit. During the first week of July they would contact us, and tell us that they had found a match! The chances, they told us, of the semen having originated from anyone other than the person they identified were approximately one in seventeen million. The name of the donor was, of course, 'J. Crerar'. The news was relayed to us by a very excited Brendan McArdle. Here was, if ever it was needed, vindication of the stance he had taken, despite all the opposition. It was news that would herald never-before-seen developments in criminal-investigative procedures throughout the country. As we sat there attempting to digest this development, Kevin Derrane's warning, written almost twenty years earlier, rang in my ears: 'Would recommend that his story be checked'.

It was decided to move quickly against Crerar. The one thing that we all feared was the possibility that news of this development would leak out, and drive our target underground. All our background work over the previous few months now kicked into gear. Crerar, we were aware, still worked in the security business. The Black and Decker factory where he had been working on the night of Phyllis's disappearance had long since closed, and he now worked in the security-control room of the Aga Khan's huge Sheshoon stud farm on the Curragh.

At 7.25 AM on the morning of 13 July 1999, as Crerar drove out of his place of work, his car was stopped by Gardai. Detective Garda Mark Carroll, a long-serving local detective, approached him and told him that he was arresting him for Phyllis's murder. At first, Crerar sat, stunned, mouth agape, unable to speak. As Mark pulled the car door open, though, Crerar reached across and grabbed a religious statuette off the dashboard. He blessed himself with it, before putting it into his pocket as he stepped out of the car. I could not believe my eyes. It was a surreal moment, on the one hand, knowing what this man was capable , and, at the same time, observing him invoking help from the mother of God! He was taken to Naas Garda Station, arriving there at 7.45 AM.

While Crerar was being 'lifted', another arrest was being made in Kildare town itself. Patrick Bracken claimed to have spent the night of 22 December working in the security hut with Crerar, except for a period of about thirty minutes after 11 PM. This, we now knew, could not be true. We were unsure of whether he had taken part in the abduction and murder of Phyllis, or was, for some other reason, giving Crerar an alibi. When told he was being arrested in connection with her murder, Bracken told John McManus, 'I did not kill anybody'. He too was taken to Naas Garda Station.

Following his arrest, Crerar was asked if he would voluntarily donate a further sample of blood, saliva and pubic hair. He readily agreed, and these were taken by a local doctor. To avoid the suggestion that there could have been any cross-contamination, Dr Maureen Smyth would herself prepare a DNA profile from these donated samples. She then compared them to the profile from the DNA extracted by Dr Greenhalgh. The results of her tests on the new donated samples were even stronger than those of Dr Greenhalgh. His figures had been based on the much larger English population. Based on the population of Ireland, Dr Smyth would say that the chances that the semen could have come from anyone other than Crerar were one in seventy-six million!

★

During his interview, Crerar had said that he did not know Phyllis Murphy. He further denied that she had ever babysat for himself and his wife, a rumour that we would later discover was rife in the community. He changed his original story, somewhat, when he told Gardai that on the night of 22 December, he and Paddy Bracken had started work at 8 PM, adding that Bracken had left the factory almost immediately and gone drinking, leaving him on his own. He had not returned until after 10 PM. This was another example of Crerar's preparation of a defence, just in case Bracken did not stick by the original story of the two of them being together for the early part of the night. He refused to answer most of the questions put to him, saying that he was acting on legal advice not to do so, at one stage telling Gardai that he wished to 'stay mum'.

Coming to the end of his period of detention, Crerar made a truly bizarre comment. After refusing to make any comment about the DNA findings and conclusions, he had added, 'I wish to God this never happened'. At another point, he turned to Bernie Hanley, one of the interviewing Gardai, and said, 'Jesus, what is going to happen?'

While being interviewed after his arrest, Patrick Bracken admitted to Gardai that he had lied to them in his original statement. He now said that John Crerar had not arrived at the factory until almost 9 PM. Crerar parked out on the road, and appeared to be fixing something under the bonnet. He had then driven away, and had not returned until nearly 11 PM. When asked why he had lied in his original story, he said that he was afraid that Crerar would lose his job had he let it be known that he had not turned up for work until 11 PM. He said that when Crerar did come in at 11 PM, he slept in a chair for the rest of the night. Bracken said that when he had heard about Crerar being questioned in connection with the murder, he had immediately regretted telling lies to cover for him. Describing how he felt after telling the truth after all these years, he said it was 'a load off his mind'.

Security man James O'Donnell, who had previously told Gardai that he had seen Crerar arriving at the factory gate at 8.05 PM on that Saturday night, was also re-interviewed. He now told us that he had not seen Crerar, and had lied because he himself would have been sacked for leaving the premises without being properly relieved by the incoming shift. Bracken, he added, had been on his own at that time when he was leaving.

Two further major items of circumstantial evidence were also established during our new enquiry. It emerged that Crerar had regularly performed static security duty at the Turlough Hill electricity-generating station, only a short distance from where Phyllis's naked body had been so casually dumped. Furthermore, other security colleagues told us that they could vividly recall seeing him washing out the boot of his car behind a shed in his workplace in the weeks after Christmas. In one instance, he had been seen pouring a kettle of hot water directly into the boot. Like the dumping of the body in the open in the hope that predator activity would conceal any evidence, he once again displayed a certain level of forensic awareness.

★

Crerar was charged that same evening with the murder of Phyllis Murphy. Throughout the day, as word spread that a person had been arrested for the twenty-year-old murder, an angry crowd of local people began to congregate outside the garda station. Rumours were rife about who the person being held was. The name of anyone unfortunate enough to be on holiday or not at his normal haunt on the day was added 'to the pot'. At one stage, it appeared as if the numbers gathered outside would overwhelm those of us inside the station. The crowd only withdrew when it was announced later that the man would be appearing in court on the following day.

Additional Gardai were drafted in on the following morning to police the courthouse. When Crerar arrived in a Garda convoy shortly before 10.30 AM, the angry crowd almost breached the hastily erected barricades. He was led into the courthouse in handcuffs, with his head covered.

At each subsequent court appearance, Crerar would go to great pains to prevent the media from taking his photograph. At the same time, escorting Gardai had to ensure that he was not physically assaulted. Things would come to a head when, on one occasion, as Crerar was being led into the courthouse, a member of the public breached the cordon and approached him in a threatening fashion. The escorting detective who was handcuffed to Crerar had, in an involuntary gesture intended to prevent Crerar from being assaulted, pulled down his hand, exposing Crerar's face to the media. This led to an official complaint being lodged against the Garda by the camera-shy Crerar, a complaint that was not upheld.

Crerar's trial opened at the Central Criminal Court the first week of October, 2002. The jury of six men and six women would sit through almost four weeks of evidence and legal argument, and deliberated for almost two days before finding him guilty of murder. On a personal level, I would have to say that it was the longest two days of my life. I cannot imagine, for one moment, what it must have been like for the family of Phyllis Murphy. Throughout the trial, they reacted with dignity and silence as the grim details of the brutal assault to which she had been subjected were outlined. As her killer was led away to commence his sentence, they cried quietly as they gathered together, remembering a sister so savagely taken from them and who, even in death, had been denied a basic dignity, by a neighbour whose wife and children were well known to them.

This case is a classic example of how misguided loyalties and an abuse of friendship can lead to a perpetrator of the worst crime imaginable being helped to avoid censure, ensuring an absence of closure for the secondary victim, be they parent, sibling or partner. Lies told to cover up wrongdoing in the workplace gave Crerar a cast-iron alibi that, for almost twenty years, remained unshakeable. I often wonder if the truth would ever have come out, if the scientific evidence had not been established. It is certain that he himself was not ever going to come forward and admit his crimes. One wonders just how many similarly unsolved cases are on the books, waiting for one person to admit that they had lied for whatever reason and, in so doing, had allowed a murderer to walk free.

This is the reality in so many of the Operation TRACE cases. All it takes is just one family member or friend to put their hand up and say they had lied – for whatever reason – and had provided a murderer with a false alibi.

John Crerar was brought to justice for the murder of Phyllis Murphy through a combination of old-fashioned police work, devotion to duty and an understanding of the power of modern-day forensic analysis. Kevin Derrane followed his policeman's instincts, and nominated Crerar for further investigation, and Christy Sheridan and Finbar McPaul ensured that the exhibits which would, in time, prove central to the solving of this case, were not swallowed up in the system. This, and the dogged determination shown by Brendan McArdle and Dr Maureen Smyth, together with Tony Hickey's foresight, all ensured that, despite official penny-pinching and intransigence, this case was finally resolved. Each of them must have felt immensely proud of the part they had played that November morning, as Crerar was led away to face a justice that he had evaded for so long.

Antoinette Smith

A day away from the stress and strain of trying to rear two young daughters on her own would cost twenty-nine-year-old Antoinette Smith her life. On 11 July 1987, after leaving her two daughters Lisa and Rachel with her estranged husband Karl, Antoinette travelled from her home at Kilmahudderick Court in Clondalkin accompanied by her friend and neighbour Mary Winters*, on the 56 bus into O'Connell Street in the city centre. The girls intended to take the night off, and it was arranged that Karl would keep his daughters in his mother's home.

Antoinette and Mary had gone into a record shop on nearby Westmoreland Street, where they bought two Bowie souvenir T-shirts. They slipped them on in the toilets in Burgerland, on O'Connell Street. The logo read 'Slane 87, David Bowie, Big Country'. Prior to this, she had been wearing a blue T-shirt that bore the logo 'No Problem', which she placed into a black Texaco bag she was carrying. It would be on this same Westmoreland Street that, some twelve hours later, Antoinette would last be seen alive. After buying their T-shirts, both girls had gone to the nearby temporary CIE ticket office, where they bought bus and concert tickets for the David Bowie open-air concert in the grounds of Slane Castle. Avid Bowie fans, both girls had been looking forward to this day for many months.

Antoinette had previously arranged to meet her brother Cyril at around 5 PM at the public toilets of the concert venue. However, she had been enjoying the concert so much that the meeting completely slipped her mind. During the concert, the two girls had purchased some food from one of the franchised chip vans. By coincidence, they knew the two men, Gerard and Tony, who operated the van: they normally operated the chip van in the Kilmahudderick housing estate, and both females were regular customers. They had a brief conversation, and had then gone back to the concert.

When it was over, Antoinette and Mary travelled back on one of the specially allocated concert buses into Dublin city. They left the bus opposite the old Dublin County Council offices on Parnell Square just after 11 PM and walked the short distance to a disco on Parnell Street called 'La Mirage'. They had been drinking steadily throughout the day, and had a few more drinks in the club. Mary later told Gardai that they were both 'fairly drunk'.

Sometime around 1 AM on the Sunday morning, two male acquaintances of theirs arrived at the disco. Tom Murphy* and Tom Doyle* were both from the Ballymun area. Murphy was an occasional boyfriend of Antoinette's, since her separation from her husband, Karl, in January of that year. She had obtained a barring order against Karl from the courts. Murphy had stayed over in her home on a few occasions. To complicate matters further, Murphy had, during that same period, had a one-night stand with Mary, while Doyle and she had been having a casual relationship.

★

The four of them stayed together until the disco had finished. Antoinette had danced a number of times with Doyle and, at the end of the night, had invited him back to Mary's home with her where she was staying that night. He had declined, saying that he and Murphy intended to go home to Ballymun. Murphy would later describe Antoinette as being 'very merry'.

As they were leaving the club, an argument developed between Antoinette and Mary. There are two versions as to its cause. Mary maintains that she had grown angry with Antoinette over her insistence that they bring Murphy and Doyle back to Mary's house. She had also suggested that Mary sleep with Murphy while she would sleep with Doyle. Doyle claimed that the argument arose when Antoinette suggested that they go home, but that Mary wanted to go on to a club in Leeson Street.

Whatever the reason for the argument, it ended with Mary throwing the key of her house at Antoinette and storming off. The argument was witnessed by one of the bouncers working on the door of La Mirage. In one of those many twists that life can bring, the key that Mary threw at Antoinette that night would ultimately be used to identify her skeletal remains.

After Mary left, Antoinette had remained talking to the two 'Toms' for about ten minutes. They walked as far as the taxi rank on O'Connell Street, where the two men had taken a taxi home to Ballymun. It was then around 2.30 AM on Sunday morning, and the two men had watched as Antoinette continued walking alone down O'Connell Street towards the bridge. This would be the last ever verifiable sighting of her. At that stage, she was wearing dark blue denim jeans and the grey 'Bowie' T-shirt. She was still carrying the black Texaco bag, which contained her blue 'No problem' T-shirt, her make-up and a change of clothes consisting of shoes and jeans. It is also believed that she was wearing a fine gold chain, and clip-on earrings.

On Tuesday 14 July, Karl Smith called to Clondalkin Garda Station to report his wife missing. He told the Garda on duty that she had last been seen alive some sixty hours earlier. Unbelievably, he was asked to return the next day with a photograph of her, and a description of her clothing. It is not known why a worried husband reporting that his wife had not been seen for almost three days was told to go away and come back the following day. It meant that another twenty-four hours passed before alarm bells were sounded.

When Karl Smith called back to the station on Wednesday, he was accompanied by Mary Winters, who recounted the events of the previous Sunday morning. At that stage, a missing-person investigation was initiated. Despite intensive investigations and a high-profile publicity campaign, no trace of the missing mother was established.

★

On Sunday 3 April 1998, a family out walking through bog land just off the Kilakee Road, in the Glendoo area of the Dublin Mountains, discovered what appeared to be human remains in a collapsed gully bank. The actual body dump site was about three-quarters of a mile off the Military Road, and about a mile from Glencree. A rough track led off the road to the site. It would be 9 AM on Monday morning before Gardai would begin a formal examination of the scene, notwithstanding the fact that they had been informed of the discovery of the body as early as 7.30 PM the previous evening. It appeared that an attempt had been made to conceal the body in the gully, but that the rain from the previous winter had washed the sods away, leading to the collapse of one side of the makeshift grave.

When the body was being examined *in situ*, it was discovered that two plastic bags had been placed over the head, with the inner bag tied tightly around the neck. Considerable difficulty had been encountered when, during the subsequent post mortem, an attempt was made to undo this knot. Given the damage caused to the body due to decomposition, it proved impossible to establish any positive indication that strangulation had been the definitive cause of death. No evidence of skeletal injury or blunt-force trauma was found. As a consequence the cause of death could not be definitively established, although the State Pathologist, Professor John Harbison, who carried out the actual post-mortem, would comment that had the bags been placed over the head during life, then they could almost certainly have caused death by asphyxia.

Formal identification of the remains proved to be very difficult. A trawl of missing-persons reports was carried out. There were certain indicators that led to the conclusion that the body was that of Antoinette Smith. A key found in the pocket of the jeans that was still on the body opened the door of Mary Winters' house. This was that same key that Mary had thrown at Antoinette as they parted after leaving La Mirage some nine months previously. In addition, the upper half of the body was clothed in the remains of a partially decomposed T-shirt bearing the 'Bowie' logo, while another T-shirt with the 'No Problem' logo was found a short distance way.

DNA evidence that could help to positively identify the remains was, of course, not available. However, there was one issue that, in most people's eyes, conclusively proved that the body was that of Antoinette. During his examination, Professor Harbison had discovered that the female victim was wearing a wig, and that beneath the wig she was completely bald. At the time she had gone missing, Antoinette had been wearing a wig, which she had purchased in March of 1987. The wig found on the remains was positively identified as being the one manufactured specifically for her by a specialist firm in March of 1987. She had lost all of her own hair at thirteen years of age due to a medical condition, and had worn a wig ever since.

★

The investigation into Antoinette's disappearance was now, some nine months later, ratcheted up to become a full-scale murder enquiry. Given the passage of time since she was last seen alive, this proved, initially, to be a difficult task. A re-enactment of her final known movements was shown on the old *Garda Patrol* television programme on Monday 9 May 1988, with an actress dressed in the Bowie-concert T-shirt, filmed on O'Connell Street late at night. This re-enactment led to one important witness coming forward, stating tat he had evidence which he believed to be extremely relevant.

Taxi driver Eamon Cooney* told Gardai that sometime around 3.30 AM on the morning of Sunday 12 July 1987, he had been working in the Dublin city centre area. As he drove through Westmoreland Street, just off O'Connell

Bridge, he had been hailed by a male pedestrian. When Eamon stopped his car, his intended passenger had opened the rear passenger door and stepped into the car. At the same time, the rear driver's door had opened, and another male, accompanied by a female, got into the back of the taxi. When he had first stopped the car, Eamon had not initially noticed the additional passengers. He had assumed his fare was on his own, and was unable to speculate on where the male and female passengers had been prior to them getting into his taxi. The female sat between the two men. The male who had flagged him down told Cooney that they wanted to go to Rathfarnham, on the outskirts of the city.

Cooney described the female as being in her late twenties, with dark, collar-length hair, and added that he could clearly recall that she had been wearing a T-shirt similar in style to the 'Bowie' one. She was well spoken, with a Dublin accent. What was most noticeable about her, he stated, was the fact that she had a very prominent, protruding tooth on the right-hand side of her mouth. Indeed, this had been a feature relied upon by Antoinette's brother when he attempted to visually identify her skeletal remains. The male who had hailed him first was described as speaking with a pronounced Dublin accent. In contrast to his much taller companion, who said very little, the first man was described as acting like a 'hard chaw'.

From the parts of their conversation that he overheard, Cooney gathered that the trio had been together in the Abrakebabra restaurant on Westmoreland Street, and that they now intended to go to a party in the Rathfarnham area. Although all three had drink taken, he said that they weren't drunk. He made one other very important observation. He told Gardai that, from their body language, there was no suggestion that the female had any romantic connection with either of the two men. However, it did appear that she knew them 'well'.

On the drive towards Rathfarnham, the smaller of the two had done most of the talking. At one stage, he had asked Cooney what he would do if they decided to rob him. His companion had responded with the comment to 'leave it out'. When they reached Rathfarnham village, he had, on their instructions, dropped them at one of the slip roads just off Butterfield Avenue. All three walked in the direction of the Rathfarnham Inn public house.

★

Another witness also came forward with equally important information. Adrian Crowley* said that at around 5.30 AM on 12 July 1987, he had parked his van in the car park at Cruagh Wood. This area is about two miles, as the crow flies, from where the remains had later been found, in the Glendoo Mountains. Adrian brought his three dogs into the woods, and let them run loose. The trail he took led uphill. As he neared the top, a lone male had appeared 'out of nowhere'. On seeing Crowley, the male had stopped briefly, and had then continued walking along the path towards him. As they passed, he had greeted the man but had received no response. He appeared to deliberately turn his head away so that his face was not exposed. The male continued walking downhill towards the car park.

Adrian became concerned about his van, which, at the stage he had left it, was the only vehicle in the car park. He decided to turn back. He called to his dogs, and then headed back downhill. He briefly lost sight of the man. When he next observed him, he saw that he had been joined by another male. Adrian could not say where this second man had come from either, but they had both increased their pace when they realised he had seen them. They continued to walk quickly in the direction of the car park. When Adrian arrived at the car park, he could not see either of the men. When later asked by Gardai about his recollection of the events of that morning, he was adamant that he had not heard any other car driving away – a sound that would have carried for miles in the stillness of that summer morning. This suggested that the two men either had no form of transport, or were hiding nearby until Adrian had left the area, before driving away themselves.

However, another witness claimed that later that same morning, he had exercised his dogs in an area in the Glendoo Mountains, only some five hundred metres from where the remains were eventually found. The dogs had not caught any scent and he would have expected them to detect a body had it been lying nearby.

The presence of these two men at Cruagh Wood was considered significant. It is unlikely that they were in the area as sightseers or hill climbers. What is equally significant is the fact that, despite all the publicity that surrounded both Cooney and Crowley's sightings, not one person has come forward to say that it was possible that it could have been them that the witnesses were referring to, and that there was a perfectly innocent explanation for their actions. Equally, no one has come forward to say that it was possible that they themselves were the person or persons whom Eamon Cooney had picked up in Westmoreland Street that morning.

As the investigation progressed, a number of persons were identified as POIs (Persons of Interest) to the investigation. These males were interviewed, their alibis checked out and then, eventually, they were eliminated as POIs. In one instance, it was discovered that one person who became a POI had emigrated to America shortly after the disappearance of Antoinette. At the request of the Gardai, Kansas State Police formally interviewed this male just a few days after the discovery of Antoinette's remains. He provided them with a strong alibi and was, as a consequence, quickly eliminated as a POI. A separate POI was interviewed by the British police, and immediately afterwards returned to Ireland and presented himself at Tallaght Garda Station, where the investigation was being run from. He, too, was eliminated as a POI.

Gardai also learned of another male who, since the acrimonious break-up of Antoinette's marriage, had been a regular late-night caller to her home. This male was interviewed, and claimed to have had, at best, only a passing acquaintance with her. However, from a number of statements taken from friends of Antoinette, it emerged that they were having a relationship. On the face of it, his omission of this detail suggested that he might be withholding other details. Whilst some members of the investigation team were suggesting that he should be arrested immediately, Detective Superintendent John Courtenay, who was in charge of the team, recommended a more 'softly-softly' approach. The man was intercepted by two senior detectives while leaving his place of work, and was interviewed sitting in their car. He readily admitted to having had an ongoing affair with Antoinette. He told them that he had last been with her on the Thursday night before she disappeared, and that they had arranged another date for the following Tuesday night.

When asked why he hadn't told Gardai this at the start, he responded that he had been interviewed on that occasion in the presence of his wife, and had been unable to tell them the truth! His alibi had been checked out, and he had been cleared of any involvement. This incident was further proof, if it was needed, of the calibre of John Courtenay as a policeman. During the troubled times of the seventies, eighties and nineties, he headed up the Murder Squad. His professionalism, expertise and dedication were an example to all of us who ever had the privilege to work with him on serious-crime investigations. The methodical and thorough manner in which all his investigations were conducted stood the test of time.

About three weeks before she disappeared, Antoinette told a friend about an incident that had occurred the previous weekend. She said that she had been dancing in La Mirage, and at the end of the night had been approached by a stranger who, she was aware, had been watching her all night. The stranger had offered her a lift home in his car, and she had accepted his offer. He had driven up the quays, as if heading for Clondalkin, but at the last minute had turned into the Phoenix Park. He had, she claimed, then driven to a secluded area. He become very aggressive and, fearing for her safety, she had consented to have sex with him. When they finished, he drove her back to O'Connell Street.

A female friend told Gardai that Antoinette had pointed out a male to her in La Mirage who, she claimed, had tried to rape her in the Phoenix Park. Antoinette had given a slightly different version of the incident to this friend. She told her that the man had been driving a van, and that when he stopped in the Phoenix Park she had struck him with her shoe. She claimed to have been able to jump out of the van, and that he had then driven away.

A few nights later, while having a drink in a pub in Dolphin's Barn, Antoinette had pointed to a number of customers seated at the bar and told her male companion that the 'bastard' who had raped her in the Phoenix Park was among them. However, she did not actually identify the male she alleged had attacked her. She would tell another male friend that she had been picked up by a man in a pub on Drimnagh Road, and had been raped by him in the Phoenix Park.

★

Gardai were unable to establish if the incidents as referred to by her friends were one and the same, or referred to more than one assault on her. The fact that one of the alleged assaults had occurred just a few weeks before she disappeared was, of course, treated as significant. They were, however, unable to progress the matter any further.

The brutal murderers of this bright and vivacious woman have never been brought to justice. Antoinette's death is now the subject of a full review by the Garda Serious Crime Review team. This review is concentrated, for the most part, on the forensic examination of her clothing and other items.

Allowed to lapse for many years, the investigation into the murder of the young mother received fresh impetus due, in no small part, to the tireless campaign waged by her two daughters.

Inga

At first, I could not understand why the ViCLAS profilers were suggesting that we should include the abduction and murder of the young German tourist, Inga Hauser in our case profiles. I knew that there was a tenuous connection, in that Inga had gone missing just three days after Antoinette Smyth's remains had been located. All similarities ended there, however, as Inga had disappeared almost immediately after arriving on the ferry at Larne port in Northern Ireland, on 6 April 1988. Her body was located some two weeks later in Ballypatrick Forest Park near Ballycastle in Antrim, Northern Ireland.

When I pointed out that both the crime itself, and the scene where her body had been located, were situated outside our jurisdiction, and her case was, therefore, probably of no relevance to us, they replied that if there was a predator stalking and abducting girls, then something as vague as a line on a map drawn purely for political expediency was unlikely to deter him. They added, anyway, that the area where she was last seen alive was only some seventy miles from Dundalk, where Ciara Breen had disappeared from: of even greater relevance, was the fact that her actual body dump site was a little over one hundred miles from Dundalk, considerably less than the distance between the locations where Ciara and Fiona Sinnott had gone missing. This, to me, was a salutary lesson in my personal failure at that time to see the bigger picture! The access to files, statements and reports that were afforded us, in both this and in Arlene Arkinson's case, by the then Royal Ulster Constabulary (now the PSNI), was without precedent, and should be acknowledged.

Inga, an eighteen-year-old student from Munich, Germany, was at that time back packing alone across Europe, travelling by public transport. She had taken the two-hour ferry journey from Stranraer in Scotland across to Larne, Northern Ireland, arriving just before 10 PM, on the night of 6 April. It is believed that she intended to take the train from Larne into Belfast city centre, where she would stay overnight in a hostel, before starting out on a sight-seeing tour the following morning. Although the train station is just a few hundred yards from the ferry port, no witness could later be located who recalled her

158

walking to the station. More significantly, not one of the four-hundred-odd passengers and crew on the ferry, the *Galloway Princess*, could recall seeing her disembark on foot! This was all the more unusual considering that Inga was an attractive girl, who would stand out in any company.

After two to three days, her family back in Germany began to become more and more concerned when they hadn't heard from her. She had, up to then, stayed in touch with them by phone every other day. Their fears intensified when she failed to keep an appointment in London with a friend on 11 April. Her parents immediately visited Northern Ireland, and alerted the police. A full-scale search was launched, but no trace of the missing teenager was found.

★

Then, on 20 April, just two weeks after she had arrived in Northern Ireland, her family received the news that they had long feared. Inga's partially clothed body was found in Ballycastle Forest Park by a forestry worker. This public park, one of the largest in Northern Ireland, is bisected by the main A2 road, which runs from Cushendall to Ballycastle. It is set in the north-east corner of Northern Ireland, and is some thirty-odd miles from Larne Port. A six-mile-long scenic drive winds its way through the forest, offering, in places, amazing vistas of the causeway coastline and, when the park is open during the summer season, attracting countless visitors.

The location of the dump site would imply that her attacker had a certain local knowledge. The entrance and exits from the park onto the Cushendall road are about half a mile apart. Inga was located close to the exit from the park, which would suggest that whatever transport was being used had entered via the main entrance, and driven along the quiet road looking for a place to dump her body.

No attempt had been made to bury or even properly conceal the body. It had been left lying face-down in some high gorse bushes, where it would not be immediately visible to anyone using the roadway. It would, however, be clearly visible to anyone taking the nature ramble through the forest. Given the number of visitors to the park, even in the closed season, it was inevitable that she would be found quickly. It was almost as if her assailant was not concerned that her body would be located.

In addition, no attempt was made to conceal her identity. Her passport and travel documents were left at the scene. The casual manner in which the body was disposed of, together with the apparent lack of concern over its potential recovery, speaks volumes for the attitude of her assailant. The reference in the press reports of the time to her being found in a 'shallow grave' were far from the truth.

Inga's clothing and personal items were carelessly strewn around the body. These included all of her documents and her expensive camera. The film in the camera, when subsequently developed, showed photographs that she had taken on her trip through Scotland. There were none of Northern Ireland, which would suggest that the opportunity to take photographs of her time in the country had never presented itself to her. There was no trace evidence located to show that the physical and sexual assault that had been perpetrated on her young body had occurred at or in the vicinity of the body dump site. This would suggest that she had been killed elsewhere, and dumped in the forest park.

Post-mortem examination revealed that the teenager had been sexually assaulted before her death. There were blunt-force trauma injuries to her head and face, consistent with her having been struck a number of times during a frenzied assault with an unidentified weapon. A most unusual feature of the assault was the fact that her neck had been broken. Following a fatal sexual assault, a pathologist will regularly find evidence of manual strangulation, whether by hand or with a binding. This is usually either through visible ligature marks or internal bruising on the neck or in the petechiae spots, that is, tiny ruptured capillaries, often found in the eyes or on the face. The investigators considered this injury to be extremely significant.

One of the lines of enquiry that the neck injury generated was an attempt to establish the type of person either capable or trained to inflict a blow that could break his victim's neck. The suggestion that was considered straightaway was the possibility that her assailant could have been a soldier or other military personnel, trained in the art of unarmed combat. It was further suggested that Inga might have met up with a 'squaddie', that is a British Army member, returning to the North of Ireland on the ferry to resume duty. Coming, as she did, from a country that was awash with military from all over the world, it was felt that Inga might have struck up a rapport with him and trusted him sufficiently to take up any offer of a lift or accommodation.

However, this line of enquiry did not yield any tangible results. The wiser heads amongst the investigating officers believed that in the then-current political situation, any unarmed British soldier would be travelling incognito, and would not have wanted it to be known that he was a member of the British Army, viewed by a certain section of the population to be a force of occupation. Only two weeks previously, two off-duty British Army corporals, David Howes and Derek Wood, had mistakenly driven into the funeral cortège of Irish Republican activist Caoimhin Mac Bradaigh, on the Anderstown Road in Belfast. Mac Bradaigh had been murdered some days earlier in Milltown Cemetery by UDA volunteer Michael Stone. Howes and Wood, despite discharging a loaded firearm into the air in order to frighten off their attackers, were dragged from their car and beaten to death in front of press from around the world.

When local priest Father Alex Reid attempted to intervene, he too was threatened with violence. One of the photographs that will always be remembered by those of us who lived through those troubled times was that of Father Reid kneeling beside David Howe's bloodied body, administering the last rites. For this very reason it was felt that, if indeed there was a soldier on the ferry, then the chances that he would identify himself as such to anyone, even a fellow passenger as pretty as Inga, were remote.

Although not then quite nineteen, Inga would have been considered fairly worldly wise by those who knew her, and would not have taken chances with her personal safety. She had travelled across Europe and up through England and Scotland by train, and did not try to hitch-hike on any part of the journey.

The fact that there was no reported sighting of her leaving the boat after it docked would suggest that she had taken a lift from a person she had met while en route from Scotland to Northern Ireland. Something – or someone – had influenced her during the two-hour sailing to set aside all of her inhibitions, and accept a lift from off the boat.

There were a number of different theories considered here. If, as suggested, she got into a car with a stranger or strangers, then there must have been some external factors that caused her to feel sufficiently relaxed and safe in the company of her perceived benefactor or benefactors. One suggestion was that the driver was an older father – or grandfather-type figure, whose appearance and demeanour had caused her to let down her guard, with drastic consequences.

Another theory favoured by some of the investigating team was that there was another woman in the car when Inga got in, either driving or as a passenger.

Such a presence would, undoubtedly, have reassured the youngster. If that is the case, then we can only speculate upon the role that this female may have played in subsequent events. Was she a willing participant in the defilement of the young victim, or was she so in fear of the aggressor that she did not intervene to stop it? One would imagine that if the latter were indeed the case, then, with the passage of time, the control the culprit had over this other person must have weakened significantly, unless, of course, she too had fallen victim at some stage in the intervening period to his homicidal impulses.

At the time that Operation TRACE began to look at the possibility that Inga's case could be linked to some of the other disappearances, it was generally accepted by both a number of the investigators and the media in general, that the youngster had been held somewhere for a number of days by her abductor or abductors, and that she had only been murdered shortly before her body was recovered. The notion that their daughter may have endured days of relentless torture while being held captive only added to the anguish and pain felt by her parents and sister. The pathologist who had performed the post-mortem examination, when asked to express his opinion on this matter, suggested that, given the condition of her body and the complete lack of predator damage, it had lain in Ballypatrick Forest for hours and not days prior to discovery.

This theory would, however, be rubbished in tests carried out some years later. Advances in forensic entomology, that is, the study of insect activity at crime scenes which can indicate Post-Mortem Interval (PMI), showed, when applied in Inga's case, that her body had lain *in situ* for a number of weeks. It now appears likely that she was murdered, and that her body was dumped within hours of her arrival in Northern Ireland. This development, naturally, has a huge significance in determining the reliability or otherwise of alibi and other evidence.

Foreign-body samples removed during the examination of her body provided a partial DNA sample. As with Phyllis Murphy, advances in this science at that time were minimal, and such a sample, based as it was, for the most part, on blood grouping, was of limited value. A number of suspects and POIs were asked to provide blood samples for comparison purposes, but these proved to be of little value.

In 2005, the recently established cold-case unit of the Police Service of Northern Ireland would reopen Inga's case. Further crime-scene evidence, not previously checked, was submitted for DNA analysis based on the advances that had been made. Detectives now have a full DNA profile of the man who sexually assaulted the young backpacker. This has been compared on the various

DNA databases, without success, both at domestic level and internationally. At local level, almost two thousand males have donated samples that have been checked without success. These include passengers and crew on the *Galloway Princess* on the night, dock workers, local taxi drivers, railroad staff and anyone else who might have been in the vicinity when the ship docked.

With the development of familial DNA cross-referencing, there is no doubt that, in time, the identity of the donor will be established. The British database alone contains millions of DNA profiles of persons who have come into contact with the law. Testing for familial similarities, as in siblings, cousins and other relatives, can provide huge indicators in the identity of crime-scene donors. It is hoped that it will, in time, provide closure for Inga's family. As with so many of the other cases that we have looked at, her father sadly died in 2006, without receiving any closure in his daughter's murder case.

Before leaving Inga's case, I would like to briefly mention the murder of another young backpacker, also from Munich, which occurred on 25 September 2001. Bettina Poeschel, a trainee reporter with a German newspaper, had spent a number of weeks with friends staying in hostels in and around Dublin, and was due to return home the very next day. She impulsively decided to leave her friends in Dublin city, and travel alone to Drogheda to view the world-renowned Newgrange tomb before leaving Ireland.

Unfortunately, on her arrival in Drogheda, twenty-eight-year-old Bettina found that she had missed the bus which would have taken her from Drogheda to Newgrange. She decided to make the short journey on foot. This, again, is another one of those seemingly innocuous decisions that can have such dire consequences. I am thinking, in particular, of Jo Jo, when she decided to remain on the road looking for a lift, of Antoinette deciding to stay behind when her friend Mary left the disco, or of Annie running and catching the bus in Sandymount.

On that bright autumn afternoon, as Bettina strolled past an area where improvements were being made on the main Drogheda-to-Donore road as part of the new M1 motorway project, she was seen and greeted by a number of the workmen. She returned their good-natured banter with a smile. She had no idea, of course, that one of those men was a convicted predator, who had already served time for the manslaughter of one female. On seeing that the girl was alone, he followed her in a work vehicle until, on a quiet stretch of the road, he seized his opportunity, and abducted, raped and strangled the defenceless woman to death.

★

When news of the disappearance of Bettina broke, a full investigation team was set up. At that stage, Operation TRACE had been 'stood down', and we had all been transferred back to our main stations of operation. Immediately on hearing that another female had gone missing from our roads, Tony Hickey hastily reassembled the unit, and sent us to Drogheda to assist in the investigation.

It would be almost a month before Bettina's body was eventually located, hidden in dense undergrowth just off the Donore Road, a short distance from where she had last been seen. This was actually the second time that this area had been searched. Certain Gardai involved in the original search had expressed reservations about its thoroughness and effectiveness. This led to the local Divisional Search Team, who were trained exterior-scene searchers, being deployed to carry out a further search. Having hacked through dense undergrowth, they located her body, concealed beneath bramble and thorn bushes some distance from the roadway. In order to allow the body to be properly viewed and photographed *in situ*, a huge swathe of the undergrowth had to be cut away.

During his subsequent post-mortem examination, the State Pathologist was unable to give a definitive cause of death, due to the extensive damage the predator had done to the body. He had no doubt, however, that the partially clothed trainee reporter had suffered a violent sexual assault. He would also comment on a foreign substance that he had found on both the body and on her clothing. This was later identified as Jeyes fluid. Someone with a certain level of forensic awareness had poured the disinfectant on her lower region and her underclothing, to destroy any trace evidence that might be found. Equally it was suggested that the disinfectant had been applied some time after death had occurred, which meant that the perpetrator had revisited the body at least once as it lay in the ditch.

Despite these amateurish efforts to destroy any trace evidence, a DNA profile was completed on semen taken from the body, and the donor was later identified as one Michael Murphy, a native of Rathmullen Park in Drogheda. In a subsequent interview following his arrest, Murphy would tell Gerry O'Brien, the local Garda Inspector, where he had hidden his victim's red shoes! Murphy was well known to Gardai. At just twenty-two years of age, he had, on 20 October 1983, strangled local sixty-six-year-old dressmaker Kitty Carroll. He was sentenced to twelve years' imprisonment for manslaughter, which, given the circumstances of the crime, was an amazing verdict. In 1993, he received a further three years for armed robberies. Then, in November of 1997, he had assaulted two females he had met out walking in Drogheda town centre. As predators go, he is almost without parallel. Like his namesake, Larry Murphy, who at the time of Bettina's murder was just starting his own prison sentence, Michael Murphy refused to fully engage in any of the sex offenders programmes. He is now serving a life sentence.

Patricia

Like every other business, Christmas Day is considered to be one of the quietest days that the Gardai will have all year. Even hardened criminals seem to be bitten by the spirit of the season and, for that one day at least, the majority of them succumb to the 'goodwill to all men' theory and refrain from committing crime. For that very reason, the Garda on the 6 AM to 2 PM shift at Tallaght Garda Station on Christmas morning 1991 could not possibly have expected that the man who arrived at the counter in the almost deserted public office at 10 AM was about to report a disappearance that would, in time, become a brutal murder, a crime that, for some twenty-three years, would remain unsolved.

The concerned caller introduced himself as Patrick Doherty, and said that he lived at nearby Allenton Lawns with his wife and two young children. He added that his wife Patricia, a serving prison officer, appeared to be missing. When questioned further, he said that she had left their home shortly after 9 PM on the night of 23 December. He was upstairs, and she had called out that she was going to get some last-minute Christmas shopping in the nearby Old Bawn shopping Centre. He had then heard the front door closing.

According to Patrick, his wife had left the house earlier that same afternoon to keep an appointment at her local hairdresser. Having finished there, she had then gone shopping, at first to the nearby Old Bawn Centre, then from there to the Square Shopping Centre. She had, he added, arrived home shortly before 9 PM. He said that it was at that stage that she had announced that she was going back down to the Old Bawn Centre, as there were some last-minute errands she had to run. He had not seen or heard from his wife since that time.

Given that his wife had, at the time he was making this report, been missing for some thirty-seven hours, a period which included both Christmas Eve and Christmas morning, Doherty was asked why he had not reported her missing earlier. Her absence during that period must, it was suggested, have caused serious upset for their two children, then aged just ten and eight. He told Gardai that his wife had worked for a number of years as a secretary at a local school, but a few months previously had secured employment as a prison officer at

Mountjoy Prison. In her new job she had to work long and irregular hours, with her shifts often running into one another. When she had not returned home that night, he had assumed that she had been called into work and was delayed there. Although he was surprised by her continued absence and failure to contact either himself or their children, it was only when she had not turned up or contacted the children for Christmas morning that his growing unease had turned into serious concern. He rang the prison and was told that she had not been in work for the previous few days. He said that on hearing this, he had rung some of Patricia's siblings, only to discover that they had had no contact from her either.

★

The delay in reporting Patricia as missing was significant, as it meant that, with the limited resources available to Gardai what with holiday, special leave and other commitments, it would be several days before a full enquiry team could be put together, and a full missing-persons enquiry initiated. Enquiries with relatives and friends quickly established that this sort of behaviour was completely out of character for the twenty-nine-year-old housewife and devoted mother. It was even more unlikely that she would have walked away, and left her son and daughter, especially at such a magical time of year for children. For this reason alone, it was suspected, almost from the outset, that the circumstances surrounding her disappearance were suspicious. Many of the investigating Gardai secretly believed, even at that early stage, that she had been the victim of foul play. They argued that had her leaving been voluntary, she would, at the very least, have attempted to get some kind of message to her children either directly or through an intermediary.

Patrick Doherty had claimed that his wife had left their home just after 9 PM, so Garda enquiries were initially concentrated around the family home and extended along the Bohernabreena Road, leading on to the Old Bawn Shopping Centre. House-to-house enquiries with her neighbours failed to reveal a single person who had met or seen the well-known housewife during the night of 23 December.

One witness came forward and told them that sometime around 9.20 PM he had observed a female who fitted the description given of Patricia, walking along the footpath opposite Bridget Burke's pub heading in the direction of the shopping centre. He described her as wearing a full-length brown mac and a gold scarf. This single sighting appeared to confirm the details of her movements as earlier supplied to Gardai by Patrick.

Given the nature of her new job, one investigative lead that was followed was the possibility that she might have been killed by or on behalf of some prison inmate whom she had fallen foul of. Even from their prison cells, certain of the more notorious gangland bosses were known still to hold sway over their empires outside. However, enquiries in the prison quickly dismissed this suggestion. Patricia was very popular and well liked, both by her fellow workers and the general prison population that she came into contact with.

★

One witness claimed to have seen a female who resembled Patricia, getting into a red car near the entrance to the shopping centre. If this sighting was correct, then it could be suggested that Patricia had left the house to keep a prearranged appointment with some other person. This, in turn, raised another scenario, and the possibility that her disappearance might have been related to some romantic liaison or relationship was canvassed. In a number of other well-documented disappearances, it had been found that sudden and unexplained departures had often arisen as a result of extra-marital relationships. This, however, was found not to be the case with Patricia. When her friends and acquaintances were canvassed with this scenario, they dismissed it out of hand. She was described as a devoted mother who lived for her two children. She would not, all who were spoken to agreed, have given them up for any man.

No one has ever come forward to say that they were either the driver or the passenger of this red car, and serious doubt has, in the intervening years, been cast upon the authenticity of the sighting. Very little further information was received from members of the public by the team. The trail seemed to end there. The searches for Patricia continued for a number of months, but no further trace of her was found. There were numerous appeals in the media, with her husband giving a number of interviews during which he asked for his wife's safe return.

Some six months after she was last seen alive, a grim discovery was made in the mountains overlooking her home. On 21 June 1992, Eamon Quinn*, a local man, was out cutting turf in bogland, in an area known as the Glassamucky Breaks, near Featherbed Mountain in the Dublin Mountains. This was Eamon's first day that year to start back cutting turf. He walked about a hundred yards off the track to where he knew, from previous years, that there was a suitable bank that would yield a good harvest of turf.

Not too far from where Eamon began digging that day is a stone monument, known as the Lemass Cross. This stone was erected some years ago, to mark the area where the body of Noel Lemass, a prominent anti-treaty activist and brother of the future Taoiseach, Sean, had been located some seventy years earlier. Lemass had been part of a plot to blow up all the main arteries into Dublin city, effectively isolating it. However, the plan had been foiled and he was one of five officers who had been captured in nearby Glencullen. He managed to escape but was eventually hunted down and killed by pro-Treaty soldiers, who unceremoniously dumped his body in the mountains.

Glassamucky Breaks is less than a mile away from where the body of Antoinette Smith had been located some four years previously.

Eamon found that the part of the bank he had selected towards the end of the previous summer had, during the intervening winter, collapsed, exposing a narrow fissure. He saw what appeared to be a brown coat discarded in the exposed bank. On closer inspection, he found that it was covering the body of a female. Nearby lay a pair of ladies' shoes. Eamon ran to his car, drove to the nearest house and raised the alarm.

★

Gardai responded to his call, quickly arriving at the scene. The area where the body lay was preserved, pending the arrival of forensic experts. It was viewed *in situ* by the State Pathologist, Professor John Harbison. A wide area of bogland, in the vicinity of where the body had been located, was also cordoned off. As in the case of Antoinette Smith, whose lonely gravesite had been located less than a mile away, visual identification was virtually impossible, given the passage of time, predator activity and climatic influences.

Within days, however, the body would be identified through dental chart comparison as being that of Patricia. Although not considered to be a definitive proof of identity, this simple procedure is nevertheless viewed as an important initial comparison test. The clothing on the body was also identified as being similar to the clothing she had been wearing on that December afternoon. A key taken from her coat pocket was found to open the door of the Doherty family home, at Allenton Lawns in nearby Tallaght. This was, of course, the same simple test used in helping to identify Antoinette's remains.

During a fingertip search of the cordoned-off area, a ladies' watch was also located, which was subsequently identified as being Patricia's property. The spot where the watch was located was almost one hundred yards from where the body lay. It was considered unlikely that it could have been moved from the body as a result of any predator activity, and the search area was then further widened. More items of clothing, including a headscarf, were then located and identified as her property. This would suggest that whoever had dumped the body had also scattered her personal property over a wide area, possibly to avoid future identification. They had obviously not considered the significance of a small thing like a front-door key!

During his post-mortem examination of the skeletal remains, Professor Harbison had been unable to definitively establish the actual cause of death, due, as mentioned earlier, to the advanced state of decomposition. He could also not find any evidence of physical injury or blunt-force trauma. In his summary, he suggested that the possibility existed that she had been strangled. He did not find any evidence of rape or sexual assault, but neither could he exclude the possibility that such an assault had occurred.

Investigating Gardai would adopt a far more reasoned approach to her death. They were satisfied that, given the extent of the decomposition of her body, Patricia had died shortly after she disappeared. A ballistic re-enactment proved that it was extremely unlikely that she could have accidentally fallen into the bog hole, and become trapped. The finding of items of her personal property scattered over such a wide area added further weight to the theory that her death had been murder, a conclusion that had always been at the forefront in the missing-person investigation that had preceded the finding of the body.

★

Once again, the passage of time between her disappearance and the finding of her body would seriously hamper the investigation. While everyone remembered the appeals for help in finding the young mother over the previous Christmas, it was proving very difficult to get people to recall any suspicious person or activity they might have witnessed around the relevant times. A full reconstruction of her last-known movements was subsequently broadcast on RTÉ television. Although a large number of persons would contact Gardai with information, no useful leads were ever obtained.

Gardai have always suspected that the murderer was well known to Patricia. The pain her children must have endured during that Christmas in 1992, as they waited for some word of their mother's whereabouts, is unimaginable. It is almost certainly the case that Antoinette's murder was a crime of opportunity; once again the victim seems to have been in the wrong place at the wrong time. Patricia's last-minute shopping trip is an activity that most parents can empathise with. No reason or motive has ever been established for the callous murder of the young working mother. This lack lends further credence to the belief that, at least for her killer, the death was 'personal'.

In recent months there have been renewed appeals to members of the public, asking for their assistance in solving this unexplained murder. As with Antoinette, Patricia's murder is now being reviewed by the cold-case unit.

Arlene

At fifteen years of age, not only was Arelene Arkinson our youngest missing-person investigation to be reviewed but, furthermore, her case, like that of Inga's, was different, given that her disappearance almost certainly occurred either on the border with Northern Ireland, or outside the jurisdiction altogether. Arlene, a native of Castlederg, County Tyrone, went missing on 13 August 1994. On that night, she was babysitting her sister Kathleen's young daughter, Jolene, while Kathleen was enjoying a rare night out at the local bingo hall. Arlene's friend, Annie*, had phoned the house and told her that her and her boyfriend, Jerry*, were going to a disco in the Palace Hotel just across the border in Bundoran, later that same night. She had added that they were travelling with her mother, Lilly*, and Lilly's new partner, Bob*.

Arlene had met Bob, a native of southern Ireland, on a few occasions in Annie's house, and did not particularly like him. However, she told Annie that she was thinking about going, and they agreed that Annie would call by the house on her way to the disco. Kathleen had arrived home around 11 PM, and was followed a few minutes later by Annie. At that stage, the youngster decided to go to the dance with her friend. As Kathleen thanked Arlene for babysitting and bade her farewell, she was not to know that this would be the last time she would ever see her younger sister.

Arlene only discovered when she got into the van outside her sister's home that Lilly was not travelling with them, and it was only Bob accompanying them to the disco. It has been suggested that Arlene voiced her disquiet at the absence of the other adult, but agreed to travel after being reassured by her friends. The three youngsters enjoyed the night out in eac other's company. However, throughout the night, Bob at all times hovered in the background, never taking his eyes off the two young females as they danced and joked together.

At the end of the night, Bob had driven the three youngsters back to Castlederg. Both the driver and the other two teenagers would later claim, when questioned by police, that they had dropped Arlene off outside her family home first, and had then driven on to Annie's house, where Bob had spent the rest of the night with Lilly. Arlene's father would later tell police that she never came home that night. For his part, the evidence of Annie and Jerry provided Bob with a cast-iron alibi for the period during which Arlene had gone missing. She was never seen alive again.

All those people in and around the small community in Castlederg who had allowed the soft-spoken stranger into their homes and lives were not to know that Bob's full name was Robert Lesarian Howard. Nor could they have suspected that he was a notorious sex offender who was more commonly known as 'The Wolf Man of Wolfhill'. He was quite proud of this nickname, and regularly introduced himself to fellow deviants as the 'Wolfhill Werewolf'.

★

Howard was – and is – one of this country's most prolific sex abusers, with a catalogue of assaults on vulnerable females that stretches back over a period of some forty years. His victims throughout that time had ranged in age from preteen to early sixties. He is currently serving a sentence of life imprisonment, imposed on him in October 2003, for the abduction and murder of fourteen-year-old schoolgirl Hannah Williams, in London in 2001. Her trussed and bound body, wrapped in a blue tarpaulin cover, was found almost two years later by workmen carrying out excavations connected with the building of the Channel Tunnel, which runs between England and France. A portion of the noose used to bind her was still present on the body. The trial judge, when sentencing Howard, recommended that he should never be freed.

Howard was one of six children born in 1944 to a local farm labourer and his wife, in the quaintly named village of Swan, in the remote rural area of Wolfhill in County Laois. He was, from an early age, thought of as 'different' by the local community. His father, it is suggested, was a very strict disciplinarian, who regularly beat the young Howard. The boy spent much of his early life sleeping rough in barns and outhouses in the area, to avoid his father. Inevitably, given these circumstances, he drifted into petty crime. He first came to the attention of the Gardai in the mid 1950s, when, then aged twelve, he was arrested for burglary, and sent to St Joseph's Industrial School in Clonmel, County Tipperary. He was released from there in 1960 at sixteen years of age. However, he would not be long out of the industrial school before he received a sentence for another burglary offence.

A few years later, he was convicted in an English court after breaking into the bedroom of a six-year-old child, whom he had then attempted to sexually abuse. Unbelievably, he had actually broken into this same child's bedroom on a previous occasion, and told her that he was a doctor. He had then sexually abused her. Before leaving, he had left his 'calling card' by urinating into a container beside his victim's bed. On the second occasion, however, the child's parents had been alerted by her screams. Howard had been arrested, and sentenced to the local borstal. Stories of the duration of the sentence he received for this crime vary, with some sources suggesting it could have been as short as two weeks.

Within four years, he was back in court again. On this occasion he received a sentence of six years, for the assault and attempted rape of a female whose home in Durham he had broken into. During the vicious assault, she had managed to escape from him. As she fled naked through the streets, he ran after her. He cornered her in a nearby garden, and there tried, again, to force himself upon her. Her screams for help were heard by neighbours, who came to her rescue. This did not deter Howard, and he had to be physically restrained by locals to prevent him from continuing to sexually assault his victim.

For a few years after serving that sentence, nothing was heard of the Wolfman. However, in 1972, he resurfaced in Youghal in County Cork. At that stage, he was staying in a local boarding house under the name of Leslie Cahill, and was securing whatever casual work was available. Then twenty-eight years of age, he broke into a neighbouring house. The occupant, a sixty-year-old female who lived alone, awoke to find a man standing over her in the bed. He bound and gagged his victim, and then subjected her to a night-long litany of sexual and physical abuse.

The following morning, leaving her bruised and battered, he calmly booked out of his lodgings, and took the train to Dublin. His victim, meanwhile, managed to escape and raise the alarm. Through some thorough police work by local Gardai, he was traced and arrested shortly after arriving in Dublin. He was charged with a number of counts arising out of the assault and false imprisonment of his elderly victim, and sentenced to a total of ten years' imprisonment.

By the time he was released from this sentence, Howard, still not yet forty years of age, would have spent almost half of his life in the custody of the State, either here or in England, with the majority of that time being served for sex-related offences. His taste in victim had undergone a considerable sea change, from a child of just six years to a sixty-year-old woman. He was not, however, finished. There was one further group of vulnerable females that he had not previously targeted but whom he would now turn his attention towards.

After release from prison, he moved into a flat in Dublin city centre. He alternated between there and Scotland. In the early nineties, he moved into rented accommodation on the main street in Castelederg, County Tyrone. What attracted the predator to this quiet little town is not clear. Given the unrest in the general area during that time, it did not appear to be the ideal location for a Catholic from southern Ireland, especially one with Howard's bizarre and violent sexual desires, to settle in.

Notwithstanding this, by 1993, a local sixteen-year-old girl, Amy Cullen*, was found running almost naked through the streets of Castlederg. When brought to the local police station, the distraught teenager recounted a horrifying tale of being duped by a man she knew as Bob Howard into visiting his flat alone. She said that he had told her that another male, whom she liked, was in his flat waiting to meet her. Amy claimed that for over two days she had been held prisoner in the flat, where, bound and gagged, she had been continuously sexually assaulted. She added that he had fashioned a noose, which he then placed around her neck and over a hanger in a wardrobe into which he had locked his young victim each time after sating his sexual appetite.

On her third night of imprisonment, Amy had jumped through a bedroom window and escaped while Howard slept. He was arrested and charged on a number of counts arising from that incident but, unbelievably, would in time receive only a suspended sentence. Given the long history of violent assault on females that dotted his background, it is difficult to accept the leniency of the sentence imposed on him for this heinous crime. Though his victim was only fifteen years of age, his defence was that any sexual activity that had occurred between them had been consensual. He did, however, put up his hands and admit an offence of unlawful carnal knowledge with a minor. This magnanimous gesture was accepted by the courts, in order, they stated, to save his young victim the ordeal of having to give evidence against him. In a psychological assessment presented to the courts during his sentence hearing, he was described as possessing an 'extremely courteous demeanour'.

★

His victim later claimed that she had encountered huge difficulties on the night she had made her escape from his clutches, in trying to get the local police to believe her story of abduction, assault and false imprisonment. The system, it would appear, had let her down not once, but twice.

Whilst awaiting trial for the assaults on Amy, Howard, despite his long criminal record and non-national status, was given bail. It was on one of the nights when he was 'out', awaiting sentence for this brutal crime, that he had driven the three youngsters to the disco in Bundoran, taking Arlene on a night out from which she would never return. It is surely symptomatic of his attitude to the police and the judicial system that, while on bail for the alleged sexual assault of a juvenile, he would be openly attending discos with children of a similar age to his last victim.

As I previously said, the two teenagers who had been with Arlene at the disco on that night told the police that they had dropped her home first, and he had then driven them back to their mother's house, thus giving him a cast-iron alibi for the time of her disappearance. They would later admit that they had been telling lies under duress, and give evidence on oath in open court that he had dropped them off first, and then driven away with Arlene in the van with him. They added that they had not seen her alive after that date.

As with all predators, Howard would first ingratiate himself with the local parents of the children he was actually targeting, and from whose numbers he would ultimately select his victims. Through this friendship, Howard had in turn come to be accepted within the local teenage community. On the night that Arelene had gone missing, he had offered to bring the two fifteen-year-olds – Annie and Jerry – to attend a disco in the Palace Hotel in Bundoran, just over the border. Annie's mother agreed to let them go with him. When Annie asked Arlene to go with them, the youngster was not to know that, by so doing, she had delivered her right into Howard's clutches. She would not survive the night.

No one had thought to question why a fifty-year-old man would want to go dancing with teenage children. To the youngsters, he presented himself as always having plenty of money, and as being available to drive them anywhere they wished to go. He was considered by some of them to resemble the movie actor Nick Nolte and, unlike most of the adults that were known to them, moved easily in their circles. What they could not have known was that this was all a façade, and that he was gradually grooming them with the intention of sexually abusing them.

Following Arlene's disappearance, although he appeared not to have been involved, local parents began to realise the threat that Robert Howard presented to their children. Already charged with the sexual assault of one teenager, he was now suspected of being involved in the disappearance of a second child. For his part he very quickly realised that it was time to move on before some of the local vigilante groupings meted out their own brand of justice on him. The house of one of the teenagers who had given him an alibi, and in whose home Howard had been living with the child's mother, had already been petrol bombed.

★

He returned to Dublin and, in early 1995, moved to a small rural village in Wexford. He did not, however, remain for very long in the area. His notoriety had preceded him, and he very quickly came to the attention of the local Gardai, who paid frequent visits to the house he shared with a couple he had befriended. What this couple could not have known when they opened their house to him was that he had almost immediately begun grooming their innocent teenage daughter. Pat McQuaid, one of the local detectives, later told me that they had been alerted to his presence in the community by locals who distrusted the soft-spoken stranger, who continuously attempted to ingratiate himself into the company of their young children. Gardai regularly called to the home to check on his movements.

Within weeks, the place would become too 'hot' for Howard, and he left the area. In a move which shows just how easy it was, and undoubtedly still is, for sex fiends to relocate in these islands, he moved to Drumchapel, on the outskirts of Glasgow city. He was housed by the local housing association, after he claimed to be on the run from terrorists in the North. The location of this flat could not have been more suited to a man of his increasingly aberrant appetites, given that it overlooked the playgrounds of two local schools. He was not long living there, however, when he was 'outed' by a national newspaper which, in a lengthy article, highlighted the dangers he posed to young children. Concerned parents surrounded his flat, demanding his immediate eviction. Howard made his escape out the back window. He then moved on to London. Once again, he disappeared from public view.

In April of 2001, the pretty fourteen-year-old schoolgirl Hannah Williams was snatched by an unknown assailant off the streets of the London suburb of Deptford. Two other young teenagers disappeared from the same area over a period of months. In their cases, the bodies were never located. Some two years after she had been reported missing, men working in a cement factory in Northfleet in Kent, associated with the building of the Channel Tunnel, found Hannah's bound and gagged body buried in the factory grounds. Post-mortem examination would reveal that she had been sexually abused.

Hannah had left her home on the afternoon of 21 April 2001, to go to a local shop. On her way, she received a call on her mobile phone. The male caller was ringing from a mobile phone that Hannah recognised as belonging to a female friend of her family. The caller told her that Evelyn*, the owner of the phone, had asked him to ring her. He said that Evelyn wanted to meet her immediately. The caller, who was using the phone (without, it should be added, Evelyn's knowledge), was none other than Robert Howard. Hannah was never seen alive again after taking that call. Following the discovery of Hannah's body, police moved quickly. Howard, whom they had always suspected of involvement in her disappearance, was arrested and charged with her murder.

During his trial, evidence was given by another local teenager that she had been brought, by Howard, to the same area where Hannah's body had been located. She claimed that he had tied a noose around her neck and assaulted her. However, she managed to escape from him. Evidence was given by Amy of her ordeal at his hands, while being held prisoner in his flat in Castlederg. Members of Arlene's family would also give evidence to the jury of her being in his company on the night she had disappeared. This is known as 'similar fact' evidence, and refers to the modus operandi or preferences of a predator whilst carrying out similar crimes for which he is facing trial. It is routinely used in Crown Court prosecutions in England, but is, unfortunately, not recognised by the Irish courts.

There was other damning evidence offered against him during the course of his trial. Blue tarpaulin, similar to that wrapped around Hannah's body, was linked to his girlfriend at that time. More importantly, while Howard denied knowing the youngster, she was readily identifiable on a home video found during a forensic search of his house, enjoying a day out with friends. It is disturbing to think how often Howard must have sat staring at this same video and reliving the moments that had preceded her death at his hands.

Howard was convicted of the murder, and sentenced to life imprisonment. He is presently detained at Frankland Prison, Durham. Though serving a life sentence and now in his late sixties, this predator has not given up hope of some day being freed on parole. His earliest parole date hearing is scheduled for 2018. In order to qualify for this type of release, Howard has to engage with the prison psychologists in the sex-offender programme. A condition of this engagement is that he must openly disclose and discuss all the intimate details of any sex crime he has committed. In order to comply with this requirement, Howard freely admits and discusses the vicious assault on his elderly victim in Youghal in the early seventies. No mention is ever made by him of the death of Hannah Williams or the disappearance of Arlene Arkinson. Arlene's name does not even come up in the private conversations he has with some of his closest associates in the prison, like-minded deviants who would share and enjoy his perverted desires. Howard, even at this stage in his life, continues to 'play the system' while, at the same time, trusting no one. In 2018, Howard, if released, will be seventy-four years of age. Despite his advanced age, in my professional opinion, he still poses a threat to any female of any age that he chooses to target.

During my time in An Garda Síochána, I have crossed paths, in a professional capacity, with the 'Wolfman' on a number of occasions. When he moved to Dublin first in the mid-nineties, he had lived for a while at the Morning Star Hostel, a hostel for homeless and transient men, run by the Legion of Mary at Morning Star Avenue, North Brunswick Street, in the city centre area. He had no sooner arrived there that, with his finely tuned predatory instincts, he started searching for a vulnerable partner. He began a relationship with Mary Doyle*, a single woman who lived in the nearby Regina Coeli Hostel. Despite all the admonitions and warnings she received from her friends, Mary fell head over heels in love with this strange man who was in possession of insatiable, perverted appetites.

The couple married, and moved into a small Dublin Corporation flats complex at Lindore Buildings on Church Street. Mary subsequently attended regularly at the Bridewell Garda Station, to which I was then attached, and complained about being assaulted by Howard. Although we spoke to him on a number of occasions, Mary would refuse to make a formal complaint about the physical abuse he was subjecting her to, and he was never prosecuted. Like many a victim in a similar position, she truly believed that he loved her, and that he would, in time, change.

After a few months, Howard began to befriend a local, intellectually challenged fifteen-year-old called Kerry White*. Both Kerry and her family were well known to me. She later told me that she had been completely swept off her feet by Howard. He showered her with gifts and money and, more importantly, continuously told her how much he loved her, and added that he was prepared to leave his wife for her. The besotted young teenager readily agreed to run away from home with Howard. He brought her in his car to a caravan that he had borrowed, which was parked on a site near Lough Neagh in the North of Ireland.

Kerry later said that when they arrived at the caravan, it was as if Howard underwent a complete personality change. He had bound her and, over a period of days, repeatedly sexually abused her. She was kept prisoner in the caravan.

Meanwhile the extended White family back in Dublin were growing more and more concerned about Kerry and, through their own sources, learned the location of Howard's caravan. A number of them quickly headed north. To this day, I do not know what transpired in that small caravan on the picturesque shores of Lough Neagh. Kerry, until her untimely death a few years ago, always refused to tell me. Whatever the family members did or said to him I do not know, but I never saw Howard back in Dublin after that visit! They returned to Dublin with her. The only comment Kerry ever made in relation to her 'rescue' was that she would have been 'more than surprised' had Howard ever shown up in her neighbourhood after the meeting with her family.

Years later, the facts of this case would be fully investigated by the Northern Ireland police. At their request, Kerry accompanied a number of Gardai from the Bridewell Station to the North to identify certain scenes to the investigation team. In a comprehensive report subsequently submitted to the Chief Prosecution Solicitor's office in Belfast, a recommendation was made that consideration should be given to charging Howard, arising out of his false imprisonment and sexual assault of Kerry, who, at the time, was just fifteen. Unfortunately, Kerry was not considered a reliable enough witness due to her intellectual impairment, and no charges were ever brought.

★

Following the conviction of Howard for the murder of Hannah Williams, the Police Service of Northern Ireland began to build a case against Howard for the murder of Arlene Arkinson. I was appointed by the Garda Commissioner to carry out all investigations connected with Arlene's disappearance on the southern side of the border. It would also be my job to rebut any suggestion that Arlene could be alive, and now residing in the Republic. With the assistance of colleagues in the Criminal Assets Bureau, I was allowed to trawl through social welfare, financial, medical, passport, driving licence and all other official records, for any mention of Arlene that would show if she had ever registered, made any claims or payments, or received any medical treatment in this jurisdiction, in the years since her disappearance. In June of 2005, I attended as a witness at the Crown Courts in Belfast on the twenty- first day of Robert Lesarian Howard's trial for the murder of Arlene Arkinson.

The trial had been preceded by a two-year news blackout of Howard's conviction, in relation to the Hannah Williams murder. It was feared that knowledge of his conviction would make it impossible for him to receive a fair trial. In addition, the Northern Ireland police were barred from giving 'similar factual evidence' as was given at his London trial. During Hannah's trial, for example, the evidence of his having previously brought another victim to the body dump site, trussed up in similar fashion to Hannah, formed one of the foundations of the case. Such evidence could not, however, be given in Northern Ireland. This led to the ridiculous situation where all the evidence of Howard's predatory activities that had been considered relevant at the trial in England was barred from the courts in Belfast. The Arkinson family would be left to rue the fact that, whereas their evidence in Hannah's case was considered to have been of vital importance in the securing of a conviction, but that now that they, in turn, needed it, Hannah's family were barred from giving similar evidence in Arlene's trial. Amy's abduction and treatment at his hands could not be given as evidence either.

Throughout the trial, Howard would maintain a stony silence. He never once glanced in the direction of Arlene's family. As each witness entered the witness box and gave their evidence, he sat looking straight ahead in the direction of the Judge. His defence team would suggest that Arlene had been a 'troubled' teenager who had, in all likelihood, simply run away from home. The family's hopes that they were finally to receive some justice and closure for their sister's murder were dashed when the jury returned a ten-to-two majority 'not guilty' verdict against Howard, after some twenty-three hours of deliberation. There was uproar in the court from her family members. The numerous members of the media, all of whom were aware of this predator's other crimes, could only sit there in amazement as the decision was announced.

Later, while sharing a cup of tea in a nearby restaurant with some PSNI colleagues prior to my return to Dublin, we were approached by a number of members of the public who had been following the trial, and were berated for not allowing the jury to hear the sordid details of Howard's murky past.

★

The 'Wolfman' is, as I have said, currently serving out his sentence in Frankland Prison. He is a voracious reader, and spends hours on end in his cell reading crime novels. As a sexual predator, he is unsurpassed in this jurisdiction. He preyed on the most vulnerable of all women, initially targeting children, then a much older woman. His depraved taste then turned to teenage girls, whom he physically subdued, then bound and gagged and, only then, sexually violated them.

The searches for Arelene's body continue to the present day on both sides of the border. There have been a number of attempts by the family to have an inquest held into her death, for the purpose of finally having her formally categorised as a victim of murder. Howard's defence team have, on a number of occasions over the years, successfully injuncted the Coroner's office, and prevented an inquest proceeding. It is anticipated that, were it to proceed, it could take upwards of two months to be fully heard. To date, the PSNI have supplied in excess of a quarter of a million documents to the Coroner. It is probable that Howard will be directed to attend and give evidence, but I firmly believe that he will resist any such move.

Arlene's father, Willie, died in 2008, without ever having seen his daughter, or her body, again. Although he had lived to see Howard stand trial for her murder, he died without ever being granted any closure in her case. Arlene's mother had died in 1990, when her daughter was just eleven.

Marie

Surely one of the most difficult tasks that an adopted child must face is reconciling the desire to trace their birth parents with the very real concern that, in so doing, they may cause unnecessary hurt to their adoptive parents. Having made the decision to proceed with their search, there then exists the possibility that the birth mother may not share the same need, or that she may, in fact, be untraceable. Marie Kilmartin had been forced, by her family, to place her child for adoption. When her daughter finally learned who her birth mother was, she also discovered that she had been dead for almost ten years. Her birth mother had been the victim of a brutal murder – a murder that, to this day, remains unsolved. Tragically, she had attended Marie's funeral in June of 1994, not knowing that the 'distant' family member, whose death she was there to honour, was actually her birth mother. Indeed, it must have been very difficult for many of those there on that day not to tell the fourteen-year-old youngster the truth, and allow her to mourn her own loss properly.

From an early age, Marie's parents, her two brothers and her sister were always very protective of her. Along with a very low IQ, there was an air of vulnerability about her that they feared would leave her open to being taken advantage of. The Kilmartins were considered to be a reasonably wealthy family. The father, Fred, owned a Ford car dealership franchise in the midlands. She was first hospitalised in Saint Patrick's at seventeen years of age, where she was diagnosed as suffering from manic-depressive psychosis. Despite the care and affection that was showered on her by her family, Marie, who, at almost twenty years of age, was still considered to be particularly vulnerable, became pregnant in 1979. At that stage she was working as a child-minder in an orphanage in Moate.

Due to concerns surrounding her mental health and ability to cope with her pregnancy, Marie was committed to Saint Fintan's Psychiatric Hospital in October of 1979. The medical advice given to the family at the time suggested that she would not be capable of rearing a child. It was recommended that, in the interests of both the mother and the child, the baby should be placed for adoption. On 29 March 1980, Marie was transferred to the General Hospital in

Portlaoise, where she gave birth to a daughter that she named Rose Marie.

Following the birth, Marie was transferred back to Saint Fintan's, where she was detained. She would be forced to leave her newborn baby behind to be adopted by a relation. Marie did not consent to her baby being placed for adoption. Her daughter would be twenty before she finally learned that Marie had been her birth mother, almost the same age as Marie herself had been when she had given birth. Marie remained a patient in St Fintan's for a number of months after the birth.

★

On her discharge from the hospital, she did not return to the family home in Ballinasloe, but moved into rented accommodation in Portlaoise town. A nurse, Aine Doherty*, who had befriended her while she was detained in St Fintan's, moved in with her as a carer/companion. This must have been a very difficult time for Marie, and it is certainly a mark of her inner strength that, despite occasional relapses, she survived both the loss of her daughter and estrangement from her family. Eventually they both moved into a bungalow that her father bought for her at Beladd on the Portlaoise/Stradbally road. Both women quickly settled into their new home. Marie got on very well with her new neighbours in the quiet estate, and was very highly thought of by all of them.

As a result of her medical condition, Marie suffered from a mild form of agoraphobia. While comfortable in the immediate environs of her home, she would seldom venture out alone into Portlaoise town. She had developed an inherent fear of men, and was also afraid of the dark, both of which severely restricted her social outings. Eventually, she secured part-time, voluntary work at a drop-in centre for senior citizens in the town. This was an environment where she felt both safe and needed. She got on well with both the staff and the clients in the centre, and was happy there, assisting in the cooking and serving of the lunches. Marie would, however, never walk the mile or so home from work alone, and would always take a lift, either from one of her co-workers or in the minibus attached to the day centre.

On 16 December 1993, the staff in the centre held a Christmas party for all the residents. Marie came into work at around 11 AM, after running a few errands and doing some shopping. Normally on the same day as the clients' party, staff and volunteers would get together in town after work for their own party. When they finished work at 4 PM, she got a lift home from two of her female colleagues.

They asked her if she would come to the party later, and she said that she might join them in the pub. Her friends knew that it was highly unlikely that she would. They declined her offer of coming into the house for a cup of tea, and then waited until she was in the house and had closed the front door behind her. This was a very important part of the daily ritual for those taking Marie home. It would also mark the last time that Marie Kilmartin would be seen alive.

When Aine arrived home shortly after 6 PM, she was surprised to find the house in darkness. Marie was not at home. The shopping she had brought home with her was lying on the kitchen table. This brings to mind the circumstances that attended the disappearance of Annie McCarrick. She too had more or less abandoned her shopping inside the house, not bothering to unpack it. In both instances, it can be safe to assume that they intended to return later to do so. Initially believing that Marie might have gone on to the staff party, Aine was not, at that stage, unduly concerned.

★

By 8 PM, a few telephone calls quickly confirmed that Marie had last been seen shortly after 4 PM, and that she had not turned up for the party. For some reason, Aine did not follow up on this marked change in Marie's established patterns. Indeed, it would only be the following morning, Friday, before the disappearance was reported. Aine told her neighbour, Mary*, the wife of the local Detective Sergeant, and she in turn rang her husband at Portlaoise Garda Station. A missing-person report was then filed.

Given her medical condition, her agoraphobia and her fear of the dark, Marie's disappearance was treated as suspicious from the outset. A full-scale search was launched. Appeals were made in the local media, and people who were known to her were contacted. An examination of the house quickly revealed that no foul play had occurred there. The investigation very quickly appeared to be going nowhere.

Tom Jones, an experienced detective attached to the Portlaoise Garda Station, decided to do a check on the landline phone in the house. He discovered that, shortly before 4.30 PM on Thursday afternoon, at a time when it had been established that Marie was in the house alone, a telephone call had been received. The call had lasted for over two minutes, and there were no follow-up calls or activity on the phone after that. The duration of the call would suggest that an actual conversation had occurred between Marie and the caller.

It was further established that the call had been made from a public telephone kiosk on the main Portlaoise-to-Dublin road, on the outskirts of the town. This phone box is just a short distance from St Fintan's Hospital, where Marie had, of course, spent a number of months as an in patient. It is also located near to Portlaoise Prison, the high-security prison used for the incarceration of subversive prisoners. A check on the telephone activity in this kiosk quickly revealed that, other than the call to Marie's home, no other calls had been made from it in or around that time. Earlier and later calls were fully checked out, and were found not to be relevant to the enquiry. Technical examination of the telephone kiosk did not provide any investigative leads.

Over a period of days, Gardai maintained a presence near the telephone kiosk, interviewing pedestrians and motorists, trying to establish whether they had been in the area on the afternoon of the 16th. On 24 February 1994, following the broadcasting of an appeal on the RTÉ Crimeline programme, a female came forward, and said that, in or around the time that the call was being made, she had walked past the phone kiosk. Her attention had been focused on passing traffic as she was attempting to hitch a lift to Monasterevin, some six miles from Portlaoise. She had been in town to collect her social-welfare money. The witness had a vague recollection of seeing a male either entering or exiting the telephone box at the time she passed by. She described him as being about thirty years of age with dark hair. Given the door height of the kiosk, she estimated him to have been between five foot six inches and five foot nine inches in height. This male has never been located.

★

It would appear that Marie had, on receipt of the telephone call, immediately left the house, not even waiting to put away the few bits and pieces she had brought home with her. Once again, it is important here to recall her medical and mental condition. Considering that it was almost half four and already dark when she received this phone call, one can only speculate on what it was that had persuaded her to leave the safety and security of her own home to venture out into the dark. This was, by any measure, a huge step for her to take, and reflects the importance she had placed on either the caller or the contents of the call. She would certainly not have gone out to meet a stranger. House-to-house enquiries would establish that she had not been picked up in a car.

This is a very relevant factor in determining who murdered Marie Kilmartin. Here was a woman who was afraid, most days, to venture out alone, leaving her house on a dark winter's evening, almost certainly in response to a request made in the telephone call she had received. We can be in no doubt of the seriousness with which Marie greeted this call. The step she took in leaving the house was, for her, huge.

A number of scenarios as to the possible identity of the caller have been considered over the years. These were subdivided into several categories, which included:

(A) Someone from her past with whom she may have been, at one time, very close
(B) Someone with whom she had been having an affair or other relationship
(C) A person with whom she was comfortable, whom she trusted implicitly and in whose company she felt safe
(D) A female whom she believed to be non-threatening

What this actually implies is that Marie Kilmartin, when leaving her house on that dark December evening, had an appointment to meet a person who was known to her. To date, this person has not come forward, and it must, as a consequence, be accepted that she met her death at the hands of someone who was known to her – a very unsettling prospect.

★

At 8.50 PM on Friday evening, 10 June 1994, while Garda Tom Flynn was off-duty and watching a football match in a field in the townland of Barnanaghs (locally referred to as The Borness, an area about ten miles from Portlaoise town), he was approached by another off-duty prison officer, Thomas Deegan. Deegan told him that he had found what he believed to be the body of a female submerged in a bog hole, at an area called Pims Lane, just a short distance away on the main Portlaoise-to-Mountmellick Road. He had earlier been cutting turf in the surrounding bogland. Tom Flynn contacted Portlaoise station, and Garda Phillip Lyne arrived at the scene shortly afterwards. Once the presence of the body was confirmed, the area was sealed off and preserved.

The area where the body lay was situated on the left-hand side, towards the end of Pims Lane. There was an area opposite the drainage ditch where the body lay, which was often used as an unauthorised dumping ground for household rubble. The ditch itself was partially concealed by undergrowth. At that time of year, the ditch contained very little water. Significantly, this was also an area that had not been dredged since the previous summer. Regular callers to this section of the bog would later tell Gardai that they recalled, as early as the previous November, seeing a child's buggy dumped on the illegal dump site.

On Saturday morning, the State Pathologist, Professor John Harbison, called to Portarlington Garda Station. He was taken, under escort, to the scene, to view the body *in situ*. He was assisted there by members of the Garda Technical Bureau, who had earlier that morning been dispatched to assist in the removal of the body and the retrieval of forensic evidence.

What was immediately apparent to all who attended at the grisly scene on that fine summer's morning was the fact that the body of the unfortunate victim had been carefully placed, as opposed to just dumped, into the drainage ditch. It was lying on its back, with the feet raised higher than the head. The positioning of the body would tend to suggest that the person who had placed it into the drainage ditch was very strong, or alternatively, had had help from an accomplice.

A ladies' overcoat, later identified as having been worn by Marie when she was last seen alive, had been draped across the body, like a blanket. On the chest had been placed a six-inch cement block. When the ditch had, over the winter, filled with water, this block would have forced the upper part of her body downwards, causing the legs to rise upwards. The block was intended to prevent the body from floating up to the surface of the water, an act that displayed an intimate knowledge of the bog movements over the seasons. However, as Professor Harbison would later state, the forcing of the upper part of the torso downwards would cause Marie's body to appear to be almost 'standing on her head'.

The shell of a child's pram, previously observed by witnesses on the other side of the lane, together with a Kosangas 'Super Ser' room heater, had then been placed across the bog hole. Were it not for the alert witness, the body could well have lain there for years without detection.

The ViCLAS profilers insisted that this case that this case had to be considered relevant to our enquiries, given that the body of Marie – as with those of both Antoinette and Patricia – had been concealed in a bog hole, notwithstanding the considerable distance between the various dump sites.

To facilitate the removal of the body, and to avoid the loss of any potential forensic evidence that might have been present, it was decided to dig a second ditch parallel to the ditch in which the body lay, and to gently slide it onto a body bag.

The post-mortem examination was carried out that same day, in the morgue at Tullamore Hospital by Professor Harbison. Given the damage that being submerged over that period of time had caused to the body, it was impossible to arrange for a visual identification. Formal identification of remains before he commences his examination is considered to be vital to a pathologist, for continuity at any subsequent proceedings.

Four rings, a watch and a gold chain were found on the body. All were identified as being Marie's property. Various work colleagues identified the clothing as that worn by Marie on the day that she had disappeared.

Formal identification of the remains as being those of Marie Kilmartin was made through dental comparison. An impression of the body's teeth was taken by a forensic dentist, and was found to be a perfect match with the records on file with her own dentist.

The body was fully dressed when located, which more or less ruled out sexual assault as a possible motive. Her clothing and underclothing was all intact. While one might consider the possibility of a culprit dressing his victim after an assault, it is a task that is almost virtually impossible to do properly. Trying to dress a corpse is a huge task; time and again it has been found that buttons have not been fastened in the correct sequence and even that underclothing has been put on the wrong way around.

Professor Harbison would find no evidence of sexual assault in his examination of the body. He concluded that a bilateral fracture, which he had found to the thyroid cartilage, could be considered as evidence of manual strangulation, and the possible cause of death. No evidence of ligature damage was present. In addition, the body was intact, with no trace of any blunt-force injury being present. For instance, if a blow to the head had killed Marie, he would have expected to find evidence of this, even at this late stage. The neck injuries were consistent with death having been caused by manual strangulation.

Given that at least six months had passed between Marie being first reported missing and the finding of her body, there was little likelihood of a technical examination of the area in the bog yielding evidence as to the identity of the culprit, or everything that would suggest that the fatal assault had occurred in or around where the body had been located. Nevertheless, a full examination was carried out. No such evidence was found. What was considered significant after these searches was the fact that several items known to have been in her possession on that day were not located. Despite extensive searches at the scene and its environs, no trace was found of Marie's glasses, or her handbag. This prompted the question as to whether they were retained by the culprit as 'souvenirs', or lost at the primary assault scene.

One of the theories that quickly gained favour with the investigation team was that it was highly unlikely that a fully conscious Marie would have voluntarily accompanied anyone, no matter how much she trusted or knew them, to that bleak and lonely spot on a dark winter's night. This would, in turn, suggest that the thirty-five-year-old was murdered, or at least rendered unconscious elsewhere, and that her body had been taken by the culprit to the bog, where he had, in a gesture which heaped indignity upon brutality, attempted to hide it in a bid to prevent its recovery.

This generated another angle that investigators attempted to follow up on without success. Was the cement block that was used to weigh down the body – as with the broken pram – an item of opportunity, located by the culprit as he went about in the dark, looking for a suitable place to hide the body, or had he brought it with him in the car or van he had used to transport the body for that express purpose. Similarly, the provenance of the gas heater shell has never been established. The question of the type of vehicle that was used by the culprit is also raised; a body would take up considerable space in any saloon car. A larger type of car or a van would be far more suitable for this chore.

It is conceded that the area was regularly used as an unofficial dump site. However, the task of gathering these items together to throw on top of the body would have taken some time, time which left the perpetrator at some risk of being disturbed.

There was, of course, a third alternative, one that some consideration must be given to also. It is quite possible that the bog hole where Marie's body had been hidden had been preselected by the culprit. This would suggest that, at the time the culprit made the telephone call which lured Marie out of the safety of her home, they intended to kill her and bring her body to the bog hole, which had already been selected, alongside the items used to conceal her body. This would display a degree of cold-heartedness that is seldom seen.

Another clue that the choice of dump site revealed was that the perpetrator had to be a local person, or at least a person with considerable local knowledge. It is generally accepted that Marie was murdered shortly after meeting up with the person from whom she received the telephone call. It would have been almost completely dark at that stage. Only someone who knew exactly where they were going would have been able to drive the sixteen kilometres from her home at Beladd, to the bog at the end of Pims Lane. When revisiting this area many years later as part of the Operation TRACE review, I could not help but think that at any time it would be a bleak and lonely spot, but at night in the middle of winter it must be particularly intimidating. Any stranger staggering around, carrying an item as large as a body, would run the risk of ending up at the bottom of a bog hole themselves!

Some two weeks after the finding of the body, Gardai made two arrests. One of the males was fifty years of age, and the second man was in his early twenties. The older of the two had previously worked near the centre where Marie worked. He had left this job the day after she had disappeared. He would have been well known to her, and, it was rumoured, had often given her a lift home from work.

★

A sixteen-year-old girl, with whom he was having an affair at that time, would tell Gardai that, on one occasion, they had had sex on an inflatable mattress in the rear of his van, while it was parked in Pims Lane, just a short distance from where the body would eventually be located. This had occurred about ten days before Marie went missing. It would further emerge, through various enquiries, that this male used to cut turf on a bank in Pims Lane, less than a hundred and fifty yards from the body dump site.

The girl also told Gardai that, within weeks of Marie's disappearance, she and this much older man had run away together. They had posed as man and wife, and moved into a flat at Chapel Street in the nearby town of Durrow. While they were together, he had, she added, regularly spoken about Marie Kilmartin. He referred to her as a 'bitch' and appeared to be resentful of her parents' wealth.

On another occasion he had, she said, given her a present of two rings, as a token of his affection for her. However, within days, he took them back, and she had not seen them since. When she asked him about them, he told her that he had lost them.

On Tuesday 23 September 2008, as part of an ongoing review of this case, two other men, aged forty and sixty, and a woman, also in her sixties, were arrested and detained for questioning in relation to Marie's murder. This was part of a planned operation, and the older man was taken to Portlaoise Garda Station, with the female and the younger man being detained in Tullamore

Station. It was believed that these two were in possession of important information concerning the murder. They would be released without being charged, shortly before 11 PM that same night, while the older male would remain in custody at Portlaoise until the following morning, when he too was released.

Both sets of arrests are considered relevant to the final outcome of this investigation, an outcome that could be affected were their details to be released in any public forum other than a court of law.

Marie's daughter, Aine, has waged a public-awareness campaign over the years to ensure that her mother's case is never forgotten. To mark the thirteenth anniversary of her disappearance, she spent the day distributing leaflets appealing for information throughout Portlaoise town. She has done a number of television and radio interviews, asking that anyone with information as to the identity of the perpetrator come forward. Her campaign is ongoing. In a newspaper interview, she appealed directly to the people 'who know what happened to my mother'. Through her direct involvement, the *Crimestoppers* programme has now joined the appeal, and they have offered a substantial reward to anyone coming forward with information.

Both of Marie's parents, Fred and Rose, together with her brother Noel, have since passed on. However, the search for the truth behind Marie's brutal murder is being carried on to this very day, by the daughter she never knew.

Stokes, Power and Colgan

There were two further crimes that, it had been suggested, we review in order to broaden the search parameters of the ViCLAS analysis fields. In both instances, the culprits had been made amenable and, in one case, the victim had actually survived her ordeal. One crime concerned the brutal rape of a young sex worker by two males, while, in the second, the victim was beaten to death by her assailant, who would later call into a Garda station and report the crime. What was considered significant in both instances was that the location of both crime scenes was within walking distance of the body dump sites of both Antoinette and Patricia.

On 30 December 1994, almost three years to the day since Patricia Doherty had last been seen alive, and a little over a year after Marie Kilmartin went missing, Valerie*, a young drug addict working the 'beat' in the Fitzwilliam Square area of Dublin's south inner city, would make a decision that would almost cost her life. Her need for a heroin fix made her both careless and vulnerable, and she agreed to get into a car with two male occupants, something that, under normal circumstances, she would not contemplate for an instant. It was late. The streets were, for the most part, deserted, in that lull in festivities that can occur between the Christmas and New Year celebrations. Driven by her heroin addiction and that of her partner, she had no other option but to be out on those lonely streets at that time of night.

The silver estate car that pulled up just at the entrance to the darkened laneway where Valerie was standing was driven by thirty-year-old Thomas Stokes, a settled traveller from outside Newbridge in County Kildare, the same town from which, some four years later, nineteen-year-old Deirdre Jacob had disappeared.

★

By 1994, Stokes was well known to Gardai, having already served prison sentences in this and other jurisdictions for violent crime. As recently as 1989, he had been convicted by the English courts of attempting to burn down a house in which he had locked his estranged wife. This crime was all the more shocking given that Stokes had himself previously lost close family members in a fire. He received an eight-year sentence for this crime, but later managed to convince a parole-board meeting that he was a changed man, resulting in him being free on that December night to commit further serious crimes.

His travelling companion was also of a similar disposition. Andrew Power, though then only in his early twenties, had already built up a reputation for himself as a violent and aggressive criminal. He had a prior conviction for sexual assault in England. Given the disparity in their ages, Stokes was nominally, at least, the leader of this pair of predators. Power, however, was his equal in his capacity for violence. They made a formidable team as they cruised the streets that December night, trawling for a victim. They were intent on abducting a woman – any woman.

They did not know, at that stage, what their chosen victim's ultimate fate might be. That they were going to snatch a female off the streets and have sex with her was a given, but whether or not she survived the ordeal hung in the balance. It was completely dependant on what they felt like when they had finished with her. For them, their ultimate victim was the classic example of someone in the wrong place at the 'right' time.

They had a conversation with Valerie, who agreed to perform oral sex upon them in turn. She got into the front seat of the car, and gave them directions to a local car park where she normally brought her clients. They ignored her directions, and took off at speed. She realised then that she was in serious trouble. Ignoring her screams and pleas for mercy, Stokes drove out of the city, through Rathfarnham village and into the mountains. On a deserted road beyond Powerscourt and Enniskerry, the area, incidentally, in which Annie McCarrick had last been seen alive less than two years previously, Stokes stopped the car. They folded down the back seat of the car and dragged their hapless victim into it, tearing her clothes from her body.

Over the next three hours, Valerie was subjected to a callous and vicious sexual assault. Oral sex was followed by violent, penetrative sex, both vaginal and anal. Her assailants appeared to be 'getting off' on watching each other perform, shouting words of encouragement, and suggesting even more deviant acts. Power had bitten her on the shoulder so deeply that he had broken the skin. At one stage, to her horror, they took time out from abusing her to fondle and play with each other. They also continued to refer to each other by their first names, a fact that convinced her further that she was not going to survive the ordeal.

★

During penetrative sex, they both wore condoms that they had removed from their victim's handbag, conscious, no doubt, of both the risk of sexually transmitted disease, and of leaving any trace evidence. This forensic awareness was fairly unusual for the times, the year being 1994. They joked about using her own condoms while they abused her. These same condoms, carelessly discarded next to where the car had been parked, would subsequently be recovered by Gardai examining the scene. Dr Maureen Smyth would extract DNA from the semen it contained. This would, in time, lead to Stokes being identified as the donor. His defence would be that the semen-filled condom had been planted by Gardai!

Finally sated, they both climbed out of the back of the car, leaving their semi-conscious victim sprawled across the seats. Having adjusted their own clothing, they stood leaning against the car, smoking and talking quietly. Valerie instinctively knew that this was the moment that would decide her fate: that a decision was being reached as to whether she would live or die. A wrong move, a shout for help or a plea for mercy might be all it would take to push them over the edge and decide to finish her off, leaving her battered and defiled body to rot on that barren hillside.

During their whispered conversation, Stokes walked around to the rear of the car and lifted the tailgate. Through partially closed eyes, she saw him take out the wheel brace, and, holding it down by his side, then close the door and return to speak with Power. They appeared to reach a decision then, and both of them got back into the front of the car and, with Stokes driving, pulled out onto the road. From where she lay, Valerie watched the roadway ahead. She was certain that they were going to take her further up the mountain and kill her. To her astonishment, she realised that they were actually heading back towards the city.

Stokes stopped the car just off Grange Road in Rathfarham village and dragged Valerie out of the car, forcing her to lie on the ground, and warning her, at the same time, not to look at the car number plate. He jumped back into the car, and drove away at speed, leaving her semi-conscious on the roadway, where a passing motorist found her moments later and called for assistance.

Stokes was arrested by Garda Desmond Quinn as he drove through Cork city the following Saturday afternoon, for a moving-road-traffic violation. He gave a false name and address to Des when he was arrested for the offence. Under this fictitious name, he appeared in Cork District Court on Monday morning, where he immediately pleaded guilty, and received a short prison sentence. He was transferred to Portlaoise Prison. Stokes was convinced that Gardai were not aware of his true identity and, more importantly, had not linked him to Valerie's rape, which was receiving widespread press coverage. He intended to serve out his sentence and then disappear for a while.

★

He did not know, however, that Desmond Quinn, a thoroughly competent and professional policeman, had already passed on details of his arrest to the team investigating the rapes. The significance of the type of car that his prisoner had been driving when arrested had not been lost on him. Stokes' car was impounded, and subjected to rigorous forensic examination. Doctor Sheila Willis of the state Forensic Science Laboratory would identify a head hair lifted from the rear seat as being Valerie's. She also identified fibres found on her clothing as having originated from the car-seat covers. In addition, she would find fibres from Valerie's clothes on the back seat of the car. This two-way transference was considered sufficient proof that this was the car that the rape had occurred in.

Immediately upon his release from prison, Stokes was arrested for rape. Valerie would bravely view an identification parade, in which a supremely confident Stokes had agreed to participate. She stood directly in front of him, and, pointing at him, identified him as her assailant. Stokes denied any involvement in the crime when interviewed. At his subsequent trial, the stone-cold rapist would spend over a day in the witness box giving evidence on his own behalf. In a carefully modulated voice, he would attempt to convince the jury that not only was he innocent of the charges put to him, but that he was, in fact, the victim of a carefully orchestrated campaign by the various organs of the State to get at him because of his work for travellers' rights. The jury took less than four hours to find him guilty of all the various charges. While sentencing him to life imprisonment, Judge Moriarity described Stokes as being both 'devious' and 'dangerous'.

It would be almost two years before Adrian Power was located and arrested for his part in the crime. At his trial, great play was made by his defence counsel on the disparity in ages of Power and his accomplice, Stokes. They suggested that undue influence had been exerted upon him by this much older and more controlling figure. The degree of consent or otherwise shown by the victim to the various sex acts that had taken place in the car on that December night was also raised. In Powers' case, the jury would be back after little more than an hour with a guilty verdict. However, the sentence that he would receive for his crimes would be just ten years.

During his trial, Stokes had produced a witness who claimed that he had spent the night of the alleged rape in her house in Kildare town. She told the jury that Stokes had slept in her bed while she had spent the night on a lumpy sofa! To back up this alibi, she produced a diary with an entry referring to him having spent the night. However, when it was admitted as evidence and given to handwriting experts, they found that a portion of the relevant entry had been crossed out, and that the obliterated entry appeared to refer to his having stayed in her house on the night before the rape, and not on the actual night itself.

The witness, however, was not for turning, and was adamant that Stokes had been with her until after 9 AM on the morning of 30 December, despite all evidence pointing to the contrary. One could not be faulted for thinking that this witness must have had a criminal background, or was someone with whom Stokes had had dealings throughout his long criminal career. This could not be further from the truth. The witness was a professional in the health care industry – an unlikely conspirator.

Incredibly, a witness put forward by convicted rapist Phillip Colgan, another deviant who also used the Kilakee Road as a body dump site for his own female victim, was herself a woman in full-time employment, with a long career in the field of education.

When he was just nineteen years of age, Colgan had broken into an old folks' sheltered accommodation unit, near his home in Donaghmeade, north Dublin. There, at knifepoint, he had subjected an eighty-year-old woman to a night of repeated rape and sexual assault. When taking his leave of his frail victim before daylight the following morning, Colgan, in a final indignity, forced her to hand over her life savings. His haul amounted to the princely sum of €140.

Less than a week later, he struck again. On this occasion, he tricked a foreign national, a nineteen-year-old female, into accompanying him back to his home to attend a family party. When they arrived at his house, she discovered that it was actually empty. Before she could make her getaway, he sexually abused her. Colgan had, within one week, started on the slippery slope to full-blown predator, with his choice of victims being vulnerable females, ranging in age from nineteen to eighty. As a result of diligent police work, he was quickly apprehended and charged. In July of 1992, he was sentenced by Judge Paul Carney to a total of eight years for the rape of his eighty-year-old victim. The sentence meant that Colgan was free to reoffend by 1998!

He served out the bulk of his sentence in Wheatfield Prison. There, he successfully completed the much-vaunted Sex Offenders Rehabilitation Programme. Colgan, as we shall shortly see, is living proof of, in my opinion, the complete uselessness of all such programmes. He also found true love while in prison. Pauline*, a qualified teacher who also gave music lessons to prison inmates, became infatuated by Colgan's charm and good looks. Convinced that he had mended his ways and that, in her, he would find the contentment and self-belief that he had so obviously lacked throughout his youth, she vowed to wait for him until he was released from prison. When he walked out of prison during the summer of 1998, Pauline was waiting outside the main gate for him. She brought him back to her house at the Crannagh Castle estate in Rathfarnham and, after a whirlwind romance, the happy couple were married in September that year. Just two days later, on the other side of the city, the Garda Commissioner would brief the press about the establishment of a specialist taskforce set up to examine the cases of a number of missing females.

Colgan would lie low for a number of months. On the outside, Pauline and Phillip looked like any other newly married couple. Despite their disparity in age – Colgan was still only twenty-five years old – they appeared happy and content. Colgan began to slowly but surely weave an aura of respectability about himself. They were popular and highly regarded amongst their neighbours. It seemed almost as if he was trying to show the world what a changed character he was. However, beneath this façade, dangerous fantasies, spawned, perhaps, from time spent in prison mentally reliving his past exploits, bubbled away. Far from being reformed or cured, he had just become much more conscious of avoiding detection as he went about selecting his next target.

On the night of 1 March 1999, almost a year after his release from prison, and just six months after his wedding day, Colgan struck again. He had spent the early part of that night drinking in pubs and clubs around the south inner-city area. To the casual observer, he was just another male out on his own enjoying a few quiet drinks and soaking up the atmosphere in and around Temple Bar. In reality, he was on the hunt for a fresh victim. Before that night was over, an innocent female would be battered to death near Kilakee Woods, with her naked body casually discarded in a ditch.

By 2 AM, he was driving through the streets of Dublin, on the hunt for a suitable victim. As if following in the footsteps of Stokes and Power, he headed towards Fitzwilliam Square. Colgan knew that if he was going to find a lone female anywhere, it would be on the streets and laneways that bisected the square.

He would later tell Gardai that, as he drove along Nassau Street, he saw a female walking on the footpath. She was alone, and was heading in the direction of Saint Stephen's Green. As in all such cases, there is usually only one version of the events as they unfolded that is available to Gardai and to the courts. In this incident, the version would come from Colgan. It was, of course, structured in such a way so as to play down any act of criminality, and portray his actions in the best possible light.

The female whom Colgan claimed to have met was twenty-three-year-old Layla Brennan, a girl who had, at one stage, developed an addiction to hard drugs. In recent months, she appeared to her family to have overcome her addiction. A native of Clondalkin, Dublin, she was residing in the city centre with friends the night she was targeted by Colgan.

He would later say that he had stopped his car to offer the girl a lift, only to discover that she was 'on the game'. She had, he claimed, straightaway offered to have penetrative sex with him for money. In a moment of weakness, he agreed and, following her directions, had driven to a laneway beside the rugby pitch in Ballsbridge. Colgan would say that he had, at that stage, changed his mind about having sex with her, fearing the damage that such an act could do to his marriage. He said that he informed his passenger that he had changed his mind about having sex with her, and offered to drop her back to Nassau Street.

On hearing this news, she had, in his version of events, become very aggressive, and demanded that he pay her the money they had agreed upon. When he refused, she had begun to remove her clothing and allegedly told him that she knew his car registration number, and intended, if she did not get the money, to go to the police to report that he had raped her. She then, he said, opened the passenger door and attempted to get out of the car.

He described himself as having panicked in response to her threat to involve the police. With his record, he knew that her story would be believed, and that he would receive a long prison sentence if he was convicted. He was also concerned, he said, about the effect that such an allegation could have on his marriage. He had hit her in the face, momentarily stunning her, and then pulled her back into the car. She began to scream. To stop her, he had started choking her.

Neighbours in the nearby apartment complex would later tell Gardai that they had been awakened by the sounds of a female screaming, but had been unable to ascertain where the noise was coming from. The girl began to struggle and to strike out at him. She scratched him across the face and hands. He, however, managed to overpower her. In his own words, he then removed her bra and, wrapping it around her neck, had started to choke her with it. She stopped struggling, and only then did he realise the enormity of what he had just done.

Colgan claimed that he transferred his victim's body into the boot of his car, and had driven off towards the Dublin Mountains. When he reached the Killakee Road, he slowed down, watching for a turn that would take him off the main road. After a few minutes, he pulled onto the hard shoulder and, in the darkness, half carried, half dragged Layla some thirty to forty yards through the heather and gorse bushes. To his horror he discovered that, though unconscious, she was still breathing. He almost stumbled down a steep incline that had been almost invisible in the dark. Settling Layla's inert body on the edge of the incline, he pushed and shoved her down the hill.

Colgan then returned to his car, and retrieved the car jack from the boot. Returning to where she lay at the base of the incline, he struck a number of blows to the head. He would claim that he had then taken her clothing and placed it, along with the jack, in a bag that he had brought from the car.

Later that same night, when asked by his wife about the injuries clearly visible on his face, he would tell her that he had been assaulted by two Gardai who had stopped his car. He hid the bag containing his victim's clothes in the garage. Over the next few days, he refused to leave the house. Never straying too far from a television or radio, he waited to hear news that a body had been found.

Colgan said that his biggest concern was that while he had been pushing Layla's body down the steep incline, he had heard the sound of a passing car briefly slowing down, as it drove by where he had parked his own car. He knew that when word about the body finally got out, this other driver might very quickly put two and two together.

★

In desperation, Colgan turned to the woman who loved him, no doubt hoping that, rather than lose him, she would provide him with an alibi should the need arise. She had spent the previous two days constantly asking him what was wrong, and to tell her what happened. He was so confident of her infatuation with him and the power that it gave him over her, that he decided to come clean and tell her what had happened.

Whatever the response he had hoped for, he certainly did not get it. Barely able to conceal her revulsion, she insisted that he go to the Gardai, tell them what he had done and point out the location of the body to them. Her repugnance, and refusal to help, took him completely by surprise. He was unused to women not responding to his charms, and to being refused anything. He would spend that Thursday night mulling over his choices. He now had a witness to whom he had, in a moment of weakness, confessed his crime. He realised that this, coupled with the person who had seen his car in the mountains, would be enough to convict him.

I have no doubt that, at some stage during that long night, the thought must have crossed his warped mind that, if he disposed of Pauline, he just might be able to walk away. However, he also realised that were she to disappear, it would open a whole new can of worms for him.

The following Friday morning, Colgan and Pauline walked into the public office at Rathfarnham Garda Station. He told the station orderly that he wished to speak with a detective. When asked about the nature of his enquiry, Colgan told the astonished young Garda behind the desk that he wanted to talk to them about a woman he had killed. He and his wife were ushered into a waiting room, and were quickly joined by two of the local detectives. In a calm, detached voice, he told them that he had killed a girl a few nights earlier.

Gardai now found themselves in a unique position. Here they had a man admitting to a murder, a crime that had not been reported, and which they did not know of. Nevertheless, Colgan's admissions were treated seriously. He went on to describe where he had disposed of the body, and where they could find both the murder weapon and the victim's clothes.

Pauline sat beside him throughout this initial statement, encouraging him to tell the truth. Other Gardai were quickly directed to the area where Colgan claimed to have disposed of the body, and they got back via radio, in less than half an hour, to say that they had found the naked body of a female, who appeared to have suffered horrific head injuries.

★

The post-mortem examination would cast serious doubt on the version of events given by Colgan. For instance, bruising to the vaginal area was found – marks that were consistent with attempted forced penetration. More chillingly, it was established that his victim had been dressed when she was battered to death, which meant that the removal of her clothing had taken place after she had been killed. It takes a certain depraved mind to strip a dead body. One can only speculate as to what perverse desire drove him to strip his victim. Only Colgan can ever answer this, but he probably never will.

A full murder investigation was then initiated. Colgan was formally arrested, and held in Rathfarnham Garda Station. This was a most unusual case, in that Gardai now had both a perpetrator and a victim, but still had no idea as to who she was. Recent reports of missing females were trawled, but no one fitting the description was found. A full description of the body, including the clothing that she had been wearing, was broadcast on both national radio and television.

The fact that Layla was not living at home meant that her family were initially unaware that she was missing. Her father Richard, however, on hearing the description of the girl that was given in the television appeal, immediately suspected that it might be his daughter. He drove to Rathfarnham Garda Station, and there he spoke to some of the investigators. He was taken to the City Morgue, and identified the body of his daughter to the Gardai.

Following his arrest, Colgan began to make some radical changes to his earlier admissions. It was obvious that the enormity of what he was facing – as opposed to what he had actually done – was hitting home with him. Ever the survivor, he now began working on his defence, a defence so bizarre as to be almost believable. He told Gardai that he had been forced, at knifepoint, to kill Layla! He claimed that during the course of that night he had met a male foreign national in one of the bars that he had visited. They had had sex – a sexual preference Colgan had developed a taste for while in prison. Later that night, at his new friend's insistence, they had picked up a prostitute. After having sex with her, the man had then forced him, at knifepoint, to kill her.

During his subsequent trial for murder, Colgan would embellish this story even further, before a jury in the Central Criminal Court. His defence would be that the foreigner he had previously told Gardai about was actually a homeless Scotsman called Wayne. After having penetrative sex in his car, they had driven aimlessly around, and Wayne had spotted Layla, who was known to him. He told Colgan that Layla owed him a lot of money, money he had given her to purchase drugs, and asked him to pull in beside her. In the ensuing conversation, Layla had, he claimed, agreed to have sex with both of them in order to write off her debt.

She had directed him to drive to the laneway beside the rugby pitch. This is a regular feature of admissions made by criminals where, in an effort to give an element of credence to their lies, they will intersperse some truths within the fiction that they were spinning. From the evidence already presented, he was aware that Layla's screams for mercy had been overheard in that area. Colgan recounted Wayne saying that he would have sex with her first, and, at Layla's insistence, that Colgan would leave the car, and return only when Wayne was finished. He said that he had gone to the top of the laneway, and waited there.

On returning to the car some minutes later, he was met by a distraught Wayne, who told him that when they were having sex, Layla had tried to 'dip' him, that is, to take money out of his pocket. Wayne said that in the fight that ensued, he had killed her. On looking into the rear of his car, Colgan said he could clearly see that Layla was dead. She was lying across the back seat with her bra tied tightly around her neck. Both of them had panicked at that stage, and began arguing about what they should do.

Colgan said that he feared that his wife would learn of his homosexual encounter, which would become public knowledge were an investigation into the girl's death ever launched. As she sat in the courtroom listening to this tale, Pauline must indeed have been wondering just what she had gotten herself into.

Colgan said that they had decided that the only hope of their avoiding arrest was to dispose of the body of their victim. They placed it into the boot of the car, and Colgan drove out beyond Rathfarnham village and onto the road at Kilakee. Between them, they carried her body some distance off the road, and rolled it down a steep incline. Wayne had taken the wheel-brace out of the car, and Colgan described how, as he looked on in horror, Wayne had repeatedly smashed the wheel-brace across her head. He had then turned and begun to attack Colgan. After a violent struggle, he managed to wrest the wheel-brace from Wayne's grasp and, in a move borne of desperation and self-preservation, he had struck him with the wheel-brace, knocking him unconscious to the ground. Placing Wayne's body into the boot of his car, he had then driven further into the mountains, where he had disposed of it. He refused to reveal to the court the location of this second body.

As defences go, it was rather unique. On the one hand, here he was offering an explanation as to how Layla had met her death in his car, how trace evidence from the victim would come to be found there and how his wheel-brace had been used to inflict the fatal blows. A crime, according to him, had been committed, but not one that he had taken any part in. The second part of his defence was equally unusual. Here he was, making an admission in a public forum, to having taken a life. However, he would only ever face censure for this latter crime if a body was located, or if Wayne was identified. He had also, in the same process, painted Layla as a heroin-addicted prostitute and a thief.

★

His trial took place under the old rules, whereby juries were required to give a unanimous decision. All it would have taken was for one of the twelve to be swayed by this most unusual defence. The jury retired at the end of the second week of the trial to reach their verdict. They were back within only three hours, to the surprise of all those gathered in the packed courtroom. They returned a verdict of guilty to murder. They had obviously been influenced by the comments of Senior Counsel for the Prosecution Maureen Clarke, who described Colgan as a 'cold, dispassionate and clever liar'. She had described his version of the events as sounding like a 'Halloween story', both a comment on his story, and a reference to the time of year.

Almost two years to the day after Colgan received his mandatory life sentence, another predator, John Crerar, who, like Colgan, thought he could get away with murder, would start his own sentence.

Neither Power, Stokes nor Colgan were ever linked to the disappearances of any of the TRACE target females, nor, indeed, to the disappearance of any other female. Nevertheless, given their modus operandi, their targeting of lone females on the open road and their selected crime scenes, they were considered relevant as POIs, and had to be 'Traced, Eliminated or Implicated'.

Larry Murphy

Operation TRACE would be in existence for some eighteen months by the time that a crime was committed that caused widespread fear and panic amongst the population as a whole. As more and more details of the incident emerged, the revulsion felt by the population deepened. The fact that this nauseating and revolting crime had been committed by someone who appeared to be a hard-working, happily married member of our own community who had never come to the attention of the Gardai, only made it more difficult to accept in the minds of most people.

Shortly after 8 PM on Friday evening, 11 February 2000, Michelle Conway* closed her ladies' clothes shop*, located just off the main street in Carlow town. Bidding a good night to her co-workers, she had turned to walk the short distance to the nearby apartment-complex car park, where she parked her car every day. It had been a busy day, and the twenty-eight-year-old was looking forward to a quiet night in, in front of the television. It was that hour on a Friday evening when the 'weekend buzz' had not quite started. The area she walked through to her car would be thronged in another hour or two with revellers heading for the bars and nightclubs in town. A busy midland town, Carlow also had a huge student population attending the local DIT.

Michelle had the cash from the day's takings in her handbag. It had been a very busy day, and the money amounted to €600. She followed the same route every day. As she walked along the quiet February street, within a stone's throw of the busy local Garda station, she was not to know that she was being targeted and stalked by one of Ireland's most dangerous sex predators.

Larry Murphy had spent most of that same afternoon in and around Carlow town. He had told his wife, Mags, that he had an appointment with his solicitor and would be home late. He had parked the family Fiat Punto in the public car park, just off the town centre. The non descript family car, complete with child's seat in the back, was unlikely to draw any unwanted attention. The spot where he had left his car had been carefully pre-selected by him, with his hunter's eye for detail. It was slightly off the main parking area, in a darkened corner that was not overlooked by the nearby houses and apartments. More importantly, there were no CCTV cameras covering the immediate area. The first parts of his plan were now in place. He had a ready alibi in the unlikely event that someone who knew both himself and his wife happened upon him as he strolled around the town. Secondly, he had carefully selected and established the transfer area for his victim. He walked towards Michelle's shop, knowing well her habits and routine.

★

Michelle entered the car park, situated behind an apartment complex adjacent to her shop, where she had parked earlier that day, and approached her car. Unbeknownst to her, Murphy was quietly walking directly behind her. At that stage, hers was the only car parked in that corner of the car park. Just as she opened her car door, he moved in, and shouted at her to hand over her handbag. She turned to face him, and, believing that he was about to rob her, tightened her grip on her bag. Catching her off-guard and standing in the open doorway of her car, Murphy struck her in the face with his fist, breaking her nose. She fell backwards into her car. With lightning speed, he followed in after her, roughly pushing his stunned victim across the front seat, and into the well of the passenger seat. He dragged up her jumper and removed her bra, which he then quickly tied around her wrists to immobilise her, while, at the same time, pushing her further onto the floor of the car.

In a further act that, undoubtedly, shows the level of planning that had gone into the whole venture, Murphy then removed his victim's shoes The psychological effect that this little action can have on an adult in a public place is amazing. Try it for yourself; you will be shocked by how vulnerable such a simple act can make you feel.

The assault had taken mere seconds, and his hapless victim did not even have the opportunity to cry out. The blitz nature of the attack had left her completely stunned and defenceless. It bore all the hallmarks of the perfect 'snatch'. Speaking, later, to residents of the apartments that overlook the car park, Gardai would learn that not one of them had heard or seen anything untoward that night. One female witness would make reference to a shadowy figure she had observed in that same corner of the car park a few nights previously. Whether or not this had been Murphy checking out his hunting ground we do not know.

Using the keys he had taken from his victim, Murphy had then driven out of the car park. What is remarkable is that, given the nature of the assault he had just committed, coupled with the presence of his semi-conscious victim lying stuffed into the seat well beside him, he had been able to drive in a normal manner to the area where he had parked his own car. The coolness he displayed in this manoeuvre, fraught, as it was, with the possibility of detection, is almost unbelievable. It says a lot about him, his mindset and personality, that he could behave so normally after such an act.

On reaching his own car, he transferred his victim, who was then beginning to show signs of regaining consciousness, into the boot of his vehicle. The transfer went smoothly and, again, was not witnessed. Ignoring her pleas not to lock her into the dark boot, he told her that he had to, because if he didn't she would start to make noise. He had removed a local GAA headband that was hanging from the rearview mirror, and stuffed it into her mouth as a gag. He then slammed shut his car boot, a movement that must have had a huge psychological impact on his captive, shivering with shock and pain, in total darkness. Murphy had then parked her car carefully, so as to avoid it looking suspicious or out of place, had locked it up and then taken the keys away with him.

Driving at an easy, sedate pace out of Carlow town, Murphy could have been taken for just another commuter heading home after a hard day at the coalface. With the car radio tuned to his local radio station, he hummed along to the country and western music playing in the background, beating out the time on the steering wheel. By this stage, his victim had regained full consciousness, and was kicking out at the boot lid, trying to scream through the gag he had put in her mouth. Murphy's response was to turn the music up in order to drown out the noise she was making.

Undoubtedly, this was an extremely pleasant journey for this very sick-minded man. The first part of his carefully planned scenario had gone without a hitch. His chosen victim was now totally in his power. Whether she lived or died over the next few hours would be entirely his choice and his decision. Make no mistake about it, these moments of anticipation must have held almost as much pleasure for the hunter/predator as the actual act. He could now relax and, at his leisure, enjoy the 'fruits of his labour'. In subsequent interviews, Murphy would deny that his victim had been pre-selected, claiming that it had been a chance encounter. This version is not accepted by the investigating Gardai, who saw, first-hand, the level of planning involved.

Contrast his mindset with what must have been going through his victim's mind as she lay, bound, gagged and in considerable pain, in total darkness, in the boot of the car, with the music blaring in her ears. In the space of a few short minutes, her life had been changed forever. A hard-working young woman,

Michelle had, over the years, built up a good business for herself. She was engaged to be married to Eoin*, her partner of six years. She now found herself at the centre of a terrifying ordeal – an ordeal that had, in reality, just begun.

Driving along what was, in the opinion of many Gardai, a well-rehearsed route, Murphy would have been only too well aware of the terror and trauma that his bound-and-trussed victim must be going through. His intention was quite clear. Having abducted, physically assaulted and isolated his victim, he was now assured of her compliance in the next part of his plan.

After leaving Carlow town, Murphy had driven a distance of some twelve kilometres to the townland of Beaconstown. This was an area well known to Murphy. Indeed, he had lived in a house just a short distance from where he now parked his car when he was first married. This house had belonged to an aunt of his. Turning up a dirt track, he brought the car to a gentle stop. He turned off the lights and ignition, and sat there for a few moments enjoying the anticipation of his next move. The area was in total darkness, with not even the sound of a passing car to be heard. This was hunting country, and the darkness and silence were his allies. He felt comfortable, and at home.

Alighting from his car, he stood at the closed boot door for one further moment, before inserting the key and slowly lifting the boot lid. He dragged his terrified victim out, and roughly pushed her around the side of the car to the front passenger door. Being fully aware of the necessity to totally dominate his victim and thus ensure total compliance, he tore off her clothes and pushed her onto the passenger seat.

Maintaining almost complete silence, he raped her, ignoring her pleas for mercy. Indeed, her tears and screams of pain would only have served to further heighten the pleasure of the moment for him. When he had finished, he dragged her back to the boot of the car and forced her, still naked, back into it, again without uttering a word. Slamming down the boot lid he paused, briefly, and listened in the dark, like a marauding animal, ready to kill to defend his trophy. Satisfied that he was in no danger, he returned to the driver's seat, and started the ignition.

Murphy then drove on to Spinan's Cross in Kilranelagh Woods, a distance of some twenty kilometres. This, again, was an area well known to Murphy, and one of his favourite hunting grounds. He pulled in off the road, into a lay-by. Directly over his head, in the tree under which he was parked, was a 'hunter's hide' which he regularly used. He would often sit for hours in the sturdily built structure, high up in the branches, and watch as the animals passed underneath, carefully selecting his target. To a hunter like Murphy, this was considered a very special, almost sacred area. This time, however, instead of staking out his target, he had brought it with him. If Murphy was to have a killing ground, then this was it.

Spinan's Cross also had another huge significance to him. His family house, where his pregnant wife and two young sons were waiting for his return, was just a few short miles away. The circuitous route he had taken from Carlow town, via Beaconstown and Kilranelagh, had been carefully selected, and actually brought him ever closer to home.

Crouched naked and cowering in the darkness of the boot, with her hands still tied behind her, Michelle must have sensed Murphy standing beside it with the key in his hand. This time, he threw the lid open violently. Grabbing his helpless victim by the hair, he dragged her out of the boot. In a complete frenzy, he again pushed her into the front passenger seat. Not content with the first vaginal rape, Murphy would now sodomise his captive, and then force her to perform oral sex on him. While carrying out this protracted abuse he kept demanding in a harsh, threatening manner that his defenceless victim 'make love' to him.

Michelle could see the changes in Murphy's temperament, and very quickly realised that her life was in grave danger because of the extreme violence he was now displaying towards her. In spite of her revulsion and pain, she decided to stop struggling, believing that her only hope of survival now lay in placating him.

To his sick mind, the fact that she had stopped struggling carried new significance to him. He would later, while being interviewed by Gardai, admit that the sexual intercourse that had taken place at Beaconstown had amounted to rape. However, he added, any sexual encounter that had taken place between them at Spinan's Cross had been consensual, even at her instigation!

On this occasion, after ejaculation, Murphy attempted to hold her in a tender embrace. Michelle waited, hoping he would drift off asleep. To her horror, he now began to give her intimate details about himself and his family. He told her that he was a tradesman, who was married with two young sons, and that his wife was due to give birth to their third child shortly. He added that he lived locally. Looking at the child's safety seat fitted into the back of his car, she must have wondered if, come tomorrow morning, this animal would transport his children, as if the events of the last hour had not taken place. Equally, the idea that his pregnant wife would then be sitting in the same seat in which he had brutalised her must also have crossed her mind. He then grew silent, as if playing over in his head the information he had just revealed to her. Michelle became aware of the enormous significance of this conversation, and realised that he would only be sharing this information if he did not intend to let her live.

Any hopes that she harboured of him falling asleep were quickly dashed when he again pushed her out of the car, and began to drag her towards the boot. She pleaded with him, begging him not to put her into the boot, promising that if he let her stay in the car, she would not attempt to escape. As he dragged her towards the boot, she somehow managed to free her hands. As he opened the boot lid and began to shove her back into it, she reached in and shrewdly grabbed an aerosol spray can of paint that was in the boot. Whipping off the can lid, she pointed it straight into his eyes and depressed the plunger. To her horror, nothing happened.

I would later see this can after the technical examination was completed. Printed on the side of the can were the words, 'Shake well before use'.

This attempt at defending herself infuriated the already volatile Murphy. Pushing Michelle back into the boot, he grabbed a plastic bag and pulled it over her head, at the same time wrapping his hands around her throat. Fighting back bravely, she managed to partially swing her legs out of the boot. While still attempting to strangle his victim with one hand, he began to remorselessly slam the boot lid down across her legs. In desperation, she pleaded with him to stop. Her pleas fell on deaf ears and seemed only to enrage him all the more. Her attempts at defending herself appeared to have totally infuriated him, almost as if the mere idea that she might have wanted to get away were an affront to his manhood!

Growing gradually weaker, Michelle began to black out. Murphy continued to tighten his grip around her throat. So engrossed was he in trying to take his victim's life that he failed to notice the sound of an approaching vehicle. It was only when the beams of the twin headlights swept around the corner, lighting up the tableau at the rear of the car, did he realise that he was no longer on his own. Murphy froze momentarily, and then, in his cowardice, pushed Michelle roughly to the ground, slammed shut the boot lid, jumped into the front seat of his own car and drove away at speed, leaving his naked victim behind him.

★

Lying on the ground, Michelle was unaware that her abductor had fled. From the corner of her eye she now observed not one but two males approaching her.

She was not to know that these two men were actually the occupants of the car that had interrupted Murphy as he tried to strangle her. Again, fearing for her life, she jumped up off the ground and ran towards the tree-line that was lit up by the car lights. However, she stumbled into some barbed wire set back in the trees, and became enmeshed in it. The two men ran towards her, shouting that they were only trying to help her and that her assailant had fled. Gently extricating her from the wire, they wrapped their own coats around her, and sat Michelle gently into the rear of their car, assuring her that she was now safe. They drove her directly to Baltinglass Garda Station, where medical assistance was sought for her. Michelle's physical ordeal was now, finally, ended.

At the Garda station, the two men recounted what they had observed at Spinan's Cross to Gardai. Not only were they able to give a description of Michelle's assailant to Gardai, but they were actually able to put a name to him! A few weeks previously, one of the men, Trevor Moody, had been in the Glen Lounge pub in the village of Donard, when a sister of a man in Trevor's company had pointed out Larry Murphy, who was also drinking in the pub. She said that she had been in the same pub the previous week when Murphy, who had been drinking alone, began to stare at her and follow her around. At one stage during that night he had reached out towards her. She believed that he had intended to sexually assault her, and she had moved out of his reach. She added that Murphy had a very bad reputation amongst the local females as a man to avoid. He often stood at the bar counter, and would continuously stare at a particular female, to such an extent that she would actually leave. All who knew him would go to great lengths to ensure that they were never alone in his company.

On the night of 11 February 2000, Trevor had been out hunting with his lifelong friend, Ken Jones. They had been 'lamping rabbits' in and around Kilranelagh forest and, when finished for the night, had decided to return home via Spinan's Cross. This was a route they normally took home. Their unexplained decision ultimately saved Michelle's life.

When they had come across Murphy's parked car and had observed the two figures standing near the boot, they had initially thought they were witnessing a violent physical confrontation between a couple. Given the particularly savage circumstances, they decided to intervene and prevent the situation from escalating further. As they pulled up, they were amazed to see the male fling the female, whom they could now see was naked, onto the ground, and then jump into the car and drive away at speed. Trevor had immediately recognised Larry Murphy, and had commented to Ken that there was something 'very wrong' going on. They jumped out of the car, and ran to help the distressed woman.

After leaving Spinan's Cross, Murphy had not, as one might expect, driven home. Instead, he had gone to the Stratford Arms pub, a short distance from his home, where he purchased a bottle of whiskey. The pub was very busy at the time, and he was observed by several people moving around inside. They later described him to Gardai as appearing 'no worse than his usual self'. It is hard to believe that he could have controlled his emotions and temperament to the extent of being able to walk into a public house, full of his neighbours and acquaintances, after the series of violent assaults which he had just perpetrated.

It is the opinion of some of the investigating Gardai that he had the presence of mind and survival instincts, even that soon after committing the crimes, to begin setting up an alibi for himself. Anyone who knew him and had seen him in the pub on that particular night would readily remember him walking around with a bottle of whiskey. Murphy remained there for about ten minutes. He then drove home. When he arrived back, his wife, Mags, was already in bed asleep. He slipped in quietly beside her, after first looking in on his sleeping children, and went to sleep.

There would be no sleep for any Garda member attached to Baltinglass Garda Station that night. Between the limited information that a clearly distraught Michelle had been able to give, coupled with the identification provided by Trevor and Ken, a full-scale Garda operation was mounted. The scene where Michelle had parked her car, and the area in which it had been abandoned, were sealed off, along with a large area at Spinan's Cross. A covert surveillance team was dispatched to Murphy's home, and they radioed back to say that the family car was parked outside the house and that the engine was still warm. They could also confirm that there was a child seat fitted in the rear of the car. The team remained in the vicinity overnight, in case the car was driven away.

Murphy was well known to local Gardai. They were aware, too, of his hunting prowess, and also of the fact that he was a listed owner of a number of firearms. It was feared that, given the enormity of the offences for which he was now being sought, Murphy might resort to violence or self-harm in order to avoid detention. An armed Garda unit was added as back-up. The necessity to ensure the safety of the pregnant woman and two small children in the same house was also uppermost in their minds.

Briefings of the various teams took place throughout the night. By first light on Saturday morning, 12 February 2000, all the separate teams were in place. The arrest team quickly and efficiently forcibly entered Murphy's home without any incident. He was secured even as he sat up in bed to check on the noise he had heard. Mags was brought by the Gardai into the children's room to reassure them. As Murphy was being led from the house, a visibly shaken Mags had turned to him and asked him what was going on, and to please tell her what had happened. Murphy, in the presence of the arresting Gardai, told her, 'I raped a girl last night'. He added that he was sorry for what he had done.

★

The family car was taken to the examination garage attached to the Garda Technical Bureau section, at the old St John's Road complex in Dublin 8, where it underwent rigorous testing. During the subsequent examination, Gardai would locate a bottle of whiskey. It had been opened, but less than one mouthful had been taken out of it. This would be identified as being the same bottle that Murphy had purchased the previous night, and proof that it had not been bought for consumption, but rather as part of an elaborate alibi he had been attempting to create.

In the boot of the car they would locate, also, Michelle's handbag. It still contained all the previous day's takings from her shop, together with all other personal items that had been in it when it was taken from her. If ever proof was needed that robbery was the last thing on Murphy's mind that night, then this was it. He hadn't even bothered to take the money from the bag. Items of her clothing would also be located in the boot. Murphy had, no doubt, intended on retaining such items as 'souvenirs' that he would use later to revisit the sordid events of that night, when all his planning had come to fruition. Gardai would also locate the aerosol can, which Michelle had attempted to defend herself with.

A particular document that was recovered in a subsequent forensic search of the garage attached to Murphy's home demonstrates his penchant for collecting 'souvenirs'. This was the written exam results of a female who we would later discover had not even realised she was missing her Leaving Certificate, usually kept in a drawer in her house. We would establish that Murphy had, at one stage, carried out some work in her home. The document itself was of no monetary value and unlikely to be missed, but held, for Murphy, some mysterious significance. Such an item would appeal to the hunter/gatherer in Murphy.

Following his arrest, Murphy was taken to Baltinglass Garda Station, where he was detained under Section 4 of the Criminal Justice Act of 1984. He could be held and interviewed about his crime, under this section, for a period of twenty-four hours. During his first formal interview with Gardai, Murphy readily admitted, in a written statement, to the abduction, assault and sexual assault of Michelle. He would deny that his crimes had been premeditated, and said that he had been taking a short stroll when he met the lady. He could not, he said, explain what had driven him to commit such an act, and expressed remorse for his actions. He described himself as hoping that his victim would recover and might, in time, even be able to forgive him for what he had done to her.

★

Of course, Murphy the predator might seek forgiveness from his victim, but, at the same time, he was never going to admit that he shouldn't have done what he did. Remorse or apology were far from his sick mind. It was at this juncture that, to the amazement of the interviewing Gardai, he attempted to differentiate between the sexual assaults at Beaconstown and at Spinan's Cross, suggesting that a rapport had built up between them, to such an extent that the sexual acts at the latter location were consensual! This bizarre suggestion no doubt reflected both his mindset, and his opinion of women. How he could convince himself of that and, at the same time, believe that he could convince everyone else also, is impossible to comprehend.

In his statement, he told Gardai that, on the second occasion that he stopped the car, it had been his intention to take his victim back to her home. However, he asserted that they had a conversation during the course of which she had told him that she wanted to 'make love to him'. He added, 'I had sex with her but it was her own choice. We made love in the car.'

This would be the only formal set of admissions that Murphy would make. The remainder of his time being interviewed would be spent in his giving monosyllabic responses to any questions put to him. In many ways, it appeared that Murphy, realising how badly he was caught, had decided to, as it were, admit his crimes only once and then, having cleared that hurdle, to compartmentalise them and move on.

Insofar as had been humanely possible, this operation had been carried out without attracting the attention of the media. However, with a prisoner in custody and with all the Garda activity – at the scenes in Carlow town, at the remote rural areas and at Murphy's home – the news gradually began to leak out. As more and more of the details of the crime became known, hordes of media personnel descended on the area. Baltinglass Garda Station became a virtual siege site, with every movement in and out of it attracting huge interest.

Murphy later appeared in the local court, charged with abduction, robbery and other offences. Even at that early juncture, links were already being made, by both the public and the media, between him and some of the missing female cases. In the weeks and months that followed, while Murphy remained in custody awaiting trial, speculation about his involvement continued to grow. The great fear all of us involved in the case had, was that an injudicious or unguarded remark made by a Garda member would prejudice his trial. As a consequence, a blanket ban had been put on any contact with the media concerning the case. Of course, this had the adverse effect of actually adding to the speculation.

One of the unique aspects of Larry Murphy's life that would emerge when we were putting together a background report on him was the fact that virtually no one person that was spoken to would either claim or admit to have been a friend of his. Information on a suspect's background is required for inclusion in all reports to the Law Officers, and is referred to as the suspect's 'Antecedent History'.

At the time of his arrest for these crimes, Murphy was thirty-five years of age, born on 7 February 1965. One of eight children born to a builder's labourer, Murphy was considered, during his school years, to be of slightly below-average intelligence. However, there was one field in which he outshone all his peers. His woodwork teacher quickly saw in him a talent for carpentry that was unique, and nurtured this in him. He would go on to become a master carpenter, known far and wide for his ability to do almost anything with timber.

There was another side to him, for which he had become equally well known. Amongst the local female population, Murphy was both detested and distrusted.

Girls and women of all ages would go to great lengths to avoid being alone in his company. He was that type of man who appeared to be mentally undressing every woman he met. It was said about him that he would even actually 'glare' as opposed to 'stare'. One female spoke of getting the impression from Murphy that, deep down and maybe even unbeknownst to himself, he actually hated women. Always standing just that 'little bit too close for comfort' for most people's liking, he would invariably manage to brush against or touch a woman in the course of a conversation. The incident at the Glen Lounge pub that had led to Trevor Moody's identification of Murphy was a regular occurrence. Even when out in the company of his wife, Mags, he behaved in exactly the same way, to the huge shame and embarrassment of his long-suffering spouse. Eventually, she simply gave up going out in public with him.

Murphy was also known to be an avid hunter. There were very few woods and hills in and around where he lived that he did not know every nook and cranny of. As the ultimate predator, he would regularly spend his time alone tracking and taking out any game or bird. He often sat for hours at a time in perfect stillness, in a manufactured 'hide', waiting for a pre-selected target to wander into his killing zone. Always hunting alone, he seldom returned empty-handed from his outings. In a sense, as our Gerry O'Connell commented after his arrest, 'It was prophetic that Murphy's actual capture was down to the good work of two fellow hunters!'

One incident of note, which could have resulted in criminal charges being laid against Murphy, occurred one night after a party in the Stratford Arms pub. Murphy had offered Veronica*, a very close friend of his wife, a lift home. Although well aware of his reputation, Veronica had taken the lift, believing that her closeness to his wife would act as a deterrent to any unwanted advances. She was very quickly proven to be wrong. Within minutes of leaving the pub, he pulled into a darkened laneway and attempted to molest her. A strong-willed woman, Veronica let him know, in no uncertain terms, that if he didn't immediately stop, she would go straight to the Gardai and also to Mags. Murphy then desisted and took her home without a further word being spoken between them.

★

We only heard about this incident after the assault on Michelle. Amongst ourselves, we had speculated that what prevented this incident from escalating any further, apart from Veronica's threats, was the fact that a large number of the people in the pub that night had been aware that Murphy was giving her a lift home. Murphy's instinct for self-preservation had served him well on that particular night. Despite his reputation among the women within the local community, Murphy did not actually have any previous criminal convictions.

Murphy's case would finally be heard before Judge Paul Carney at the Central Criminal Court, in May of 2001. On the first day of the proposed trial, all witnesses were in place, and all necessary steps to ensure Michelle's anonymity had been taken. In a move which took everyone, including his own legal team, by surprise, Murphy quietly entered a plea of 'Guilty' to all the charges as set out on the indictment laid before the court. This included a guilty plea to the charge of attempted murder. This was one of the hardest charges to prove, given the necessity to establish what the culprit actually intended as the outcome of his actions, at the time of the crime.

His plea sent shockwaves through the crowd gathered in the courtroom. On that day there was really 'standing room only' in Central Criminal Court Number 1 in the Round Hall, at the Four Courts Complex on Inns Quay in Dublin. In my almost thirty years in and around the courts, I had never witnessed such a gathering of both media and public at a trial. The crowds that gathered in the court on that day reflected the fear and loathing felt amongst the public, sentiments given further fuel as details of his crime were revealed. Following his pronouncement, what began as a ripple of sound graduated to an all-out shouting match, and all hell broke loose. It was with some difficulty that Judge Paul Carney eventually restored order in the court.

I well recall Mark Kerrigan turning to me in the courtroom, after we had heard Larry's guilty plea, saying that was a 'very shrewd' move. By pleading guilty, Murphy had ensured that his victim Michelle would not have the opportunity in the witness box to tell the world the extent of the brutal assault that he had perpetrated upon her. The details of the crime would now be presented to the court by the prosecuting Garda officer. In this instance, that would be Inspector Pat Mangan of Naas Garda Station. The real details of the crime would be, to put it mildly, sanitised. It meant that Murphy did not have to sit in the dock and listen, while surrounded by a jury of his peers, the media representatives and members of the public, as this brave young woman recounted, in detail, the extent of his depravity.

It must be said of Michelle that she behaved with great dignity during that court hearing. She had sat in the body of the court, surrounded by her family and friends, and faced her assailant without flinching. She had accepted his guilty plea without comment, and later left the courtroom with her head held high.

In the subsequent sentencing hearing on 11 May 2001, Judge Carney, while referring to the 'Guilty' plea given by Murphy, had pronounced that, due to a number of Supreme Court rulings, he had to give the defendant some credit for his plea. The higher courts had ruled that where a culprit saves his victim from having to relive the trauma of a crime perpetrated against him or her when giving evidence at trial, then the culprit must be given some credit in any subsequent sentence that was imposed on him.

I think it unlikely that the 'learned members' of the higher court, as they like to hear themselves referred to, could ever have foreseen that this ruling would ultimately benefit the likes of Larry Murphy. Far from wanting to spare his victim any further pain, Murphy's sole intention had very likely been to protect himself from the outrage that would follow a public recounting of the degradation he had submitted his victim to.

Judge Carney handed down a sentence of fifteen years' imprisonment, with one year suspended. He would also, he said, take into account Murphy's previous 'good character' in his previously law-abiding life. All of us were acutely aware that, though it appeared to be a lengthy sentence, Murphy would not serve much more than ten years in prison for his heinous crime.

Just some three weeks later, on 1 June 2001, in a separate case once again involving the abduction of a female, the culprit came up for sentence before Judge Carney. On 2 February 1999, Thomas Callan, a native of County Monaghan, had abducted a fourteen-year-old girl at knifepoint. Four months later, on 5 June of the same year, he kidnapped another girl in Carrickmacross. On this occasion, his victim, who was seventeen years of age, had been walking home late at night. He snatched the girl off the street, locked her into the boot of his car and drove to a darkened laneway just outside the town of Ardee. He took his victim from the boot, and attempted to have sex with her. Remarkably, she managed to talk him into letting her go. He even offered to drive her home, an offer she declined. Judge Carney would sentence Callan to ten years for this assault in June, and an additional fourteen years for the assault in February.

When passing sentence, Carney had commented that he would suspend the final year of both sentences, as Callan had pleaded guilty. By entering a guilty plea, Callan had, according to the Judge, saved the court's time, and given it more time to 'deal with another violent prisoner'!

After his sentencing, Murphy was taken to Arbour Hill Prison, a long-stay prison situated in the north inner-city area, which houses the majority of murderers and serious sex offenders convicted within the State. At the time of Murphy's incarceration, the 'Hill' held some one hundred and fifty kindred spirits. This might sound like a huge figure, but it is actually the case that, by 2012, roughly one in twelve prisoners out of three hundred were serving life sentences, while a similar number were serving sentences of over ten years. Given that the prison proper was situated in the Bridewell Garda district, I would be tasked by Tony Hickey liaising with the prison authorities in all matters pertaining to Larry Murphy's stay there.

Amazingly, for a man who had never 'done time', Murphy took to prison life like the proverbial duck to water. Ever the loner, confinement held no fear for him. In the first few months, he would just sit for hours on end alone in his cell, looking out through the open door, and not returning any greetings that were proffered by staff or other inmates who walked past. In the prison yard, he paced relentlessly, gaze firmly fixed on the barbed wire that topped the high outer wall, avoiding all eye contact.

One prison officer told me that Murphy would follow sufficient orders and directions to avoid being disciplined, but no more than that. With him, he maintained, you 'never knew what you had'. He said, 'He had this unsettling, far-away look – you only knew that he had been listening to you, or even that he was going to follow any instruction you gave him, after he had carried it out. His whole attitude said, "I will do it, but only because I want to do it, not because you told me I have to do it." In all my years in the prison service I have never met anyone like him.'

Amongst the other detainees, his aloofness and strange behaviour earned him a certain reputation. Even the hardened lags and lifers within a prison pop-ulation that consists of some of the most dangerous men in Irish society, treated him with a certain wariness, and would walk around him in order to avoid unnecessary confrontation. This suited him well. His years of quietly stalking game, of waiting patiently for his target to come to him, of sitting silently and unmoving, now stood him in good stead.

There were equally fellow inmates for whom Murphy's well-documented exploits earned him a grudging respect. To many of them, his crimes were no more than the culmination of some of their darkest desires. Domination and the infliction of pain no doubt fuelled many of their own fantasies. He, in their eyes, had not just dreamed the dream, but had actually lived it.

Not many months into his sentence, Murphy started to work in the prison workshop. There, amongst all the timber and tools, he finally found the missing piece that he needed to make prison life tolerable. Slowly but surely, he ingratiated himself with the officers who ran the workshop to such an extent that, eventually, he would be allowed to bring his tools back to the cell with him at night, to finish work on some project or other. The hammering and cutting sounds coming from his cell would vie with the other usual noises heard on a prison-wing floor – the sounds of loud radios and televisions, the murmur of conversations, voices raised in anger or frustration, and all the other sounds that make up prison life.

In his cell, he fashioned bookcases, bedside tables and chairs that were the envy of all the other inmates. Soon, the bolder of them would request that he make furniture for their cells. Demand for his services spread to other wings of the prison. For his work, he would be paid in one of the three principal currencies of prison life; cigarettes, porn or illicit drink. His thriving business was, if not condoned, certainly tolerated by the prison officers.

Gradually, however, he began to develop an entirely separate and far more lucrative market. The Investigation Section of the Prison Service began to take note of the number of prison officers and civilian staff leaving the prison at the end of their tour of duty, carrying items of furniture or intricately carved ornaments, all made from wood, and all of it hand made by Larry Murphy. Neither, they very quickly realised, was he supplying these items for free. Each of his creations was paid for in hard cash. Murphy, it seemed, had established the original captive audience for his sales! Following a number of reports submitted to the Prison Governor, this trade was ended. In the following months, a rumour would surface in Arbour Hill that Murphy was, once again, supplying items for sale to the prison staff, coupled with the suggestion that either a prison officer or a former prisoner was acting as 'banker' for him in his new venture. Although this allegation was never proven, it led to a total ban on the removal of any item made by Larry Murphy from the prison.

Given that the majority of the prisoners incarcerated in Arbour Hill were all long-stay, a slightly less severe regime normally operated there. This principle is adopted in similar prisons worldwide. It ensures greater cooperation between prison staff and prisoners, who, for the most part, have little to lose, and to whom a punishment handed down by the Prison Governor for some transgression or other is not really going to adversely affect their sentence. One way that this laxity can be clearly seen, is in the fact that long-term prisoners are permitted to associate more freely than short-timers. Lockdown, that time when prisoners are locked into their cells for the night, is much more flexible. It was a regular occurrence for prisoners to visit one another in their cells, and be able to walk freely along their own corridors.

Relationships (including those of a sexual nature), friendships and bonds can, as a consequence, develop much more freely. It is a regular occurrence for a prisoner, on finding himself not fitting in or not being accepted for one reason or another, to seek and be granted a transfer. Whole corridors can very quickly become 'no go' areas to the one who is not accepted. In Murphy's case, though he never mixed with the other inmates on his corridor, not one of them would suggest he be moved or, alternatively, try to push him out. They got on with normal prison life and chose to ignore him.

★

One of the high points of any prisoner's existence is the weekly visit from spouses, children, family members and friends. This was the one privilege that they all dreaded losing. These visits were an opportunity to brush up on news from the outside, to speak with loved ones and, however briefly, to mentally escape from the drudgery of prison life. The main visiting area in Arbour Hill is unique in that the only barrier between prisoner and visitor is the table between them. Unlike some of the other prisons, there are no separating glass panels or wire cages. I was often personally amazed, during the course of official visits to persons detained in the prison, by the amount of physical contact permitted between visitor and inmate. Prior to the actual meeting taking place, the visitor would have been rigorously searched in the waiting area, situated outside the main gate, to ensure that no weapons were taken into the prison.

In the case of Larry Murphy, such outside contact did not exist. In the ten years or so of his incarceration following his guilty plea and sentence, one can count the number of visits he received from family members and friends on the fingers of one hand. This lack of contact extended to letters and telephone calls. To any other prisoner, this loneliness would have driven them over the edge. Not so with Larry Murphy, though. It is an indicator of his strength of character that, at least outwardly, he did not appear to let this near-total isolation from his life prior to prison faze him. Any prison officer working with long-term inmates will tell you that this is a situation that very few, if any, prisoners could tolerate without it affecting them deeply.

Murphy never received a visit from his wife Mags or their children, for the entire duration of his custody. All the big occasions in his children's lives – all the various birthdays, communions and confirmations – and even the birth of his new child, would pass without visit or word from them. Equally, he never sought or sent out word asking for his wife and/or children to come in to see him. It was almost as if that part of his life had never existed, or that, if it had, that he had now moved on. While he was in prison, Mags was granted a separation from him, which he did not contest. Even this loss of wife and family, coming as it did on top of his loss of liberty, left him unscathed. This, if such was required, was further proof of the singular character of Larry Murphy.

There were actually those in his family who, prior to his entering a 'guilty' plea, had suggested that had the long-suffering Mags been a 'better wife' to him, his life might have been very different. This suggestion was treated with derision by the investigating Gardai. We were firmly of the view that Murphy had married Mags to lend himself a veneer of normality and respectability to anyone observing him from the outside. It was our opinion that in the level of fear, intimidation and abuse that he had subjected Michelle to, the real Larry Murphy could be clearly seen. Hiding behind what appeared to be an outwardly normal life, there lurked a true psychopathic personality, with a total lack of remorse or shame, who sought sexual gratification through the infliction of pain and humiliation.

★

While Murphy was incarcerated in Arbour Hill prison, a number of his fellow inmates were approached by Operation TRACE to establish if, by word or deed, Murphy had made reference to any other crimes that he might have committed or have knowledge of. These enquiries were invariably met with a wall of silence. A number of them attributed their lack of information to the fact that Murphy, for the most part, did not socialise or engage in what passed for normal prison gossip. However, it was equally clear that a number of prisoners were found to be uncomfortable when his name was mentioned. Indeed, the suggestion made to one prisoner that he might contact us in future if he learned anything that might be of interest to us, was quickly relayed back to Murphy! An official complaint was subsequently lodged on Murphy's behalf!

Murphy spent almost the entirety of his sentence in Arbour Hill prison. The one exception to this came about, for the most part, through his belief that he had become untouchable. The Special Investigation Unit at Arbour Hill Prison would, in mid-2008, carry out a surprise inspection of his cell. These specially trained and highly motivated officers quickly discovered a stash of cannabis resin that Murphy had concealed in some of the furniture he had made and fitted into his cell. Any other prisoner would have met this infraction of prison rules head-on, and thrown himself on the mercy of the prison authorities. However, Murphy, by then convinced of his own importance, adopted an attitude almost of, 'Do you realise who you are dealing with here?' in response to the charges laid against him.

Very quickly, the authorities reacted, and Murphy found himself transferred to Limerick Prison for one month. This punishment had a devastating impact on him. He lost all the privileges he had enjoyed as the trustee in charge of the prison workshop. He was denied access to his beloved tools, and to his special position in the workshop. On a psychological level, it shocked him to the core, reminding him that the rules of structured living applied to him too. He returned to Arbour Hill a much-chastened man.

Insofar as it could be said that throughout his time in Arbour Hill prison Murphy had formed any sort of an association or befriended anyone, then it would have to have been with fellow prisoners Frank McCann and David Lawler. A brief look at both of these gentlemen's criminal behaviour, which had led to their incarceration, explains why, in them, he could have recognised some sort of kindred spirit. It has to be emphasised, however, that he would at all times keep a certain distance between himself and others, and never allow anyone to become too close to him. Murphy considered himself too self-sufficient to open up to anyone. With the finely honed survival instincts of a true hunter, he trusted and relied solely upon himself.

Frank McCann was, outwardly, a man who had it all. Married for some five years to Esther, by 1992 the couple were in the process of adopting Jessica, who had been born to his younger sister. They had, almost since the child's birth, fostered her. McCann owned and operated the Cooperage pub in Blessington village, so named after the trade that both himself and his father had followed. He commuted daily from his large family home, in the exclusive area of Butterfield Avenue in Rathfarnham, on the outskirts of Dublin City.

In his spare time, McCann was a swimming coach with Swim Ireland, and, by all accounts, a very good one. He held the post of vice-president with that organisation. In 1992, he had been head coach to the Irish international swimming team, who competed in the Barcelona Olympics. Two of his closest friends were also heavily involved in coaching Irish swimmers. I am referring, here, to George Gibney and Derry O'Rourke, two paedophiles who used their senior positions within amateur swimming circles to prey on youngsters who had been entrusted to their care. For his part, O'Rourke would be sentenced, in 1998, to a total of one hundred years in custody, for an almost similar number of offences involving the molestation of children. Unfortunately, the sentences ran concurrently, and would amount to just twelve years. Gibney would move to America, after a High Court ruling that prevented the allegations that were made against him proceeding in the courts.

The attempts by Frank and Esther to adopt baby Jessica had dragged on for a number of years. Despite repeated enquiries from Esther, she could establish no reason for the delay. She was never informed that the Adoption Board had been in touch with the family solicitor, who, in turn, communicated only with her husband. This was a strange reaction, considering that the application had been a joint one. Finally, she managed to secure an appointment for herself and her husband with senior officials from the Board, where she hoped to have all her questions answered. The appointment was set for 7 September 1992. A delighted and much-relieved Esther immediately contacted Frank, to tell him the good news. At last, she enthused, they would have their questions answered, and might be able to move on their stalled application. She was not to know that by insisting on this meeting, she had virtually signed her own death warrant. On Monday 7 September, her body and that of baby Jessica were taken to Firhouse Church in the nearby suburb of Tallaght, before being taken to Tramore in County Waterford for burial the following day.

On the night of 4 September 1992, the Dublin Fire Brigade responded to a call of an outbreak of fire at the McCann home, at 39 Butterfield Avenue. On their arrival at the scene, they found that the fire had already taken hold, and they were unable to quell it. Despite several valiant attempts by fire service personnel, they were unable to enter the building and rescue Esther and Jessica, who were trapped inside.

★

Neighbours watched in amazement as a speeding car, driven by Frank McCann, negotiated the various rescue-tenders parked on the street, and screeched to a halt outside the house. A distraught McCann jumped out of the car, and attempted to rush into the house, in what appeared to be a brave but futile attempt at rescuing his wife and Jessica. On being prevented from running through the front door, he was then seen attempting to scale a ladder that had been placed against the bedroom window. He had to be physically restrained by Fire Brigade members, and was consoled by friends. His screams moved even the hardest hearts amongst those gathered at the scene. Sobbing hysterically, he spoke of having rushed home from work to be with his family, only to find his house in flames. McCann was then taken by ambulance to hospital, where he made a remarkable recovery, and discharged himself.

McCann's attempts at disguising himself as a grieving spouse and father did not fool members of Esther's family. They were well aware that a serious rift had developed between husband and wife. Rumours had also surfaced of a possible relationship between him and a sixteen-year-old girl, who worked as a lounge girl in his pub. There had been a series of curious incidents in the family home preceding the night of that fatal fire, including a number of gas leaks in the house, that had been reported to and investigated by the gas supplier.

All these matters were made known to Gardai, and a full-scale murder enquiry was launched. For his part, McCann would claim that both himself and his family were the victims of a campaign of terror and intimidation arising from his running of the pub. This intimidation was, he claimed, centred upon a campaign to get him to pay 'protection' money, and ranged from threatening phone calls to graffiti being scrawled on the outside of his pub.

Garda investigations would quickly establish that there was a side to McCann that did not sit well with his role of grieving husband and father. They would discover that the mother of a young special-needs girl had lodged a complaint in April of 1991, that her daughter, a keen and accomplished swimmer, had become pregnant, and that McCann was the father of the child. It was this issue that, in fact, was stalling Jessica's adoption process. He had been informed of this development by his own solicitor. McCann was aware that, were Jessica to find out about this affair, his marriage would be over. In addition, his position as national swimming coach would prove to be untenable. For these reasons, she had to die. The fact that Jessica, an innocent child, also had to perish, was irrelevant to McCann. In the overall scheme of things, to his mind, Jessica was no more than 'collateral damage'.

★

The Garda investigation into the deaths of Esther and Jessica was thorough and prolonged. It eventually established that McCann had, prior to leaving for work on the night of the fatal fire, set up a 'ticking time bomb', after tampering with a gas cylinder. The resulting explosion destroyed the family home so completely that, even had the emergency services been on hand, they would have been unable to rescue the two females trapped inside. Esther's body was located at the top of the stairs. She had died attempting to crawl along the landing to rescue baby Jessica, who was found dead in her own bedroom.

The comprehensive Garda investigation was led by Detective

Superintendent Tony Sourke, one of the country's top detectives. Gardai were aware that, in McCann, they had the right man. Their task was to ensure that he did not walk away on a technicality. The thorough investigation even included a staged re-enactment of the explosion and fire, under laboratory conditions, in England! McCann was detained for interview in November of 1992. Even while he was detained for questioning about the brutal murders of his wife and Jessica, his colleagues in the Irish Amateur Swimming Association had re-elected him as president of the Leinster branch of that organisation! It says a great deal abut McCann's meticulously curated public persona that his peers chose to ignore rumours, even then, linking him to the deaths of his family.

While being interviewed by Gardai, he would tell them that the problem with the young girl who alleged that he had indecently assaulted her was a mess that 'had to be sorted out'. He would tell them, also, that it had actually been his intention to kill himself in the fire. Given the complexity of the case, a full file was required by the Law Officers before a decision about the laying of charges could be made. When released from custody the following day, McCann immediately signed himself into Saint John of God's, a psychiatric institution on the outskirts of Dublin city. True to form, in his brief stay he quickly struck up a relationship with a female patient there.

In April of 1993, Frank McCann was formally arrested, and charged with the murders of Esther and Jessica. The first trial for the murders began in January of 1994. Ten days into the trial, the case was suddenly withdrawn from the jury by the presiding Judge. The jury were informed that medical evidence had been received by the court, which cast some doubt on McCann's ability to properly follow the proceedings. What Judge O'Hanlon could not tell them, was that McCann had been found in the holding cell beneath the courts attempting to set fire to himself! Following a second lengthy trial in August of 1996, he was convicted in relation to the deaths of both females. He would be sentenced to life imprisonment, and incarcerated in Arbour Hill prison.

Like Murphy, McCann did not mix with the other prisoners. Equally, in his case, he genuinely felt himself to be superior to the more common murderers and rapists that comprised the majority of the prison population. He eventually secured work in the prison library under the supervision of another prisoner who considered himself 'special', one Malcolm MacArthur. While in custody, McCann completed a degree course in Computer Science.

★

While Murphy may have known McCann previously, as his pub in Blessington was located just a few short miles from Murphy's home, his relationship with David Lawler ran much deeper. They were actually cousins, raised within five miles of one another, and had both attended the local secondary school, Scoil Chonglais. On leaving school, Lawler had secured employment with the then Department of Posts and Telegraphs, installing telephones in homes and offices. He moved to Dublin, where he had married and settled down in Blanchardstown. Murphy, on the other hand, had stayed at home. Over the years there had been very limited contact between them, yet there lurked in both their psyches a similar twisted sexual desire and a capacity for evil seldom seen within Irish society. Again, as with Murphy, Lawler had no previous criminal convictions prior to his arrest for murder.

On the night of 21 December 1995, civil servant Marilyn Rynn had attended a Christmas party with her work colleagues from the Department of the Environment, at the Old Sheiling public house in Raheny, Dublin. She got a lift into the city centre, and had a meal before catching the late-night bus from nearby Eden Quay to her home, at around 3.30 AM. She got off the bus when it reached Blanchardstown, and took a short-cut through the Tolka Valley Park to her home, at nearby Brookhaven Drive. She was never seen alive again. Her naked body, concealed among some bushes, was located some days later, by a Garda search team deep in the Tolka Valley Park, in an area locally known as 'The Tunnels'. Her clothing lay neatly folded beside her; she had been raped and strangled. Her death shook the foundations of the local community.

The resulting investigation, led by Detective Inspector (now Assistant Commissioner) Derek Byrne, was two-pronged. On the one hand, you had the tried-and-tested investigative process, which would see over two thousand persons interviewed, and almost one thousand statements taken. A total of two hundred persons of interest (POIs), were identified. These included David Lawler, who lived only a short distance from the scene in nearby Edgewood Lawns, and had, during the course of door-to-door enquiries, admitted to having been 'in the area' on the night in question.

The account of his movements, as supplied by him to Gardai, was felt not to ring true by Detective Garda John Lyons, the experienced Incident Room Coordinator (IRC) on the case. It was decided that he would be one of those asked to provide a blood sample, for comparison with foreign bodily fluids found on Marilyn's corpse.

DNA, was then, as I made mention of earlier, in its infancy in this jurisdiction, and little was known of it. The traces of bodily fluid found on the victim were of such an incredibly high standard that it was decided to trace, implicate or eliminate (TIE) all POIs using this method. The state Forensic Science Laboratory did not then have the necessary facilities to compare and analyse samples and trace evidence. All body samples taken would be personally transferred to privately run laboratories, in both the United Kingdom and Northern Ireland.

David Lawler readily agreed to provide a blood sample, which was then taken from him by a doctor. This sample, and a number of others from other POIs, was then taken by a Detective Garda to the laboratory outside of Birmingham, in England, where it was analysed. It would later be established that Lawler had actually checked the Internet before giving the sample, and had learnt that foreign fluids left on or in a body exposed over a period of time to the elements would very quickly degrade, due to both weather conditions and predator activity. Given that Marilyn's naked body had lain exposed in the woods for two weeks before discovery, he firmly believed that any sample of foreign-body fluids found on her would have degenerated to such an extent as to be virtually useless.

Lawler spent many hours locked in his room alone trawling the Internet. The majority of the sites he visited were, of course, sex-related. His preoccupation with spending hours alone surfing the web was akin to Murphy's habit of sitting in his 'hide' in the woods.

Great play would be made at Lawler's subsequent sentencing hearing by his barrister, Mr Paddy McEntee, who suggested that in giving the blood sample, Lawler was, in effect, entering a plea of 'guilty' to the murder. This contention, I believe, is completely without foundation. It was instead a case, for Lawler, in which 'a little knowledge' was 'a dangerous thing'.

What Lawler had not allowed for, was the fact that, throughout the time the body had lain in the woods, the temperatures had been consistently at or below freezing. In many ways, as I wrote earlier in relation to Phyllis Murphy, this had the same effect as if the body had been placed in a refrigerator. As a consequence, all trace evidence on the body was actually frozen, and perfectly preserved.

The similarities between this case and that of the murder of Kildare woman Phyllis Murphy in 1979 are truly astonishing.

Lawler was sentenced to life imprisonment on 26 January 1998 by Justice O'Higgins. The court was informed that he had told Gardai, following his arrest in August 1996, that he had been 'overcome by a homicidal and sexual impulse'. The hearing lasted all of ten minutes.

Murphy, McCann and Lawler were sociopaths in the truest sense. Amongst their peers, and to society in general, they presented themselves as upright, hardworking and conscientious citizens, with relatively successful careers in their chosen fields. Underneath this exterior, however, while appearing to be able to participate in normal social relationships, they were cold, cunning and unable to experience true human emotion. The infliction of pain on others was, to them, the norm. Their acts of violence were carefully planned, the environment chosen to avoid interruption or detection and to minimise any evidence that was left behind. Any risks they took were calculated and premeditated. All three failed to show a modicum of remorse or guilt. They all exhibited a complete lack of conscience.

★

Throughout his term of imprisonment, Murphy refused to engage in any of the programmes designed to help sex offenders, despite the fact that Arbour Hill prison, which, by 2010, housed a total of 111 of the 320 persons within the State convicted of sex-related offences and then serving time, had such a programme in place and was designated as the national centre for imprisoned sex offenders. This designation meant that a full range of therapeutic interventions was available to any sex offender anxious to avoid reoffending.

Research by the American Department of Correction show that the recidivism rate for sex offenders who participated in programmes like these held in penitentiaries in Washington State was as low as 7 percent. When one considers that the normal rate of reoffending for this type of crime, in the USA, is approximately one in five, these are impressive results. The programmes are based on the premise that sex offending is usually a learned behaviour, and so, by teaching the participants to avoid instances or opportunities of sexual aggression, the likelihood of reoffending can be reduced.

In this jurisdiction, prisoners must voluntarily participate in the programme, which is designed to commence in the period eighteen months prior to their known release date. A total of fifty-eight of what were considered to be offenders in the 'high-risk' sector underwent this program. Murphy's reluctance to engage was, I have no doubt, because the central tenets of the treatment centred on disclosure, life history and offence background. Ultimately this type of programme was only availed of by those wishing to change their lifestyles and to curb their violent fantasies.

The big stumbling block to engaging in this type of rehabilitation was, as I have said, the fact that participation is voluntary. A prisoner's right to early release is not dependent, as most right-thinking people might think, on their willingness to change. The original Prison Regulations (14), which were revoked and replaced by new regulations in 2007 (15), appear to suggest that remission is only to be given to a prisoner who displayed 'industry and good conduct' throughout their incarceration. The rules further specify that no more than one quarter of the sentence can be set aside through remission. Basically, therefore, remission can be earned merely through not becoming involved in breaches of discipline while in prison. Unfortunately it has come to be viewed as a right, rather than something granted at the discretion of the prison author-ities. This is another of the main reasons why, at the time of Larry Murphy entering his plea of 'guilty' to the assault upon Michelle, my colleague Mark Kerrigan described the move as 'very shrewd'. He had, in effect, bought himself almost four years of freedom!

Murphy had therefore, throughout his incarceration, a definite release date to aim for. This was not, as many of the public believed, some point in mid-2015. In fact, he would be eligible for release as early as 12 August 2010. Had Murphy been sentenced to life imprisonment, as many felt he should have received, based on the nature of the assault, then he could only have been released at the discretion of the Minister for Justice. This release would have been 'under licence', and subject to certain conditions. Failure to observe these conditions would see the released prisoner being returned to prison.

Larry Murphy spent the months leading up to his release making various preparations. Through the Department of Justice, a Garda Inspector attached to the Bridewell Station was asked to apply for a driving licence and passport for him. It must be emphasised, here, that this is a common practice for long-term prisoners coming to the end of their sentences. It meant that, following their release, they would be free to travel out of the country. Murphy's new documen-tation was handed over to him at the prison.

These were not, however, the only arrangements that Murphy put in place for his release. Following the media blitz that had greeted the release of double-murderer Michael Bambrick from Arbour Hill prison a few short months before his own impending release, Larry Murphy was visited by two senior Garda members. They advised him that, given the media interest that still cen-tred around him and his crime, they believed that there would be a similar media frenzy waiting to greet him on his release. He was asked if there were any steps in relation to his personal safety that he required Gardai to take in order to protect him. Murphy had scoffed at this offer, no doubt suspecting some ulterior motive on the part of the Gardai. As it transpired, Murphy had his own carefully orchestrated contingency plans in place.

At around 10 PM on the night of Wednesday 11 August 2010, the prison officer on duty at the main gate of Arbour Hill observed a crowd gathering just opposite the main entrance. The Garda radio control room at Harcourt Square was contacted and, given the number of high-profile prisoners that were detained inside those walls, a number of units, included armed-response teams, were dispatched immediately to the scene. On their arrival, they quickly established that all those gathered there were from a number of media outlets, all of whom were 'jockeying' for the best vantage points to cover the prison gates, believing that the prison authorities would attempt to 'slip' Murphy out early the following morning. A Garda management plan for dealing with crowd control outside the prison, due to come into effect at 1 AM, had to be brought forward by several hours. Crash barriers were erected, and the media personnel, whose numbers were increasing by the hour, were confined to the opposite side of the roadway. The 'Siege of Arbour Hill', as it was referred to by some within the crowd, had begun.

By early morning of 12 August, the numbers had increased so much that additional manpower was needed to control the gathering crowd, which, by now, included many members of the public. As the morning wore on, there was a noticeable shift in the mood of the public gathered outside the Garda barriers. Every time the prison gate opened, a huge sense of expectation swept through the crowd. Prison vans bringing remand prisoners to courts across the country were greeted with shouts, catcalls and jeers, on the off-chance that Murphy might be concealed within one of them.

At 10.15 AM, a grey Toyota taxi pulled up just at the entrance gateway to the prison grounds. The taxi bore no company logo or telephone contact details, just a licence number on its roof bar. As the taxi stopped, the wicket gate set into the main doors swung open and Murphy stepped out. He was carrying a green hold-all. It took the gathered media and onlookers several moments to realise that the figure striding confidently towards the rear door of the taxi was, in fact, the man they were all gathered to see, the same man who had become one of the most hated in Irish society.

All hell broke loose, as media and onlookers pressed forward to get a look at him. Calls of 'Over here, Larry' mingled with shouts of 'Scumbag' and 'Killer' from onlookers. Totally unfazed, Murphy opened the rear door of the taxi, and got in. He was dressed in a distinctive New York Yankees black hoodie with 'NY' emblazoned in gold across the front. To complete the ensemble, he wore dark aviator shades, and a baseball cap. This outfit would ensure that the wearer would stand out in any crowd. It would emerge that it had been carefully selected for just that reason.

The taxi took off at a moderate speed, driving down Montpelier Hill before turning off onto the North Quays. It had taken the packed media personnel a few moments to react, and there followed a mad scramble for their cars. It was mayhem, with cars forcing their way through pedestrians and Gardai alike. Three high-powered motorcycles, with pillion passengers festooned with cameras and dangerously perched on rear seats, took up immediate pursuit. Radio contact was opened between the motorcycle drivers and the media personnel in the cars, and the carnival quickly assembled behind the taxi carrying Murphy, which was following along at a normal pace. The presence of a number of Garda traffic motorcycles helped ensure that road-traffic regulations were, to some extent, observed by over-enthusiastic reporters and cameramen.

The taxi turned onto Drumcondra Road, and headed northwards. At that stage, the call went out that Murphy was headed for Dublin airport. A large number of the vehicles in pursuit of the taxi broke away and headed for the airport, where there were a number of camera crews waiting, on the off-chance that he would go there. However, as it passed the Santry exit on the M1 motorway, still headed in the direction of the airport, the taxi took a sharp left turn onto the roundabout and then headed down Oscar Traynor Road, passing the Northside Shopping Centre, and towards Coolock village. The pursuing pack of media was further reduced by this sudden change in direction.

As the taxi approached Coolock Garda Station, it signalled a right turn, and drove into the enclosed yard. To the amazement of everyone who had managed to pursue him, including, it has to be said, the escorting Gardai, Murphy alighted from the taxi, and strolled confidently into the station.

★

The Garda on duty had already been alerted that something strange was going on outside, by the sheer volume of traffic horns and shouting that had greeted his move. Murphy had been joined by some of the staff from the other offices in the building. To the astonishment of all of those gathered in the office, Murphy strolled up to the counter and, in a loud, confident tone, introduced himself. He added that he wished to lodge a serious complaint about the manner in which he had been stalked by members of the press.

Gardai, who perform duty on a regular basis in public offices in Garda stations countrywide, are well used to weird and unusual occurrences in these same offices – anything from admissions to murder, to physical assaults to childbirth. I would suggest, however, that the sight of Larry Murphy standing at their counter complaining of harassment will be difficult to surpass.

Having lodged his complaint and demanding that it be noted, he returned to the taxi, and opened the door. One of the press photographers who had managed to stay on his tail said to me that he gave a wry smile in their direction as he got into the car. The cars full of members of the press, who had stayed with Murphy after his turn-off from the M1, had, by that stage, been joined by a number of those that he had earlier managed to loose. The enlarged cortège set off once again. As it approached the M1 junction, the taxi signalled a right turn onto the roundabout. To those following, it appeared, once again, to be headed for the airport. A large number of his pursuers overtook it, and headed towards the airport to try and regain their original vantage points. Instead of taking the expected route, the taxi turned left, and headed back towards the city centre.

It drove along Drumcondra Road, and, from there, onto Dorset Street. It stopped momentarily at the junction of North Frederick Street, and then turned left down O'Connell Street. Crossing O'Connell Bridge, it drove around Trinity College, and up towards Nassau Street. As the taxi drew near to the Molly Malone statue, the back door opened, and Murphy stepped out and walked onto Grafton Street, disappearing into the huge crowd of shoppers and tourists that fill that street on a daily basis. His pursuers were caught totally off-guard. As Grafton Street was a pedestrian-only thoroughfare, they could not follow him, and there are absolutely no parking facilities in the area. They could not park, and they could not abandon their cars.

Murphy had lost none of his hunter instincts. Moving swiftly, he disappeared into the crowd, removing his baseball cap and slipping out of his distinctive hoodie, both of which he placed into the holdall he was carrying. As I have suggested already, I have no doubt that this outfit had been carefully selected to draw the attention of any followers. By taking it off, he managed to blend in with surrounding pedestrians, while the few remaining media people who had been able to leave their cars searched the crowd in vain for the hoodie or baseball cap. Murphy had vanished.

★

Entering the Brown Thomas store from the Grafton Street entrance, he left via the rear door, and walked onto Exchange Street. While the media searched the Grafton Street area, it is suggested that he had calmly walked down through Temple Bar to the quays, where he hailed a taxi, asked to be taken to Heuston railway station and then purchased a ticket to Cork. When the train pulled in at Cork station, he darted in and out among the people gathered on the platform, occasionally stopping and turning around abruptly, to ensure that he wasn't being followed. Murphy then darted out onto the centre of the roadway. At the same time, a darkly coloured car, obviously the one he had being waiting for, pulled up beside him. He jumped in, and it immediately took off at speed.

His movements from the moment he had left the prison had, evidently, been carefully orchestrated. Murphy had lost none of his sharpness or survival instinct. He would, in fact, spend a number of days in west Cork with an associate he had met in Arbour Hill. This man, a convicted rapist, allowed him to stay in his remote cottage, while every Garda and media person in the State sought him. Speculation was rife about his whereabouts. Suggestions that he was staying in particular houses or hostels would immediately draw angry crowds. In a number of incidents, Gardai had to physically restrain crowds from storming the houses. Radio stations were inundated with calls about him. Meanwhile, he lay low in his hideout in west Cork, and enjoyed his first taste of freedom.

As the furore started to die down, Murphy, through a probation officer, contacted a senior Garda officer, and informed him that he was going to leave the jurisdiction. This arrangement for monitoring his movements had been put into place prior to his release. In Murphy's case, the regulations governing the monitoring of the movements of convicted sex offenders did not apply, insofar as his conviction had preceded the enactment of that legislation. They were, in fact, only applied on an ad hoc basis. This arrangement had been agreed in the weeks leading up to his release. Less than a week after his well-publicised release from prison, Murphy slipped quietly out of the country on a ferry. He travelled by bus and train to southern Spain, where he stayed for a number of weeks before moving on, for a time, to South America.

Murphy returned to the south of Spain in 2011, where he enjoyed a fairly idyllic lifestyle. However, during the course of a late-night incident in a local pub, his new passport was mislaid. Arrangements were put in place by the Irish Embassy in Madrid to have him issued with another one. Unfortunately, he had to return to Ireland to collect it. Though he slipped quietly back into the country in May of that year, his travel arrangements soon became public knowledge.

After staying for just three days, he again left the jurisdiction, returning briefly to Spain before going into hiding once more.

★

In November of 2012, investigative journalist Paul Williams traced Murphy to Amsterdam, the sex capital of Europe. He was working as a general handyman, doing small repair jobs in private houses in the area near to where he was living. Of greater interest, however, was the identity of the man who was sharing an apartment with Murphy. In 2001, Murphy's new-found friend, Dublin man Thomas Dolan*, had abducted two females at knifepoint in the Rathmines/Ranelagh area of the city. He had taken both of them to a nearby apartment, where he had raped them repeatedly, over a number of hours. They were eventually rescued by Gardai, who had been alerted when their screams were heard by a neighbour.

Dolan, like Murphy, had never before come to the attention of Gardai prior to the offence for which he was sentenced to ten years. He served all of these ten years in Arbour Hill prison, during the same time that Murphy was incarcerated there. The mere thought of this pair associating together in a city known for its sex industry would send shivers down the spine.

At the time of writing this, Murphy is still living in Amsterdam. There is a train of thought prevalent in Irish society today that would believe that he has 'done his time', and has paid his debt to society. He should, some argue, be allowed to live a normal life, without being harassed and vilified by the media and public. At the other end, there are those who adamantly believe him responsible for the abduction and murder of at least some of the missing girls whose cases were reviewed by Operation TRACE. Certainly some sections of the media would suggest that this is the case.

As I have already said, there is an inherent danger in assuming, without proof, that a particular person committed a crime or series of crimes. To this end, Operation TRACE has always kept an open mind in relation to the tarring of any one individual as the culprit. Over the course of our enquiries, we were regularly met with the comment, 'Sure, didn't so and so do that'. If one were to approach an investigation having already mentally assigned guilt to a particular individual, then there is a real danger that the true culprit might walk free. The charging of Dean Lyons with the Grangegorman murders is a classic example of the outcome of such a mindset, and should act as a salutary lesson to us all.

False Prophets and Divine Intervention

The media blitz which greeted the launch of our taskforce had never been seen before. It attracted widespread interest from members of the public, both within the State and, unbelievably, internationally. The first few weeks were spent answering the dedicated telephone lines, which rang incessantly. We had calls from publications as diverse as *True Detective* magazine and the *New York Times*. All these calls were carefully logged. Tony Hickey insisted that the last thing he wanted was for us to discover, after months of investigation, that the information necessary to resolve the issues we were investigating had been sitting in our own records all along.

That caution was based upon research which has shown that, given the wide trawl that accompanies all major investigations, either the identity of the culprit, or certain identifiable traits relevant to that person, will already have been established. This information is in the possession of the investigating team in the first forty-eight to seventy-two-hour period. We were, he insisted, to listen to and acknowledge everyone who contacted us. All recommendations, information, advice or suggestions received were to be 'actioned' and followed through to their conclusion.

I have already referred to the various sciences and investigative skills made available to us in our work. There was, of course, one other investigative tool that had not been available to us at the outset, but was very quickly offered in tandem with all the publicity we received: we became inundated with offers of information, advice and warnings from people who claimed to possess spiritual powers.

Within police circles, the information contributed by psychics, and others claiming to have divine powers, is usually described as having been established using the 'Martin Luther King Methodology of Homicide Investigation'. The title is based upon King's rousing civil rights speech of the 1960s, during which, while referring to the pace of the movement towards equality in American society, he uses the much-quoted phrase, 'I have a dream'. The difference being, of course, that while Mr King's dreams were driven by realism, a large number of the alleged visions that were relayed to us were driven by over-fertile imaginations.

Within hours of the establishment of Operation TRACE, we would receive, as it were, our first contact from 'the other side'. A female caller stated that she was aware of the exact location of the body of Annie McCarrick and, further-more, was convinced that the bodies of at least two of the other missing females were buried in shallow graves, in close proximity to where Annie lay. This was, of course, music to our ears. When pressed further, the caller, who gave her name as 'Liz', said that the body dump sites were just behind a newly painted red barn, in a rural area. There was a nearby tree, she said, with a forked trunk, and a stream running at the end of the field: this was where the bodies were buried.

★

At this stage, specific locations were requested from Liz. Her response was that this information had not been given to her, but might be passed on later. I began to question the origin of the information, and was assured that it had come from an 'impeccable' source. When asked just how impeccable it was, Liz stated that it was Annie herself who had appeared to her in a dream, and asked that she pass this information on to us. She described Annie as being 'troubled, upset and lonely', adding that she could not 'pass over completely into the next life' until her body had received a formal interment in hallowed grounds. Comments such as these often accompanied this type of assertion.

By end of day one we would have received four more telephone calls from other individuals, all of whom would claim to have been in touch with one of the missing persons, and all of whom had information concerning their where-abouts, what fate had befallen them, and at whose hands. Although not entirely unexpected, the sheer volume of calls received that day suggested that there were a lot more to come.

A protocol for dealing with calls of this nature was quickly established. The personal details of all the callers would be ascertained. The information would then be accepted, assessed, attributed, logged and actioned, as was every other call from any member of the public who contacted us. If the caller sought to meet with us, we would agree to do so, but on the understanding that we were there to receive information only, and that there would be no attendant media or public-ity. We would try to contact the caller with the outcome of any enquiries or searches we performed, arising from the information they had supplied.

From a practical policing perspective, this approach made perfect sense. We, as investigators, must treat all information that we receive as genuine, and ensure that it is followed through to a conclusion. This applies to all evidence that comes into our possession, no matter what the source.

Members of the public have many reasons for providing information to Gardai. These range from a sense of duty, outrage at a particular atrocity, a desire to help, a troubled conscience, a genuinely held belief or even a desire for fame or notoriety. There are as many different motives as there are types of evidence. There is, of course, the very real possibility that a culprit, in an attempt to take the pressure off or deflect publicity and suspicion falling upon themselves, might try to pass on information using any number of different means. This could be as simple as feeding misinformation to send enquiries into a different direction, or of nominating some entirely innocent person as a suspect for the crime.

Where we decided that the information provided to us by a person claiming to have received it in a dream or seance warranted a search of a particular area or a 'dig' of an identified burial site, the person who had supplied the information would not be notified in advance of the time or date we took this action. Based upon the outcome of any such actions, we would then contact the caller, and advise them that the information which they had provided had been checked out. The reason for not giving any information prior to the 'dig' or search was to avoid the possibility that the person would alert the media present to capture the Gardai acting on their prophecies.

We would actually have one instance of a person who, at their request, had been supplied with Ordnance Survey maps of a particular area in which their 'vision' had told them a body was concealed. We obtained the requisite map from the Garda Mapping Section, and handed it over. Within weeks, a photograph of our 'diviner' appeared in their local paper. The accompanying story told how, because of his previous success using his otherworldly talents, he had been 'called in' to help Operation TRACE in their search. In the photo, he is shown standing in a field with the red barn and twisted tree – not to mention the obligatory stream – in the background, and holding a map clearly displaying the Garda crest!

We considered it significant that the level of publicity a particular disappearance had received was reflected in the number of callers who referred to that case only. For instance, the number of persons who contacted us to say that Annie McCarrick had appeared to them in a dream far exceeded the total number of calls received concerning three of the other cases.

I want to preface any subsequent opinions I express on this subject, by emphasising that I have no doubt that, in the vast majority of cases, those clair-voyants, seers, mediums and shamans who contacted us then, and continue to contact the police, genuinely believe in their own psychic abilities, and are con-vinced that they have received this message or intuition from a divine or super-natural source. They are never in any doubt as to the reliability and content of their message. Some claim to have been contacted directly by the spirit of the missing person in the course of a dream, trance or seance. More will refer to pre-monitions they have had, arising from articles they have read, photographs they have seen or areas they have visited.

From my own perspective, however, speaking after almost forty years in mainstream policing, with involvement, either directly or peripherally, in a number of the largest investigations ever undertaken within this State, I have never seen any tangible results arising out of information offered from people claiming to have psychic abilities. Neither have I ever seen any murders solved, or missing persons located, as a result of this sort of information.

I have studied police procedures and practices in other jurisdictions, and have attended police colleges and facilities in Ireland, England, America, Germany and Canada, and have never seen one instance of a case been solved through psychic abilities.

★

In one particular instance, word was received by our unit that a male, who gave us an address in the midlands, wanted to pass on information about an acquain-tance of his, whom he had seen concealing a body in a nearby quarry. This caller sounded quite genuine and convincing. Two of our finest, who, to save their blushes, I won't name, were immediately dispatched to meet with the informant at his home, at 8 PM that evening. The caller had placed particular emphasis on the need for them to arrive at this time. They arrived at a large house that was in almost in total darkness, and were ushered into a small room in which they found a number of persons gathered around a table. They were brought to a set of vacant chairs, and had no sooner sat down than the remaining lights were put out, and their hands were grasped firmly by those seated on either side of them.

By this stage, our two stalwarts had realised they were in the middle of a seance. Not wishing to give offence, they decided to 'go with the flow'. No doubt because of the ethereal vibes being given off, both of our detectives had the same thought throughout the ensuing seance – how, in the name of God, would they face the rest of us if their participation was ever revealed! More importantly, how would they hide it from Tony Hickey! This, in fact, may even be the first time Tony hears of this incident.

The two detectives left the house after about an hour. In their possession, they had information pointing directly to a local farmer who had been seen by the group during their last seance, concealing one of the bodies of the missing girls in a ditch at the bottom of his garden. The following morning, still trying to figure out how best to break the news to the rest of us, they received an urgent call from their host. He sounded very upset, and wanted to know if Gardai had already arrested the farmer. On learning that his dastardly neighbour was still free, he heaved a big sigh of relief, and explained that immediately after the Gardai had left his home the previous night, the supposed spirit of the missing girl had appeared, and warned them that the story about their neighbour was, in fact, a deliberate fabrication being spread within the spirit world by a rogue spirit, intent on creating mischief.

I have written further on about the case of Larry Griffin, one of the first disappearances in the history of the State to be categorised as 'suspicious'. In his definitive work on this subject, author Fachtna O'Drisceoil[6] makes mention of a search for evidence carried out by the investigating Gardai at the home of the Whelan family, from whose adjoining public house Larry is alleged to have been seen leaving. A number of Whelan family members were detained, in connection with Larry's disappearance, while this search was carried out. This was the third time in a matter of days that Gardai searched the same house. During the course of this particular search, an apron and a piece of cloth – both of which appeared to be bloodstained – were found in the bedroom of one of the daughters.

Two previous searches had failed to reveal the presence of what was, potentially, vital evidence. In subsequent official reports to the authorities, the Garda who found this incriminating evidence, Detective Garda Thomas O'Rourke, claimed that the actual location of these bloodstained items had come to him 'in a dream'. I am not trying to cast any doubt on either Detective O'Rourke's investigative abilities or the veracity of his evidence. It is, however, the case that the High Court would subsequently find him guilty of mistreating one of the witnesses in the case, an allegation that he had vigorously denied.

★

In my experience, some of these so-called psychic detectives will push themselves, uninvited, into the midst of grieving and concerned families. They will turn up on doorsteps, canvas relatives and friends, give media interviews and generally attempt to manoeuvre themselves into the immediate family circle, all the while giving false hope and misinformation to people who are already suffering deep distress and anguish. Indeed in certain jurisdictions they offer their services to distraught families and friends in return for payment. It seems to me to be one of the lowest tricks that can be perpetrated on already vulnerable and hurting families.

One of the most high-profile claimants in this field, the American woman Nancy Myer, proudly declares on her official website page that 'Paypal is now available!' She goes on to request that, before she takes on a homicide case, she be supplied with a photo of the victim and samples of their handwriting. Oh, and don't forget to send a map showing home, workplace, last sighting area and body dump site, together with relevant dates. These are all the basic tools of any investigation and, to complete the picture, Nancy would also like you to send any available crime-scene photos! Nancy, and others like her, do not come cheap. A fee of $100, for thirty minutes, or $200 for a full hour's 'reading' applies.

These self-proclaimed psychics regularly arrive, uninvited, at family homes, with stories of body dump sites, of missing loved ones being in great danger, pain or fear, or of the involvement of some named person in the disappearance or death, all details which they claim are known to these 'psychic detectives' alone.

A number of the 'prophecies' made by those claiming to possess psychic abilities are readily understandable. For instance, when they enter a missing-person case and predict that the victim is dead, they have, at its most simplistic, a fifty/fifty chance of being correct. Couple this with the figures for child abductions by strangers in the United States, where the death rate for the child in the first twelve hours is somewhere around 70 percent, and it is easy to appear to have gotten it right. The body will, they invariably state, be buried in a shallow grave, in a remote area. Again if we break this down, it is quite logical to think that a culprit will attempt to conceal the body, which may bear vital forensic evidence that could convict them, in a remote area, so as to lessen the chances of it being discovered. In addition it is, of course, far less tiring to dig a hole capable of concealing a body to a depth of one foot, as opposed to a depth of six feet. Laziness, coupled with the fear of being observed or disturbed, can readily account for this particular prediction. And yet, these claims may be viewed as relevant, even earth-shattering, and are used to support the claim that the alleged evidence could only have come from the 'restless spirit' of the victim.

While investigators will never publicly criticise or rubbish people such as these, we will, amongst ourselves, give very little credence to any of their suggestions. Were a grieving or concerned family member to seek my advice and ask if I felt that they should avail of the services of a psychic, I would advise them to not get involved, as they run the risk of being manipulated by the mind games that are often played. I would be completely opposed to their involvement, fearing that, through unfounded pronouncements, they will only visit hurt upon the family.

I know of one Dublin family who, despite their own personally held reservations, allowed themselves to be swayed by one of the lead Garda investigators into allowing a medium into their daughter's bedroom. She had recently been murdered. The medium spent considerable time – to the parents' consternation – going through their teenage daughter's private and personal belongings, a task which even they themselves were only gradually coming to terms with.

Following her visit, this medium would later suggest the possibility of the involvement of a very close family member in their daughter's murder. This assertion was made without any evidence whatsoever, and was based, in its entirety, on a 'feeling' they had gotten during the course of reading the dead girl's private letters and diary. This suggestion must have had a dreadful impact upon the already vulnerable family. It certainly did nothing to enhance the trust between the Gardai as investigators, and the family members as secondary victims.

In recent times, I have visited the website hosted by this medium and, to my utter disbelief, found that she has the affront to claim that she, through her 'gift', had 'assisted' the Gardai in their investigation of this murder, which, fifteen years on, remains unresolved. She even goes so far as to name the Garda member to whom she had passed on her groundbreaking 'intuitions'.

★

Following the disappearance, in June 2002, of American girl Elizabeth Smith, investigators attached to the Salt Lake City Police would receive almost nine thousand calls, with information concerning her whereabouts and fate from persons claiming to have psychic abilities. Not one of their stories would prove to be even remotely correct.

On 17 November 2004, Louwana Miller appeared on the Montel Williams television show, a weekly chat show programme broadcast across America. The special guest every Wednesday night was a woman called Sylvia Brown, who claimed to have supernatural psychic abilities. She also claimed to have assisted a number of police forces in over one hundred murder enquiries. Sylvia is, it should be noted, available for one-on-one consultations with families, for a fee of $850, for twenty minutes.

Louwana was there to try to find out what had happened to her daughter Amanda Berry. Amanda, a bright seventeen-year-old, had left her part-time job at a Burger King outlet in her hometown of Cleveland, Ohio, at 7.45 PM on the evening of 21 April 2003. She rang her sister, and told her she was getting a lift. Amanda never came home. Despite a huge publicity campaign, driven in no small part by her family, Amanda was not located. Monthly vigils were held near the spot where she had last been seen, in an attempt to revive interest in her case.

It was with a sense of desperation that Louwana finally went on the show with Sylvia Browne to see if she could help her. After listening to this broken-hearted mother beg for help in locating her daughter, Browne, with no evidence whatsoever, replied, 'She's not alive, honey'. She added, 'I hate when they are in water'. When the mother asked if she would ever see her daughter again, Browne responded, 'Yeah, in heaven. On the other side'. Not content with destroying any hope that this distraught parent had of ever seeing her daughter alive again, Browne went on to ask her if she knew a nineteen-year-old youth, whom she referred to by name. This youth, according to Sylvia Brown, may have been involved in Amanda's disappearance. The name was unknown to Louwana, who would later describe herself as being '98 percent convinced' by Browne. Within a further two years, Louwana herself would be dead, carrying to her grave the grief over the murder of her daughter.

Some ten years later, on 6 May 2013, neighbours on Seymour Avenue in downtown Cleveland were astonished when a distraught woman started knocking loudly on their front door. The woman screamed that her name was Amanda Berry, and that she had been held captive in a house across the road. Police were summoned and, on entering this house, found two other females, Gina DeJesus and Michelle Knight, both of whom had been missing for over nine years. They would also find a six-year-old girl, whom Amanda had given birth to during her captivity.

★

A fifty-two-year-old male, Ariel Castro, was arrested in connection with the abduction of all three girls. He would later be convicted by the courts on various counts of rape and kidnapping, and two counts of aggravated murder.

These latter charges refer to the deaths of two infant children born to his captives. He was allowed to enter a plea of guilty to all charges, in a deal to avoid the death penalty.

Sylvia Browne was later asked how she had got it all so very wrong, when telling Amanda's mother that her daughter was dead. Far from admitting that she had made a blunder, she would defend her 'prophecy' by stating that, overall, 'I have been more right than wrong'. In what probably passes for humility in her strange world, she added, 'Only God is right all the time'.

Of course, it was not the first time that this self-proclaimed expert got her predictions wrong. In 2002, an eleven-year-old boy, Shawn Hornbeck, was abducted near his home. After a year of fruitless searching, his distraught parents consulted the redoubtable Ms Browne. She would tell them that Shawn had been murdered, and that his body was buried near two strange rocks, in a wooded area. Almost four years later, Shawn would be located, alive. He had been held captive all along by his abductor.

In 2002, Gwendolyn Krewson sought assistance from Sylvia Browne to help in tracing her daughter, Holly, who had been missing since 1995. Having consulted with her friends in the spirit world, Ms Browne told Gwendolyn that her daughter was alive and well, and working as an exotic dancer in Hollywood. Years later, using dental records, police would identify a body that had been located in 1996 in San Diego as being that of Holly Krewson.

She told the parents of six-year-old Opal Jennings that their daughter, who had been abducted in 1999, was being held in virtual slavery in a remote village in Japan. In December 2003, a body was located a short distance from her home, and would be identified as that of Opal. Forensic testing would put her time of death as being within hours of her kidnap. A local man would be charged and convicted in relation to her death.

Of course, Browne, a convicted fraudster, reliably predicted that Bill Clinton would be cleared of any involvement with his intern, Monica Lewinsky, and that President Obama would not be re-elected. Her criminal conviction for investment fraud and grand theft arose when she diverted funds which she had received from a member of the public, who believed the money was being invested in a gold-mining project. Sylvia put the money, instead, into 'psychic research'.

By her claims, Ms Browne undoubtedly put the families of Amanda Berry, Shawn Hornbeck, Holly Krewson and Opal Jennings through a great deal of additional pain and suffering.

★

A 1993 survey[7] of the fifty largest police forces across the United States would suggest that only one third of them would actually accept information from persons claiming to have psychic abilities, with only a seventh of that figure saying that they would treat the information any differently to that received from the general public. A separate survey, in 2006[8], suggests that a total of twenty-eight of the police forces in the United Kingdom claim that they would not use, and furthermore, had never previously used, psychics in their investigations.

Ms Browne's claim that she was 'right' in her predictions concerning murders and missing persons 85 percent of the time were addressed in a 2010 study.[9] In the study, entitled 'The Psychic Defective', the authors claimed that she had never been 'mostly correct' in a single case.

The operations of mediums, clairvoyants and psychics are controlled, in England, by various consumer-protection regulations. These are set out in the Consumer Protection Act of 2008. These regulations replaced the Fraudulent Mediums Act of 1951 which, in turn, had replaced the Witchcraft Act of 1734!

I will leave the definitive comment on psychic abilities to journalist Gordon Deegan, writing in the business section of the *Irish Times* newspaper, on 12 March 2014.[10] The article refers to the appointment of a liquidator to the firm behind Irish Psychics Live, a service providing psychic readings over the phone. Claiming to be 'operated by genuine Celtic psychics, the most psychic race in the world', at the height of its popularity in 2009, they charged €2.40 per minute for telephone psychic consultations. The article is entitled 'Unforeseen losses force Irish Psychics Live into liquidation'.

False Dawns and False Confessions

Of course, the establishment of such a high-profile investigation and the publicity surrounding it can also attract a totally different type of caller. At around 2 AM on the morning of 7 March 1999, the station orderly (SO) on duty at Wicklow Garda Station received what was, at the very least, a most unusual telephone call. Phone traffic at that hour of the night is limited enough in most rural stations. For the most part, it would concern more localised topics. This call, however, was anything but 'run of the mill'. The caller spoke in a high-pitched voice with a pronounced foreign accent. He asked to be allowed to speak with the policeman in charge of the investigations into the cases of the missing women. When told that he was ringing the wrong Garda station, as that particular investigation was operating out of Naas Garda Station, the caller said that he was not, at that time, in a position to make any further calls. He said that he was ringing from a location near Quebec, in Canada, and that he wanted to admit his involvement in the murder of a female in the Wicklow area some years previously. He said that her body had never been located.

The caller introduced himself as Clifford Robert Olson. He told the increasingly dumbfounded Garda that, on a visit to Ireland some years previously with a close friend called Collin, they had, in his words, 'snatched' a woman as she walked on the public road. They then brought her to a spot in the Wicklow Mountains, where they had held her prisoner for a number of hours, and subjected her to repeated rape and sexual assault. They had then, he coolly added, battered her to death with their fists and feet, before throwing her body, weighed down with some large stones, into a lake. Both of them had returned to Canada shortly after this incident.

Olson said that he had only been back in Canada a short time before he was arrested on what he called 'trumped up' charges. He had received a long sentence, which he was then serving. He gave the SO a contact telephone number, and asked that it be passed on to the team investigating the disappearances of

246

the six women. Olson described himself as possessing further, very relevant information, including photographs of some of the missing women. At this stage, a second voice came on the line, and made some comment in French; the call was then terminated.

★

All through that night and early the next morning, the phone lines between our homes, Naas and Wicklow stations were buzzing. On Gerry O'Connell's instructions, I rang the number that the caller had given earlier. My call was answered by a French-speaking male. When I enquired, in my fractured French, whether he spoke English, he immediately responded with an 'of course'. I introduced myself. I told him that I was a detective attached to the Irish police, and that we were currently investigating the disappearance of a number of females in our jurisdiction. On hearing that I was Irish, he immediately responded by telling me that his wife's grandfather was from Galway, and that they intended visiting sometime soon.

I then asked my newfound friend where he was based, and he told me that he was a prison officer attached to the Special Handling Unit of the Correctional Service of Canada at Montee Gagon, Anne Des Plaines, outside of Quebec. I told him about the strange call that had been received at Wicklow Garda Station the previous night. When I mentioned the caller's name, he responded that Olson, whom he described as an 'evil, evil little man' was serving eleven sentences of life imprisonment in the penitentiary. 'You must,' he added, 'be very careful not to turn your back on this sick person.'

My call was then transferred to the Prison Governor's office. I again introduced myself. The officer to whom I was speaking was, naturally, reluctant to reveal much information over the telephone. He confirmed that they currently had a prisoner called Clifford Robert Olson, who was serving a number of life sentences for the abduction, rape and murder of eleven teenagers. Of equal importance was the revelation that, some hours earlier, Olson had, at his own request, been facilitated with a long-distance phone call to a number that I recognised as that of Wicklow Garda Station. This call, it was confirmed, as with all such prison calls, was monitored. The recording could, under certain circumstances, be made available to us. As he was not then in a position to establish my credentials, he told me that he could not give me any further details about Mr Olson or his crimes. I informed him that arrangements would be put in train to afford me 'police to police' cooperation in any further enquiries I made concerning Olson. This process is normally set up at the highest levels between two police forces, after which a liaison officer is appointed to act as a go-between. I was assured that once this process was in place, the fullest cooperation would be afforded to me.

★

Tony Hickey then made a number of telephone calls, and by 10 PM on the next day, I was on the telephone, speaking directly with the Irish Ambassador to Canada, Mr Paul Dempsey, at the Irish Embassy in Ottawa, Ontario. Mr Dempsey made contact with the Canadian authorities, who organised a contact at the highest level in their Correctional Services, and with the Royal Canadian Mounted Police. The work done on our behalf by Mr Dempsey and his staff at the Embassy was, I should take this opportunity to say, of the highest calibre. I was assured that anything I needed would be made readily available, and arrangements were put in place which would allow me to speak directly with Olson.

Prior to doing so, however, I attempted to gather as much information as I could on him. Even if the particular murder he was referring to did not fall within the remit of Operation TRACE, it would still need to be followed through. To this end, it was vitally important that I know as much as possible about this man, to help me control and direct our conversation.

I would learn that the self-styled 'Beast of British Columbia' had been in custody since 1981 and, only the previous year, had his application for parole turned down. At that hearing, a prison psychiatrist had stated, based on evidence which Olsen had admitted to him, that he had committed somewhere between eighty and two hundred homicides. Many of these admissions were contained in video recordings made with Olson over a five-year period. He described Olsen as 'likely to reoffend'.

The crimes for which Olson had been convicted by the courts, and for which he was serving a number of life sentences, involved the abduction, torture and murder of eleven children and young persons, between the ages of nine and eighteen years, in a killing spree between November 1980 and July 1981. In the final month alone, he abducted and murdered five children. His victims were randomly selected – eight female and three male. All crimes had occurred in the suburban Vancouver area and, given that at that time the Surrey police area alone had a yearly total of two thousand 'runaways', the majority of his victims had actually been wrongly classified as such. He also preyed on the heroin-addicted street prostitutes, who numbered in their hundreds, working the Bowery/Skid Row areas of town. His choice of victim ensured that, for many months, he had flown below the radar. The authorities were slow to come to the realisation that a serial killer was at work.

His last victim, seventeen-year-old Louise Chartrand, had been picked up by him as she hitch-hiked to work. Olson had been driving aimlessly after meeting with his solicitor earlier that day, to complain about the police harassing him in connection with the disappearance of a young girl, Ada Court, from the apartment block where he lived. He would later be convicted of her murder. He had driven Louise to a local ski resort, where he had raped, and killed her, then dumped her body.

★

En route to the ski resort, he called to Squamish Police Station to try collect a gun that had earlier been seized from him. They refused to return it to him, and he left the station, threatening court proceedings against the police. As he stood there arguing about his rights as a citizen, his latest victim lay trussed and drugged in the boot of his car, awaiting whatever fate he decided to mete out to her.

Even following his arrest, Olson continued to exploit both his victims and their families. He described himself as being prepared to reveal, in return for his wife of four months receiving the sum of $10,000 Canadian per head, the location of the bodies of his victims. As a 'gesture of goodwill', he handed over one of the bodies free of charge. The various locations of a further ten bodies were then revealed, after his wife received $100,000 Canadian. He had actually murdered one of the children on 19 May 1981, just some four days after his wedding, while still on his honeymoon. There was such a public outcry when word of this grotesque deal between Olson and the Canadian authorities leaked out in the media that no further money was paid. True to form, Olson would not reveal any further body dump site locations to them.

Olson would eventually die in custody in 2012. Even then, his death was shrouded in controversy. Some months previously, it was discovered that, having been in custody for almost thirty years, he was still in receipt of social-welfare payments. These had been paid into a trust fund through all his years in custody. Only direct intervention by the Canadian Prime Minister, Steven Harper, would ensure that these payments ceased.

My first conversation with Olsen was, to put it mildly, bizarre. I had barely finished introducing myself when he interjected and said, 'I killed Carole Jordan. We met her in Ireland, we took her, we enjoyed her and then we killed her so slowly.' Trying hard to conceal the revulsion that I felt at the matter-of-fact way this pronouncement was made, I asked what he meant by 'we'. Olson then told me that, before he was locked up, he had visited Ireland with a friend called Collin. Collin had, he said, been reading somewhere about how easy-going the Irish lifestyle was, and they decided to visit the country. They believed it to be full of lone female backpackers, and persons living bohemian lifestyles in out-of-the-way places.

They had, he said, met in prison, while both were serving short sentences, and had struck up a friendship there. They soon realised that they shared a common interest in a particular type of sex and had, he said, 'fantasised about snatching a woman and playing with her'. From their conversations, they believed that they would be able to hunt more easily, and without the fear of detection in Ireland.

★

At this stage, I interrupted him. I told him that I would be taking notes of our conversation, and that any such notes could one day be used as evidence. He replied that he was aware of this and, furthermore, that he realised that the prison was probably taping the call. I added that, in order to comply with our legal requirements in relation to verbal admissions, I had to administer what was referred to as a verbal caution before proceeding. He responded, 'You do what you have to do. I know what I have done'. In accordance with the regulations governing the admissibility of admissions, I issued a formal caution. I told him, 'You are not obliged to say anything unless you wish to do so, but anything you do say will be taken down in writing, and may be given in evidence'. The last thing we needed was to be given vital evidence that was unusable because of a failure, on my part, to comply with one of the most basic of all the rules governing police work.

Olson then continued, as if I had never interrupted him. Following their release from prison, Collin and he had travelled to Ireland. They stayed in a hostel in the middle of Dublin, and were 'blown away' by the number of women who were staying there on their own. On only the first night in the hostel, they befriended a French-Canadian girl called Carole Jordan. She was backpacking across Europe, and had only arrived in Dublin that week on the first leg of her travels. She told them that she intended to hitch-hike to Roundwood in Wicklow the following day, and was going to spend a few days sleeping in a tent near a big lake. Olson told me that they could not believe their luck. Carole was a petite girl who did not look like she could defend herself, and here she was talking about visiting some lake in the middle of nowhere, and entirely on her own. She had, he said, 'selected herself to be our first'.

He and Colin took the first bus to Roundwood the following morning, and spent the first half of that day hanging around the village. Their wait was rewarded when, sometime around noon, they saw Carole climb down from the cab of a truck, and then take the road to the lake. They decided that they were going to have a bit of fun with her first, and followed her at a distance. At the lake, Carole took a scenic path that wound its way up and around a mountain. They then grabbed her, dragging her off the track and deep into the woods. They warned the petrified girl that they would hurt her if she called out. They then found a secluded spot, where they beat and raped her. 'We played with her for a day and a night. At the end, she begged us to kill her to stop the pain'. He told me that they had killed her, but added, 'We took our time'. They then stuffed her body into her sleeping bag, which they filled with rocks, and dropped into the lake. 'She is still there. We put our marker on the bank. Collin has been back to it. She waits to be found.'

I cannot describe the revulsion I felt at the matter-of-fact way this man spoke of the pain and suffering they had inflicted to satisfy their own lust. I think my reaction was clear to Olson, who, I have no doubt, was enjoying telling the story and recollecting the moment. Remember that this was a man who had handed over eleven maimed bodies, in return for cash, and who had only recently started talking about having tortured and killed upwards of two hundred people. I told him that I was not familiar with the case of Carole Jordan, to which he responded, 'Check it out, check it out, you will see that I am telling the truth'.

I told him that this information would, of course, be thoroughly checked out. I added that, as Operation TRACE was case-specific, we might not be the Gardai who would be directly involved in any subsequent investigation. However, I told him that , if he wished, I could continue to act as liaison between himself and the other policemen.

Olson said that he would only deal with the TRACE taskforce. There was, he added, a very good reason for this.

Since I was locked up, my friend Collin has been visiting me regularly. Collin still does the hunting. Sometimes Collin will use a mixture of chloral hydrate and alcohol to drug our targets. We used this when we were hunting together in the United States and in Canada. He brings me Polaroid photographs and souvenirs from the girls he picks up. I have twenty-seven such photos. Collin does good work. He knows what I want, and how to handle his women. He still goes back to Ireland; he has had many successes there. The women still walk the streets alone. Collin keeps me supplied. A few of the Polaroids he gave me are of girls he snatched a few years ago near the Wicklow Mountains. I have them still. They are in the safe in the prison's Central Registry office, sealed with all my legal papers and my videotapes. I enjoy looking at the photos sometimes.

Three of the girls in Collin's photographs are amongst the photographs of the six girls you are looking for. All show the girl before she dies, when she is dead and when he takes off their clothes. One of your missing girls was Collin's girlfriend. I know, because he told me that he was going to visit her, that he was in your country in - - -, when she went missing.

My solicitor has the stubs of all our plane tickets which will show when Collin and me were in and out of your country, and when Collin was visiting since. You can look at them, and compare them to when some of your six girls were murdered.

★

This was a startling statement. Olson, however, wasn't yet finished. He told me that Collin had buried all of his victims in the same area. He then claimed to have photographs of the actual site. According to him, Collin had buried the bodies in a place that was of special significance to both of them. This was the same spot where they had raped and tortured Carole. He was prepared, he told me, subject to whatever legal advice he received, to identify the dump sites for all four of the bodies, and to stand trial for the murder of Carole.

Olson asked for reassurance, on one point, before he would commit to any further course of action. He asked that a document be formally issued from our Justice Department, to show that there was no death penalty for murder in our jurisdiction. I assured him that this was the actual position, and that the last sentences of death imposed in this country had been connected with the murders of policemen, and in each instance these sentences had been changed to life imprisonment. I told him that I would ensure that a 'letter of comfort' in this matter would be made available to him.

I told Olson that I would require either the original or copies of the photographs he was referring to, for the purpose of establishing that the females in them were connected with our investigation. He replied that he would be reluctant to hand this evidence over, either to me personally or to any Canadian police officer, without receiving certain assurances from the highest levels of government right from the outset. He then gave me contact details for a firm of solicitors based in Maple Ridge, in British Columbia, who would verify his claims about the existence of the twenty-seven photographs. If there was to be any formal handing over of evidence, or of copies of it, he would do so, he said, only through his solicitor, and to a person from the Irish Embassy. Furthermore, he added that, as Collin was then currently travelling outside of Canada, and could even be in Ireland hunting a new girl at that very moment, there would, he said, be no handover of photographs and documents, until he knew that Collin was safe.

In a further twist – as if it could get any more bizarre – Olson also gave me the contact details of another solicitor, based on Nimitz Highway in Honolulu, Hawaii, who, he stated would provide me with information concerning a murder that Olson had committed in that jurisdiction, and to which he had offered to enter a plea of 'guilty' before their courts, in return for certain assurances being received. He was, he said, passing on this information to prove to me that he was a man of honour, who could be trusted to keep his end of any deal that we struck. It was, to say the least of it, strange to hear a man of his reputation speak of honour and trust. I had then told him that I was about to terminate our telephone call, and undertook to talk to him again within the next few days.

★

Just prior to my hanging up the phone, Olson, in a further, throwaway remark, made reference to his having been in contact with an FBI Special Investigator called Robert Keppel, whom he described as the lead investigator in the 'Green River Murders'. I was aware of some of the details of this high-profile search for a serial killer who, over eighteen years, had abducted and murdered at least fifty females in the Seattle area of Washington State. Further details would, in time, be provided to our taskforce, through contact from Detective Tom Jensen, who, at the time of our enquiry, was the coordinator in the hunt for that serial killer.

Seattle itself is just across the border from Canada, and only a few hours' drive from Olsen's hunting grounds around Vancouver. The majority of the Green River murderer victims were believed to have been involved in the sex trade, and were dumped in or around the Green River, often in clusters. One particular search, based on a sighting by a member of the public, had recovered three bodies within yards of each other, all nude and provocatively posed. The majority of the victims had last been seen alive on the infamous Pacific Highway South. They had all been strangled.

Eventually, in 2001, an ex-naval veteran, who had served in the Vietnam war, was arrested and charged with four of the murders. Gary Leon Ridgeway had been identified through DNA analysis of body samples taken from some of the victims. He had been considered as one of the main suspects in the murders all along, having first fallen under suspicion as early as 1983. However, at the request of the police, he had taken and 'passed' a polygraph test in 1984. As a consequence of this, he was, effectively, allowed to remain at large, and continue to torture and kill new victims. At his crime scenes, Ridgeway, who was extremely forensically aware, would scatter chewing gum and cigarette butts that he had picked up in bars and other places, to contaminate the scene. A plea bargain, struck by Ridgeway's defence team, would see him plead guilty to a total of forty-eight murders, after assurances that he would not receive the death penalty. As part of this arrangement, he revealed the locations of a number of his victims' bodies.

In court, Ridgeway would describe himself as having killed so many women that he was unsure of the exact number. He would state, 'I wanted to kill as many women I thought were prostitutes as I possibly could'. This three-times-married sexual predator used to regularly file complaints to the police about the activities of the prostitutes who operated in his area, while, at the same time, availing of their 'services'. In his workplace, he would often read aloud to his workmates from the Bible, and would go door-to-door in his own neighbourhood spreading its good news. Paint scrapings, unique to his place of work, would be found adhering to the scant items of clothing he left on some of the bodies. His victims were normally strangled, either manually or by ligature, after he had had sex with them. He also admitted that he would regularly revisit the areas where he had dumped the bodies, to have sex with the corpses.

★

Although serving forty-eight life sentences for murders he had committed between 1982 and 1984 (as many as one a week, during some periods), Ridgeway would again appear in court in 2011, charged with the murder of another girl, whose body had been located in 2003. This would bring the number of his victims to an appalling forty-nine. In videotaped interviews with police, he would suggest that he had murdered as many as seventy females.

The DNA sample taken from the victims (that had been identified as having come from Ridgeway) had been compared to a body sample that Ridgeway had given to police in 1987. DNA identification was, at that stage, still in its infancy. As previously mentioned, we in Operation TRACE had similar success with a sample taken from the body of Kildare woman Phyllis Murphy in 1980, which would eventually be identified in 2000. This identification would lead to the conviction of her neighbour, John Crerar, for her murder.

Olson had, following my original conversation with him, rung the office of the Minister for Justice in this jurisdiction, who was, at that time, Mr John O'Donoghue. Olson spoke with a senior official in that office. He requested that details of his conversation with myself, and the importance of the information he had imparted to me, be brought to the personal attention of the Minister for Justice. In this way, he ensured that details of his claims and admissions were known at the highest levels, thus putting additional pressure on the police to take it seriously. That office would correspond directly with the Governor of the prison.

After my conversation with Olson had finished, I sat down with my colleagues, and attempted to take stock of all the various murders he had alluded to. For starters, there were the murders of the eleven children that he had abducted in the Vancouver area, and for which he was serving eleven life sentences. We then had the statement from the prison psychiatrist at his parole hearing, who said that Olson had admitted to somewhere between eighty and two hundred further murders. He was, at the time of our conversation, negotiating a deal with the authorities in California. In return for assurances concerning his sentence, he was prepared to plead guilty to six murders. Negotiations were also ongoing in Hawaii, with a view to him entering a 'guilty' plea to one murder. To cap it all off, he was talking to the head of the special 'Green River Murders' taskforce, who were dealing, at that stage, with forty-eight unsolved murders.

★

Here he was now admitting to the murder of a French-Canadian backpacker, whom he had abducted and tortured in our jurisdiction. The various murders he had referred to in our conversation actually amounted to a total of two hundred and seventy. He was also claiming to have photographic evidence linking his friend, Collin, to the murders of at least three of our Operation TRACE targets. Certainly, nothing in my career had prepared me for dealing with a monster like Olson. As one of my colleagues succinctly put it, 'Olson has killed more people than cancer'.

Gerry O'Connell told me to stay in regular touch with Olsen, and try to maintain the rapport we had struck up in our opening conversation. At government level, a First Secretary at the Irish Embassy in Ottawa was appointed to act as a conduit, for any correspondence or photographs that Olson agreed to hand over. Arrangements were put in train to facilitate an immediate flight to Canada, in the event of any such transfer occurring. On a police-to-police cooperation level, a senior investigator in the Royal Canadian Mounted Police (RCMP) was appointed as liaison officer, to render whatever assistance might be required to me.

From an investigative perspective, our first priority had to be the securing of the photographs, followed by the aeroplane ticket stubs. I was instructed that in our next conversation, I was to open negotiations with Olson with a view to obtaining this vital evidence. However, I was to stress to him at all times that I was not entitled to make any offer, or enter into any arrangement with him. Again, all our conversations were to be preceded by me administering the official caution. Tony Hickey insisted that he be fully briefed after each conversation. Equally, if, as he appeared to be hinting, he was amenable to travelling to this jurisdiction to identify the body dump sites, this could only be arranged at the highest inter-governmental levels. Any such step would only be undertaken after the evidence he claimed to possess was received by ourselves, and then only after it had been analysed and verified as genuine. In the event that such items actually existed (and, at that stage, we had no reason to think any differently), then we were looking at our investigation taking a major step forward.

We set in motion enquiries with a view to establishing the identity of 'Collin'. The suggestion by Olson that Collin might, at that stage, be here in Ireland hunting for a new victim to abduct, torture and kill was a frightening prospect, and one which galvanised us all into action. Without causing a huge public panic, we had to identify and locate all male visitors from Canada who had travelled alone to Ireland in recent weeks. Again, we would turn to the Canadian authorities for assistance in this matter. Our concerns in this regard were lessened considerably when Olson rang us a day or two later, with the news that Collin was still in Canada, having cancelled his proposed trip to Ireland, and would be visiting him in prison within the coming weeks.

★

The one thing that Tony Hickey stressed to us that day was the importance of this information not being leaked to the media. The papers would, he suggested, be unable to resist reporting on a development as serious as this one. Given Olson's notoriety, it was unlikely that the media frenzy would be confinable or controllable. It could, therefore, seriously interfere with other avenues of investigation that were then being followed. It was also important that we not concentrate solely on this development, and risk losing sight of any other lines and leads that had been established.

There was, Tony added, also the situation in which we found ourselves, where certain members of some of the missing girls' families were having trouble coming to terms with the chilling fact that their child might have been murdered. To learn that a known sexual predator and convicted murderer claimed to have graphic images of the bodies of their daughters would have a devastating effect.

Within days of our opening conversation, I received, from Olson, what was to be the first of many letters. The paper upon which it had been typed carried a banner heading which read: 'Democracy cannot be maintained without its foundations; free public freedom of thought, belief, opinion, and expression, including freedom of the press and other media of communications, freedom of association, and discussion throughout the nation of Canada of all matters affecting the Canadian nation within the limits set by the Canadian Charter of Rights and Freedoms and by the Criminal Code and Common Law.'

This message from Olson would appear on all communication that was received from him at our office, over the next few days and weeks. As our relationship developed, I would very quickly come to the realisation that, notwithstanding his high-brow text, democracy, to this sick predator, meant the defence of his personal, and, as he saw it, God-given right to hunt, torture, sexually abuse and kill children.

Included with this first letter was an example of what Olson required as a 'letter of comfort'. It was an actual copy of a letter he had previously received. An official document, it bore the seal of the District Attorney's office of a county in California, and guaranteed Olson that, were he to be convicted of the six murders of females, which he had admitted to having committed in that jurisdiction between 1978 and 1981, any sentences he received would run concurrently to each other and, more importantly, to the sentences he was then serving in Canada. This letter was signed by the Assistant District Attorney for that county.

★

The actual text of the letter, which was addressed to Olson's solicitor, reads:

Dear - - -,

I received a letter from Mr Olson, who requested that our office agree that any murder convictions in our county relating to the six victims described by Mr Olson not only run concurrent with each other but also with the murder convictions that Mr Olson is currently serving in Canada. This office will agree to that condition.

Also enclosed was a note, signed by a very high-ranking official in the Canadian Penal System, and dated 1993. In the body of the text, permission was given to allow Olson to be interviewed by the FBI as well as senior officers from the RCMP, for the purpose of enlarging the serial-killer databases held in both jurisdictions. There is also a comment included in the letter, to the effect that the author believes that 'research' might not be the only consideration behind the various requests for permission to interview. This was considered to be a thinly veiled reference to the possibility of further, unresolved, homicides being addressed. This note was accompanied by a formal written and signed consent by Olson to participate in such interviews.

He also sent us a copy of a letter that had been sent to the Canadian authorities, from the Office of the Public Defender for the State of Hawaii. The author of the note states that he had been appointed to represent Olson in any criminal actions, and that he was to be held accountable for them in that state. They put themselves on record as being available to represent Olson in any proceedings, in any jurisdiction worldwide.

In our next telephone conversation, Olson stated that there was to be no interaction between ourselves and the RCMP, in relation to any of the crimes in our jurisdiction. A named attorney in San Francisco, California, had recently, he said, received a substantial part of the personal documentation that had previously been held in his 'Preventive Security' file at Saskatchewan Penitentiary This transfer of documentation had come about, he claimed, because of a recent ruling by the Prison Warden that Olson was not to have access to any pornographic images. He said that he had had the documentation transferred, because he feared that it would be stolen. It included the twenty-seven photographs that Collin had taken of the Irish girls. There was also a total of fifteen letters from Collin, all of which dealt with his hunting for females in Ireland, together with the airline ticket stubs. He undertook to provide me with a letter from this new solicitor, to confirm that he had received all these items, and that he would represent Olson in his dealings with us.

★

Within days, a further letter arrived at our office. As promised by Olson, there was a note from a firm of solicitors with offices in San Francisco, Los Angeles, Sacramento and Washington DC It declared, 'I have your letter and the twenty-seven nude photographs of the Irish girls'. There was also an invitation to Olson to 'plan a program' in connection with clearing the murders in Ireland, while, at the same time, ensuring that there be no repercussions from any 'overzealous boy scout policemen'. Mark Kerrigan read this last comment and remarked, with a wry grin, that 'Mr Olson seems to be getting to know Alan very well'.

On 17 May 1999, during one of our telephone conversations, Olson said that he had, through his solicitor, attempted to forward copies of the photographs to the Irish Embassy, but had been prevented from doing so by the prison authorities. I suggested that he could ask one of his solicitors from among the names which he had provided to me, to send them directly to the Embassy. This included his solicitors in Canada, San Francisco and Hawaii. As an alternative, I told him that I had been authorised to go anywhere he suggested, and to take personal possession of any items he wished to hand over. About an hour later he rang back, and said that he would authorise one of his solicitors, from outside the Canadian jurisdiction, to provide us with copies of the various photographs. It was arranged that he would notify me in advance of their delivery, so that I could be present to receive them. This news was greeted with great excitement in our unit. After over two months of negotiations, it appeared that we were, finally, about to get our hands on this vital evidence.

However, once again we were to be disappointed. Olson rang, and said that the prison authorities had expressly forbidden him from communicating with any foreign embassy. This had grown to be a regular feature of his dealings with us. On each occasion that he was due to hand over any definitive evidence, he came up with some excuse at the eleventh hour. I told him that we had received notification some weeks previously, through our Department of Justice, that this embargo was about to be introduced, but that we ourselves would not be affected, as we had already been approved at government level. This, I told him, meant that he was free to send the various items on to our embassy. As an alternative, I told him I would attend directly at either the Penitentiary or at the offices of one of his solicitors, and collect them personally. Of course, this was all dependant on whether he actually had such photographs in the first place.

At this suggestion, he became very aggressive, shouting and screaming down the phone. These tantrums had also been a regular feature throughout the contact I had been having with him over the previous two months. If he felt, at any stage during the course of a conversation, that he was not being treated with the deference and respect that he craved, he could become extremely agitated. Even over the distance of thousands of miles, it was easy to see just how volatile and explosive a character he really was. He then slammed down the phone. To quote Mark Kerrigan after this particular call, 'Alan has just been thrown out of the Boy Scouts'.

★

Two days later, Olson rang back. He said that, having consulted with his legal people, he was now prepared to travel under Irish police escort to Dublin and, from there, to bring us to Wicklow, to point out the area where he and Collin had dumped Carole's body. The other three bodies would all be buried very close by, and it should be an easy task to find them. He added that he had just that moment sent a letter to the Irish Minister for Justice, asking that a solicitor be appointed to represent him.

This offer was, I was aware, about to herald a defining moment in the Garda relationship with Clifford Robert Olson. Over the last few days, I had spoken by phone with various lead detectives in some of the other cases that Olsen had made admissions to. They confirmed that they had been contacted by Olson, who had made certain admissions to them in relation to unresolved homicides that they were investigating. These admissions were sufficient, in themselves, to lend credence to his claims. However, he also claimed to have certain physical evidence which directly linked him to the crimes to which he was admitting. As with our case, in one instance, he claimed to have photographs of the dead bodies, while in the other case, he offered to bring the investigators to a body dump site he had been using. They stated that he had never delivered on the actual handing over of the items and they now suspected that the items never actually existed.

A consensus had been reached between ourselves and those other lead detectives, following a number of conference phone calls in which Gerry O'Connell and Mark Kerrigan had also participated. It had been agreed that, were Olson to offer to travel to Ireland, as was felt he was obviously building up to, from the tone and content of his calls, then I was to request that we be given sight of the independent evidence he claimed to possess before any such move took place. This demand was to be non-negotiable. Referred to, in police parlance, as the 'put up or shut up moment', the ball would be firmly in his court.

We expected Olson, when we spoke by telephone next, to try to offer some sort of compromise, by way of delaying things regarding our requirement. After I spoke there was, for a moment, no response, just complete silence. I thought that we might have been cut off. The silence was quickly shattered. I was completely unprepared for the flow of invective and diatribe to which I was subjected. Screaming half in French and half and English, Olson appeared to have lost control of himself entirely. His curses were peppered with comments on my birthright, my lack of respect for a man of his stature and my failure to recognise that I was messing with the wrong man. 'I will make you suffer,' he screamed. 'I will make you beg me to kill you. I will take my time with you and enjoy doing you'. When he finally began to run out of steam, I interjected, and told him to think about my offer, and to come back to me when he was ready. On hearing this, he became almost apoplectic. I thought he was going to explode. The phone was taken away from him by an attending prison officer, who apologised to me and quickly ended the call. Had I been standing beside him in that prison in Quebec, instead of sitting in an office in Naas Garda Station, I firmly believe I would have been fighting for my life. That was the last we spoke.

★

In conversation with some of the other investigators over the following days, we learnt that their own requests addressed to Olson had elicited a similar response. They had found themselves unable to definitively dismiss Olson's admissions of involvement in their unresolved murders while, at the same time, having nothing but his own words to connect him with the crimes.

Within days, a telephone call from the prison authorities would go a long way towards answering all our doubts and fears. We were told that an inmate in the prison, a trustee who worked in the prison library, had come forward with certain information concerning Olson and his contact with us. This prisoner, Justine X*, was, at that stage, completing a lengthy prison sentence for serious sex offences. He told the prison officers that his role in the library allowed him almost unfettered access to the internet. In a general trawl some months earlier, he had come across mention of a special taskforce having been set up in this jurisdiction. In a discussion with Olson, whom he feared and revered in equal measure, he had mentioned Operation TRACE to him. At Olson's request, he had then established as much information as he could about the judicial system and due legal process in Ireland, together with the details of the various crimes.

Based on what he learned, they had then concocted a story which they believed they could sell to the Irish authorities. They had, he claimed, used the carrot-and-stick approach with the Irish police. The carrot, in this case, had been the suggestion of the existence of the twenty-seven photographs showing the three girls that Collin had, allegedly, murdered, alongside an offer to identify their body dump sites to us. The stick had, of course, been the suggestion that Collin was actually in our jurisdiction. The next phase of this scam would have been a further phone call, suggesting that the next victim had already been selected and was even then being groomed by Collin, who was waiting for a signal from Olson before killing her.

The invention of one victim, Carole Jordan, had all been part of this scheme. They believed that if he could convince the authorities here of the commission of that particular crime it would have been sufficient to force our hand into bringing Olson over. Once in Ireland, in what he considered a far more relaxed prison system, he felt he had a better chance of gaining his freedom, either by parole or by escape. He knew that he was never going to be set free in Canada.

I sometimes wonder, while concocting the story about killing Carole Jordan, which of his actual victims he had been recalling when he spoke of 'taking her . . . enjoying her . . . and killing her slowly'. He had gone into very intimate and precise details about the murder, leaving us in no doubt that he was describing a real event in which he had participated.

★

Our paths would cross again some nine years later. In late 2008, I attended a Cold Case Training Seminar at the Royal Canadian Police College at Chilliwack, Vancouver. During the course of a 'Lessons Learned' module, reference was made to the failures in the investigation into the disappearances of Olson's victims. The fact that he had operated for so long with total impunity, under the noses of the authorities, still rankled, and had led to wide-sweeping changes in how disappearances were logged and investigated. When I mentioned that I had interviewed him in relation to his admissions concerning a number of murders in Ireland, all those in attendance at the seminar were astounded. To the majority of them, he was just a figure from the past.

When our class ended, I was approached by the Senior Investigator, who had presented the paper on Olson. He asked me if I would be interested in taking a short spin with him. We drove to Chilliwack Lake, a distance of about four miles from the college. There, my guide brought me to an open area in the forest, where he told me that, as a very junior detective, he had been one of the search party that had located the body of Sandra Lynn Wolfsteiner, the sixteen-year-old that Olson had abducted, raped and tortured on 19 May 1981, just four days into his honeymoon. As we stood there in that idyllic spot, it struck me, most forcibly, that we as a society will never come to terms with or even try to comprehend the degree of depravity and savagery lurking in the twisted minds of people such as Olson. I was affronted that someone like him had attempted to lecture me about fair play in my dealings with him.

If the attempt by Olson to have himself charged with the murder of Carole Jordan – a crime that not only had he not committed, but that had never been committed in the first place – sounds strange, then, even more astounding, were the admissions made by Felix Maher*, the twenty-nine-year-old son of a settled traveller, from a provincial town in the Midlands.

In June 1999, a male caller rang Clondalkin Garda Station. He told the Garda member who answered the phone that he wanted to talk about the murder of one of the females whose disappearance was being reviewed by Operation TRACE. The Garda asked him if he wanted the number of Naas Garda Station, but the man said no. He then suggested that the Garda officer write down what he was about to tell him. He went on to say that on the day the girl in question had disappeared, he and his uncle Harry* had been driving around looking for scrap iron. They met a girl walking by herself on the roadway. They had at first driven past her, but Harry had then suggested that they have some fun with her. Following Harry's orders, he climbed into the back of the van, and partially opened the side door. Harry turned the van around and drove back to where they had seen the girl, pulling up beside her. She was standing at the passenger side and Harry told her he was looking for directions.

★

When the girl approached the van, the caller had opened the side door and dragged her in, giving her 'a few slaps' to quieten her. Harry had then driven off. They took the girl to a spot they used to hide stolen scrap, and took turns having sex with the girl. He said that he had intended to let her go when they had finished with her, but Harry said she would tell the police. They killed the girl, and dropped her body down a bog hole.

The Garda taking the call asked the caller for his name, but he declined to give it. He told the Garda that he would ring back, and then hung up. We were immediately contacted with details of the call, and established that it had been made from a public telephone box in the Clondalkin area of Dublin. The phone box was quickly sealed off, and technically examined. However, nothing of an evidental nature was located. On the face of it, this looked to be a promising lead, but, having been recently fooled by Olson, we decided, on this occasion, to tread very warily. The snatch method as described by the caller sounded quite plausible, though, and was a frequently used ploy by predators to take their targets from the roadside. The chances of being observed were slim, and the victim would have had very little opportunity to get away.

Unfortunately, we could only wait and see if the caller, who later identified himself as Felix*, would contact us again. About three weeks later, a Garda on duty in the public office at Store Street Garda Station in Dublin would receive a second call from Felix. On this occasion, Felix, who again, at that point, refused to give his name, said he had been involved in the murder of one of the other girls whose disappearance we were investigating. During this call, he claimed that they had snatched a second girl in the middle of the day. This time, there were three of them driving around, and he described how they had dragged their victim into the van. She had put up a 'fierce' struggle, and they had had to chase her down. She almost got away from them. As they were driving away, they noticed her handbag lying on the side of the road. They reversed the van, and one of them jumped out and grabbed the bag. The van had then been driven away, at some speed, to the same area where they had taken the first girl. This second victim was repeatedly gang-raped by the three men, and then killed. Fearing that they might have been seen by a passing motorist when abducting the girl, they then drove to a remote area, and set the van on fire. It was, he said, a van that could never be traced back to them. It had been bought 'up north', that is, in Northern Ireland, for hard cash, and Harry had given the seller a false name and address.

★

Once again, the caller would not give any personal details. He did say, though, that when he had kidnapped the second girl, he had been accompanied by his uncle and a cousin. This cousin had since died in a traffic accident. He described himself as being convinced that God had punished his cousin for the rape and murder of the innocent girl. This belief had, he said, prompted him to come forward and make his own admission of guilt. However, he feared that his uncle Harry would kill him if he was aware that he had gone to the police to admit his part in these crimes. Harry was his mother's brother, and had moved in with his family when his father died. He was a bully and a drunk, and had, from an early age, sexually abused both him and his sisters. He said that he had gone to his mother about the abuse, but that she had not believed him. Harry had, he claimed, forced him into taking part in the rape and murder of the two girls.

The caller had then told the Garda member that he would ring back within the next few days, with information about where the bodies were hidden. At his own request, he was given the dedicated phone number in our office. This second call from our mystery caller was made from a coin-box in Coolock village, on the outskirts of Dublin. Subsequent technical examination of the box would not, once again, yield any evidence as to the caller's identity.

Over the next few weeks, we waited to see if he would contact either ourselves directly, or another Garda station. Days turned into weeks and dragged on into months, without any further contact being made by our mystery caller. We went so far as to ask the caller, in a carefully worded message, to contact us, during the course of one of Gerry O'Connell's press briefings. The request that was broadcast only made reference to the 'recent telephone caller to Clondalkin and Store Street Garda Station'. This request failed to elicit any response.

At one of our team conferences, we addressed the question as to why our mystery caller had failed to continue his contact with us. Pat Treacy suggested that, given how anxious he had appeared to be to admit his part in these abductions, his failure to contact us in recent times could only be explained by his being actively prevented from so doing. There could, Pat added, be as many as three distinct possibilities preventing him from ringing: fear of his uncle Harry, serious injury or incarceration. Tony directed us to follow up on the latter possibility. Throughout his telephone calls, our caller had given us certain information to allow us to make an educated guess at his background. A trawl was made of recent prison committals, focusing on persons of a particular age and background. Given his involvement in the alleged rapes of the females involved in our investigations, we concentrated, furthermore, on prisoners who had been sentenced for sexual offences. We were still, however, unable to identify the mystery caller.

Pat's suggestion about prison time would, later, prove to be partially correct. Just before Christmas of 2000, an Assistant Chief Officer attached to one of the main prisons in the State, rang our office in Naas. He told us that he had been asked by a psychologist attached to the prison service to make contact with Operation TRACE, and to make an appointment for us to visit her office at the prison. The officer told us that he was not aware of the reason for the request, but understood that it was urgent. Pat and myself made arrangements to call to the prison the following day.

When we arrived, we were greeted by Doctor Helena White*. She informed us that she was an accredited psychologist attached to the prison service, and that what she was about to tell us had been disclosed to her by a prisoner attending one of her weekly clinics. She said that, so as not to betray client confidentiality, he had requested that she contact us on his behalf. She stated that her client had informed her, during a lengthy counselling session, that he had contacted two Garda stations, by telephone, in the months before he had been sentenced. In the course of those calls, he claimed to have made certain admissions, in relation to his own involvement in the cases of two missing females, whose disappearances she believed us to be investigating. We told her that these two calls had indeed been received, and that certain information had been passed on. We added, however, that we were not aware of the identity of the caller, nor could we comment on the genuineness of his admissions.

Dr White asked if we were prepared to meet with her client, in her presence (if he so desired), and let him recount the story he had given her. She said that, in her opinion, her client was extremely vulnerable at the moment. For his sake, the pace and content of any conversation must be dictated by either herself or her client. We established that her client did not wish to seek legal advice prior to talking with us.

By way of background information, she informed us that he was a twenty-nine-year-old single male who, prior to his current incarceration, had been 'living rough' in his hometown. He had, over the years, amassed a number of criminal convictions, and was currently serving a term of imprisonment for the abduction and serious assault of a young male. For this latter offence, he had received a sentence of twelve years' imprisonment.

The actual details of this particular crime are quite shocking. Felix abducted a young male at knifepoint, and forced him to drive the two of them around on his motorbike. He eventually ordered the youth to drive to an area outside of Athlone called Creggan Bog. Forcing his terrified victim at knifepoint to remove his T-shirt and shoes, he had then tied his hands behind his back. Felix pushed the youth into a bog hole filled with water, and then pushed the motorbike in on top of him, effectively trapping him in the bog hole, with just his head above water level. He had then walked back into Athlone.

★

Some hours later, Felix met two Gardai, whom he knew, while they were on routine patrol. The Garda members stopped and greeted him. To their amazement, Felix immediately began bragging that he had abducted a youth and left him to die in a bog hole. The members checked with the local station, and were told that no report of a missing youth had been received. However, Felix remained adamant, and both Gardai then asked him if he would show them where he had left his victim. Stepping into the patrol car, he calmly directed them to the Cregan Bog area. They drove along the bog road, until Felix told them to stop. Turning off the engine but leaving on the headlights, they stood, momentarily, beside the car. In the ensuing silence, they could hear plaintive screams. On searching the area, they found the youth still trapped under the motorbike. Both Gardai bravely climbed into the bog hole and managed to pull the youth out from under the bike. Medical assistance was sought, and he was taken to hospital, where he would make a full recovery. Throughout the rescue, Felix casually leant against the Garda car, watching, but making no comment.

Our first meeting with Felix was quite unusual. We met in one of the solicitor/client interview rooms, which meant that there were no dividing barriers between us. Felix was stripped to the waist. His entire upper body and arms bore evidence of a multitude of self-harm scars, running up both arms, from wrist to shoulder. He even had scars on his neck and throat. He was a large, imposing figure, with a surprisingly gentle voice. After Dr White had formally introduced us, Felix asked her to leave the room, telling her that there were things he had to tell us that he would rather not say in front of a female.

I will never forget Felix's opening comment. As Dr White was leaving the room, he turned to us and said, 'I only killed two of the girls. Don't try stitching me for the others'. I told him that we were aware that there were certain matters he wished to discuss with us, but that, prior to him doing so, I had to caution him that he was not obliged to say anything unless he wished to do so, but that anything he did say would be taken down in writing, and could be given in evidence. When I asked if he understood this, he replied that he did, that 'every shade he ever met always said that'. A 'shade', for those who do not know, is a slang term used within some communities to describe a Garda, with a 'shade Og' either a young or a very naive member of the force. He asked that at this, our first meeting, we not take any notes, but rather just listen to what he had to say. We could then, he said, do 'all the writing in the world'.

★

Felix told us that he had been involved in the abduction and murder of two of the females whose cases we were investigating as part of TRACE. On the first occasion, he had, as he had said, been accompanied by his uncle Harry looking for scrap metal, when they had observed the girl walking alone. They had a very lucrative trade, at the time, in stealing items such as gates and beer barrels, and selling them on to other unscrupulous dealers. Harry had, he repeated, suggested that they take the girl and have some 'fun' with her. He pulled her into the van, and knocked her unconscious. They then drove to a remote mountainous area, just outside the town in which he lived, where they stockpiled their stolen goods before selling them on. They took turns raping the terrified girl. Following Harry's orders, he then, he said, strangled the girl, and dumped her body into a nearby bog hole.

He said that when they had snatched the second girl, a cousin of his, Patsy, had been with them. Patsy had 'messed up', and the girl nearly got away. There had been a struggle, and Harry was afraid that someone driving by might have taken the number of their van. They eventually brought the girl to the same area and, after subjecting her to prolonged and violent sexual assault, killed her and disposed of her body in the same bog hole. This time, however, Harry was afraid that they might be traced through the van, which he had bought for cash outside Newry. They decided to burn it in a different location. Harry blamed Patsy for the loss of the van, and gave him a 'terrible beating'. Some weeks later, Patsy had been killed in a freak road accident. 'His head was cut clean off', according to Felix. 'It was', he added, 'the hand of God. Patsy had given that girl an awful time, doing things I've never seen before. Patsy deserved to die like that'. Patsy's death, which had occurred just weeks before Felix received his current sentence, was what had convinced him to come forward, and admit his role in the murder of the two missing women.

Pat asked Felix if he was prepared to take us to the area where they had allegedly dumped the bodies, and he said that he would. He wanted two assurances before doing so. The first was that no member of his family be told that he was talking to the police. Secondly, he requested that a named senior prison officer be allowed to accompany him. Dr White would, he added, contact us and let us know when he was ready to travel.

Felix added that, on both occasions, the snatching, abuse and murder of the females had been Harry's idea. He had taken part in the crimes only because he feared Harry, who had, throughout his youth, sexually and physically abused him. He claimed that some of the scarring on his body had been from the beatings Harry had inflicted upon him. Harry, he said, had also boasted about being involved in the taking of one of the other missing girls. He told him that he had been accompanied by a young female cousin, who had tricked the girl into getting into the van with them. The missing girl's body had been dumped into the same bog hole as the other two.

★

His fear of Harry was palpable. Even in prison and serving a long sentence, he did not, he said, feel completely safe. If it became known that he was talking to us, his life would, he said, be in grave danger. As real as this fear was, it left us in a dilemma. If what Felix was telling us about his own involvement in the murder of two of the girls was true, then it was essential that he point out the location of their bodies to us. We explained this to him, and he said that he would show us where they had left the girls so they could have a Christian burial. We told him that, between ourselves and the prison authorities, we would ensure his continued safety. Felix said that he would talk to Dr White, whom he trusted implicitly, and that she would contact us when he was ready to bring us to where the bodies were hidden. We said that when we received word from him, we would talk to the prison authorities.

Within the following three weeks, Felix was ready to leave the prison under escort to show us the body dump sites. To ensure that the purpose of our trip would not leak out, it was officially announced that Felix was being allowed visit his father's grave, to mark the anniversary of his death. He would leave the prison under escort from prison officers, and we would meet up with them en route. However, on the day we expected to meet, we received word from the prison that Felix had been moved into solitary confinement, after assaulting a number of prison officers the previous evening.

Dr White then contacted us, and told us that this incident had occurred following a visit that Felix had received from his mother the previous day. After his mother had left him, he had been found attempting to self-harm with a prison shank (a knife made from a toothbrush handle, attached to the blades of a disposable razor). Unfortunately, Dr White could not say if the incident was as a result of the visit from his mother, or had been triggered by his impending journey to show the location of the bodies to us.

For our part, it confirmed a lot of the doubts that we held concerning the truthfulness of the admissions that Felix was making to us. Notwithstanding our misgivings, we had ballistic, forensic and specialist search teams in place, to assist us if Felix was able to point out the area. The teams had been waiting in the back yard of the Garda station. Their presence, naturally, had attracted great interest, and their prompt withdrawal attracted almost as much speculation. We decided that, during our next visit with him, we would attempt to tie him down in relation to the actual details surrounding his claims.

It was almost three months before Felix contacted us again. When we met with him, he presented in a very truculent and confrontational mood. His opening greeting was to ask us if we were serious about wanting to find the missing girls, We looked at him in amazement, and told him that if, as he had claimed, he had in fact been involved in the abductions and murders, then there was a lot of detail that he appeared to have omitted in his previous conversations with us. He became extremely aggressive towards us, and had it not been for the presence of the escorting prison officers, our conversation would have ended in physical violence.

★

Felix then began, once again, to talk about his role in the abduction and murder of the two girls. We asked a number of probing questions. In a rambling tirade, it became obvious that his knowledge of the circumstances behind the actual abductions was limited to what he read in the newspapers or heard in discussions with his fellow inmates. Pat then put it formally to Felix, that we believed that he did not have any involvement whatsoever in the disappearances and that, from our enquiries, his suggestion of being abused and controlled by Harry was entirely without foundation. On hearing this, Felix had drawn himself up to his not inconsiderable height, and went as if to lunge across the room at us. He was quickly ushered back to his cell.

This, however, would not be the last occasion on which I would have dealings with Felix. Over the following years, he would make contact with other Garda members whom he had come to know throughout his career in crime. At least twice-yearly I would receive either a telephone call or a written report from some other Garda member, detailing admissions made to them by Felix, in relation to the murders of two of the missing women. The information, they would tell me, had been supplied by him during the course of a meeting they had had, at his request, in prison.

After receiving each such report, I would go to the prison and meet with him. My request to him on each occasion was quite simple. In order for his claims to be taken as genuine, he would have to give us the location of the bodies. This request led to a number of further 'false dawns', where arrangements were put in place to take him from the prison. However, on each occasion he would either refuse to leave the cell that morning or, alternatively, have been involved in some incident prior to our arrival that would see him having been returned to solitary confinement.

It eventually reached the stage that the Assistant Commissioner Operations directed that a note be placed on Felix's criminal record that, in the event of him contacting any Garda member and claiming to have any information concerning the disappearance of any of the Operation TRACE females or, indeed, any other person, that same Garda member was to make direct contact with myself prior to initiating any action that was based on requests or claims made by Felix. All such claims would, it was decided, be followed up with a visit with him in the prison.

My last contact with Felix would occur in February 2011, a few months before I was due to retire from An Garda Síochána. Prior to this meeting, he had contacted a female member based in a mid-western station, who had had dealings with him almost fifteen years earlier. He had recounted a story similar to that which he had told me some ten years previously, but with one important difference. Over the intervening years, his list of 'victims' had gradually increased, and he now claimed to have been involved in the abduction and murder of all six of the missing girls.

★

For this, my last meeting with Felix, I was be accompanied by Detective Sergeant Noel Mooney, who was due to take over my role as National Coordinator in Operation TRACE. When we met Felix, he was in a very strange and subdued mood. I introduced Noel to him, and told him that, from now on, it would be Noel who would visit him and talk to him about the missing females. I explained that I was shortly due to retire. Felix replied that he was due for release the following year, having served almost the entirety of his sentence. When Noel commented that he did not appear to be looking forward to finally getting out, he had replied that he genuinely feared going back out into society. The majority of his adult life had, he added, been spent in one prison or another. At this stage he began to cry. It was a shock to witness this giant of a man becoming so upset.

'I know', he said, 'that you don't believe me about the girls. If you would only charge me for one of them, I would get life, and not worry any more'. Turning to Noel, he pointed at me and said, 'I trust him – I hope I can trust you'. We left the prison, after reassuring him that he would be allowed out of prison if he wanted to point out a place to us, and after Noel had promised to be always ready to visit him in the prison if he sent out 'word'.

Given the nature of the crime for which he was serving the lengthy prison sentence, and the extreme violence employed in carrying it out, Tony Hickey had, almost from the outset, insisted that Felix be visited by us on each occasion he contacted us to make his admissions. The fear was, of course, that maybe, just maybe, he was telling the truth.

My last conversation with Felix essentially summed up the divide between his admissions and those of Olson. In Felix, we had a man who, through so much time spent in prison, had become totally institutionalised. Given his personality and imposing physicality, he was never going to fit into normal life. The notoriety in the confined prison society that would attach to anyone connected with the deaths of so many females, especially to a man who could defend himself, was something he craved. As an attention-seeker who would never 'fit in' in the outside world, adulation from his peers in the prison community meant as much to him as fame does to every wannabe pop singer. However, we as policemen also had to be mindful of the harm that false admissions could cause a grieving family, and the potential for misdirection that could be visited upon an investigation. Admissions made by persons like Felix have, initially, to be fully checked out, and then carefully handled.

Olson, on the other hand, had made his admissions for the sole purpose of attempting an escape from custody, or serving out his sentence in a less strict institution. I have no doubt that, in order to carry out this plan, he would have certainly attempted to plead guilty to the murder of Carole Jordan, which had, of course, never even taken place.

Both Olson and Felix condemned themselves, by the admissions they made, to their alleged involvement in the murders of the missing girls. Without those admissions, neither of them would have ever been linked to our cases.

Categorising Missing Persons in Ireland

Since the foundation of the State, Gardai have maintained statistics in relation to all reports made throughout the country, of persons reported missing to them. The Annual Report of the Garda Commissioner contains details of all those persons whose whereabouts remain unknown at the end of each calendar year. The actual numbers reported missing, year-on-year, run into several thousand. The number outstanding at the end of the calendar year is normally only a fraction of the total; the majority of those reported missing are either located, return voluntarily or have made contact with families or acquaintances.

On its establishment, Operation TRACE was supplied with a list, compiled by the Garda Statistical Unit, that contained the particulars of the disappearances of almost three hundred persons whose whereabouts had, it stated, never been established. Some of the cases dated back to 1929. We were never explained the criteria used by the unit, to decide which cases would be included. However, a perusal of the list proved to be very interesting, reflecting, as it did, both Garda and societal attitudes of the time, particularly towards females and persons with mental health issues. It was referred to as the TRACE list.

Missing-persons records had, previously, been kept at Crime Branch, Garda Headquarters. With the establishment of the Missing Persons Bureau in 1982, this task was transferred to that unit.

The disappearances of persons who have not been located by the end of each calendar year in which the report was made, were categorised and recorded under one of four separate headings. Categorisation was, of course, dependent on the outcome of the local enquiries. The category under which a particular disappearance was classified, also had a direct bearing on the extent or otherwise of a follow-up investigation. The four categories used were:

(A) Suspicious
(B) Possible suicide
(C) Believed drowned
(D) Voluntary leaving

Investigations would, for the most part, have been carried out by local Gardai. It was only in extremely rare cases, for example where a child has gone missing, or foul play was suspected, that outside resources would have been sought or utilised.

As reports of missing-persons were received, there would be an immediate distinction drawn between cases deemed to be either 'Acceptable' or 'Unacceptable'. 'Acceptable' cases were those involving children under eighteen years of age, elderly persons, physically or mentally disabled persons or persons whose disappearance had taken place in circumstances that gave rise to fears for their physical or moral safety.

Following intensive lobbying from various groups and interested parties, including, it should be said, a number of comprehensive submissions from Operation TRACE, the classifying of missing persons changed dramatically, with the introduction of three new separate and distinct categories in 2003. These were:

Category A: those cases requiring immediate attention, such as child abductions, unexplainable disappearances etc

Category B: including persons not considered to be at immediate risk, such as persons who may have had a good reason for leaving or may have left a note

Category C: includes all those considered not to be at any risk

Of equal significance, however, are the procedural changes which were put in place at the same time. Reports of missing persons must now be immediately referred to the District Superintendent, who has to take overall control of the investigation. This removes the danger of an inexperienced Garda being left to investigate a case alone. It also ensures that the approach to the first report will be completely non-judgemental and that the investigation is not hampered by a lack of local resources.

In our recommendations, we had suggested that the English model be applied, whereby the first report of a missing person received at station level is treated with the same professionalism and pooling of resources as is the report of a homicide. The new procedures now in place have not gone quite that far but are, nevertheless, a huge improvement on the old system.

Background checks on missing persons normally include relationship issues, possible physical, mental or sexual abuse, business or financial concerns and other push/pull factors. In cases involving missing females, the investigators invariably also consider other possibilities, ranging from abusive relationships to unplanned pregnancies.

★

The year-on-year number of missing-person reports, as recorded by Gardai, does not properly reflect the actual number of persons who go missing. It refers, of course, only to the number of reports received. As a consequence, persons who regularly go missing appear in the end-of-year figures as separate cases. For instance, a child or vulnerable young person in the care of the State can often leave the foster home to which they have been attached on a regular basis. The foster parent is legally bound to report all such incidents as they occur.

A 2007 report clearly shows that 43 percent of reports of missing persons, which had been received in the previous year, comprised of children in contact with the health services.[11] At the same time, the number of children who had actually gone missing accounted for just 8 percent of the overall total. In one instance, the report found that one youngster had been reported missing a total of 169 times, or almost once every two days. This skewers the statistics and, as long as this accounting process continues, will keep giving an inexact record of the problem of disappearances.

In a recent presentation to a Dáil Committee,[11] Assistant Garda Commissioner John O'Mahoney stated that, while the number of reported cases of missing persons lay, annually, in the region of seven thousand, the actual number of persons who went missing would be only half that figure.

Should an adult, who is not considered to be either at risk or vulnerable, decide for any reason to leave home, there is no legal sanction that can be imposed to prevent their leaving. Nor does any sanction exist that would take account of the efforts by various organs of the State to locate the person, even though that same person was aware, throughout, of the extent and scope of those self-same efforts.

Similarly, if the 'missing' adult is subsequently located, Gardai are not entitled to give details of their whereabouts to person'sthe concerned family, spouse or friend who made the report, without the persons expressed consent. In those instances, the person is normally requested by the investigating Garda to contact some independent person, usually a friend, to convey the news that they are not in danger to the person who had reported them missing.

In order to demonstrate the effect that the old system of recording missing persons had on the subsequent Garda investigations, we can refer, briefly, to the TRACE list, which, as already stated, contained details of some three hundred persons, whose whereabouts had not been established by the end of the respective calendar years, between 1929 and 1998. Some seventy-two of the entries refer to females, ranging in age from eleven months to seventy-five years.

The cases of the missing females were categorised as follows:

'Suspicious'	Eleven (11)
'Possible suicide'	Thirty-one (31)
'Presumed drowned'	Seven (7)
'Voluntary leaving'	Twenty-three (23)

Amongst these cases there are, undoubtedly, instances in which the missing person may, in time, have made contact with particular family members or friends, or with some other person whom they trusted, just to let them know they were still alive. It is for that very reason that I have deliberately not named any one person. There would, almost certainly, be cases where they did not want an abusive husband or partner to know they were still alive. The record shows that, over the years, a significant number of females have been reported missing by spouses and immediate family members.

A total of seventeen disappearances were simply described by the person making the report as 'believed to be living in England'. These are included in the category of 'voluntary leaving'. What is startling is that one of these cases actually involved the disappearance of a twelve-year-old female. It was even suggested that she had moved to England with a named, much older, male. In some of these same cases, it was alleged that the person had left a note for their spouse, stating that they were leaving to start a new life somewhere else.

Only eleven of the seventy-two missing-female cases are classed as 'suspicious', with eight of those disappearances having occurred between 1993 and 1998. In addition, the first disappearance of a female to be recorded as 'suspicious' does not occur until 1982, notwithstanding the fact that, by that year, as the list shows, the whereabouts of some forty females was unknown. The

TRACE list would suggest that an average of one in every seven disappearances of a female was considered as suspicious up until 1982. Between 1982 and 1998 this would rise to an average of one in every three disappearances. A number of reasons were advanced for this large difference. These range from societal changes, to public awareness, the changing perception of the role of women in society, and better training in investigative procedures for Gardai.

★

My investigative role on Operation TRACE regularly brought me into contact with detectives based throughout the length and breadth of the country, many of whom had been involved in investigations at local level into disappearances of females. They would often comment on the huge investigation that was being concentrated on our six targeted disappearances, and voice their regret that a similar commitment had never been available to assist them with their particular enquiries. They would, furthermore, ask me to outline the criteria that had been used when selecting our cases, and ask if our list could be added to or amended to take on a case that they believed might have benefited from greater scrutiny.

The general consensus in Garda circles was that our operation was, for the most part, media-driven. It was suggested that the high-profile disappearances of Annie, Jo Jo, Ciara, the two Fionas and Deirdre had each attracted wide-spread media coverage, and that it had been the press, as opposed to any investigative development or requirement, which had been influential in the selection of our cases.

I am firmly of the belief that another factor that has brought about significant change is the knowledge, on the part of the Garda, of the often unwelcome but nevertheless continuous scrutiny of their work by the media. Mirroring the changes that are occurring in society as a whole, this day-to-day monitoring of our every move and decision ensures that prejudices, personal opinions, judgement calls and complacency are daily becoming less and less a feature of our work. I am not attempting to insinuate, here, that any of these matters could or did influence the official investigation of missing-persons reports in the past, but I will argue that there is certainly no place for them in a modern investigation, where a local incident can become, within minutes, the subject of national or even international attention.

There is also the additional pressure that the families and friends of missing persons, whom we refer to as 'secondary victims', will bring to bear on any investigation which they believe is not receiving the commitment and effort it deserves. It is through their hard work that so many of today's major cases do not quickly become yesterday's statistics. I also found this to be the case in my role as a Cold Case Investigator. Families who have dedicated their whole lives to seeking justice and answers for their loved one's death or disappearance will not rest until they receive answers. Their work deserves the highest praise and support.

Having already commented on the paucity of the use of the categorisation of 'suspicious' in those cases included in the TRACE list, it has to be conceded that the very first case it contains is categorised as such.

It concerned the disappearance, on Christmas Day in 1929, of Laurence Griffin, a local postman, from Kilmacthomas, just outside of Waterford city. He had last been seen alive delivering post in the village of Stradbally, some eight miles from Kilmacthomas. Christmas Day deliveries were a feature of that time.

★

Griffin, a married man with three children and a veteran of the First World War, had spent the early part of that day delivering post in this intimate community. Many families had husbands and sons working abroad, due to the dual scourges of unemployment and emigration, and were completely dependent on the money that their letters from abroad contained.

His bicycle and rain cape were located some two days later, about two miles outside the village. To this day, his body has never been recovered, despite the personal intervention at the time of senior clergy and members of the government. The Garda investigation into his disappearance was personally led Eoin O' Duffy, then Garda Commissioner.

The original investigation culminated in ten members of the local community standing trial for the murder of Mr Griffin. The defendants, unusually, included two local Gardai!

Witnesses claimed to have seen a very drunken Thomas enter Whelan's pub in the village at around 6 PM on Christmas evening in the company of Garda Jones*. Two other Garda members, along with a number of local dignitaries, were named as having been in the pub at the same time. An altercation, it was alleged, had broken out between Griffin and a local man in the pub, during which he received a blow to the face. While falling backwards, he had struck his head and received fatal injuries.

Another witness said that the body was bundled into the back of a car, and driven from the scene, to be disposed of. As one senior colleague of mine, who had, at one stage, read the original Garda investigation file, would later tell me, it should not have proven to be a huge task to trace this car, given that the number of cars in the locality could probably have been counted on one hand.

The investigation and subsequent trial attracted a huge amount of media interest, with reporters present from both the local and national newspapers and even from certain international publications. Although the investigation was led by the local Chief Superintendent, based in Waterford city, O'Duffy kept a watching brief on the investigation, demanding daily updates on its' progress.

On his instructions, those Garda members who, it had been suggested, had been present during the alleged murder, had been escorted to Garda Headquarters in Dublin, where they were interrogated by a special team selected by O' Duffy. They continued to deny any involvement in or knowledge of the matter. They further pointed out that they could not even have been in the public house at the time, given that it was not open, it being Christmas Day. This suggestion did not impress O'Duffy.

The trial of the ten accused was set for 7 March 1930. It did not, however, proceed, as one of the lead witnesses refused to give evidence against his friends and neighbours. Given the tense political situation of the time, it has also been suggested that local sympathy and support for Griffin, a man who had fought for the hated British during the First World War, was minimal.

The passage of time would not change this mindset. Our list shows that during the mid to late forties, a new type of 'missing' person began to emerge. These were those Irish Army personnel, described as 'deserters', who had left the jurisdiction. Far from being deserters, these men had joined the English Army to fight and die on the side of the Allied forces against Hitler's Germany. Barred for years from every government job or from receiving any social-welfare payments, they would finally be 'pardoned' by the Irish government in 2013.

★

An independent team was appointed by an irate Commissioner O'Duffy, to investigate allegations that witnesses had been coerced into giving false evidence during the original enquiry. Not surprisingly, nothing came of this enquiry. All it did was reveal the oppressive nature of O'Duffy's interference in the original investigation. He went so far as to summarily dismiss a number of the Gardai who had allegedly been involved. They would be reinstated the following year, after a general election and change of government which brought Eamon De Valera into power. These would not be the only sacked policemen he would reinstate, but that is a story for another day.

The State was successfully sued by a number of the witnesses. The then Minister for Justice refused repeated calls for a commission of enquiry to be held into the whole sordid affair. He laid the blame for the failure to successfully prosecute the offenders or to locate the unfortunate Mr Griffin's body on the 'over-zealous' approach adopted by some of the investigating Gardai.

Over the years, other rumours of what had actually taken place that Christmas Day emerged. These included the suggestion that Laurence had last been seen alive leaving the local Garda station, where he had been involved in a high-stakes game of cards with a number of local dignitaries. It was further rumoured that he had won a great deal of money, and had been murdered for the winnings he had taken with him.

Whatever the motive behind Laurence Griffin's disappearance, the fact remains that neither the alleged initial involvement by members of the Gardai, nor the subsequent manner in which the matter was handled, did much to enhance their reputation either at home or abroad. In this, their first investigation into the circumstances surrounding the suspicious disappearance of a missing person, they were found to be seriously wanting.

A fascinating book on this case has recently been published by Irish author, Fachtna O'Drisceoil.

★

Amazingly, there would be a fifty-year gap in police records, before the appearance of a second 'suspicious' disappearance! It has often been suggested that the fiasco that ensued following the investigation into Griffin's murder may have caused some Gardai to hesitate before categorising any further missing-persons reports as such. One would sincerely hope that these were not the criteria used when reports were received.

Twenty-four-year-old Gerry Evans was reported missing by his father on 25 March 1979. Gerry, a native of Crossmaglen, was last seen hitch-hiking outside Castleblaney, County Monaghan. His disappearance would be blamed on increased Provisional Irish Republican Army (PIRA) activities, and would later be linked to the disappearance of another fifteen persons, all victims of the

Troubles in Northern Ireland and its overspill into this jurisdiction. They would, during the peace talks, be referred to, collectively, as the 'disappeared'.

A Committee of Investigation was set up by the Irish and British governments, in an attempt to locate the bodies of the 'disappeared': the Independent Commission for the Location of Victim's Remains (ICLVR). The ICLVR received information from a subversive source in 2010, which eventually led to the discovery of Gerry's remains in bogland at Carrickrobin, outside Hackballscross, County Louth. During the subsequent forensic 'dig', an area estimated to have been the size of four football pitches was excavated before the body was located.

The IRA eventually admitted to having murdered nine of the 'disappeared', while the Irish National Liberation Army (INLA) took responsibility for having murdered one of them.

Gerry was laid to rest in Crossmaglen Cemetery, just yards from the grave of his neighbour, Charlie Armstrong, who had been abducted by the same group in 1981, and whose body was not be located until July of 2010.

The ICLVR stands mandated by the British government to trace a total of sixteen persons, fifteen male and one female. Their appeal for assistance in their search was aimed directly at persons who had been involved in subversive activities throughout the seventies, eighties and nineties in Northern Ireland. Anyone coming forward with relevant information was guaranteed total confidentiality, and assured that their information would not be passed on to any other person. To date, nine of the bodies have been recovered.

Those bodies that were recovered include that of housewife and mother of ten Jean McConville. In December of 1972, she was abducted and murdered by a gang of IRA sympathisers. It was believed by them that she was 'touting' to the British Army. Her body, with a gunshot wound to the head, was located in August of 2003, at Shelling Hill Beach in County Louth. Her murder was described some three years later by the then Chief Constable of the PSNI, Sir Hugh Orde, as a crime for which it was unlikely there would ever be a 'successful prosecution'.

★

On 22 March of this year, seventy-seven-year-old Ivor Bell was charged with aiding and abetting others in the abduction and subsequent murder of McConville. Nineteen-seventy-two would appear to have been a very busy year for this republican activist. Bell, then the 'Belfast Brigade Adjutant', had, during that same year, been flown to London to attempt to broker a peace deal with the British government. He was accompanied on that trip by Gerry Adams and Martin McGuinness.

There remain two other members of the 'disappeared' whose bodies have not yet been located.

Columba McVeigh, a seventeen-year-old from Donaghmore, County Tyrone, has been missing since October 1975. At the time of his disappearance, he had been living for a short while in Donaghmeade, Dublin. This youth was suspected, by certain figures within the IRA, of attempting to infiltrate their organisation as a spy for the British Army, and was executed by them. Seemingly he had, during the 'interrogation', admitted as much to them. Searches are currently ongoing in the area of Bragan in County Monaghan. On our list, Columba was reported as having gone missing in 1978. More bizarrely, however, he is described as being a member of the IRA, who was believed to have moved to England. His disappearance was even categorised as 'voluntary leaving'.

The second person from the 'disappeared' that is of concern to us is Captain Robert Nairac, a British soldier attached to the Special Duties Unit of the infamous 14th Intelligence Company, whose disappearance we have referred to previously. What makes this case interesting to us from a missing-person' perspective is the fact that, despite Nairac's body never having been located, he was not included in our list.

The first female to appear on the list disappeared on 13 January 1949. Seventy-five-year-old Francis* was reported to have gone missing during the night by her friends. She was described as 'suffering from depression', and her disappearance was, as a consequence, categorised as 'possible suicide'.

A further forty missing females are listed between that year and 1977, a period of twenty-eight years. In a large number of instances, these disappearances had been reported to Gardai by the husbands of the women. The suggestion that they had 'gone to England' was regularly appended to the reports, leaving children, extended families and work behind. 1977 would be the first time the disappearance of a female was categorised as 'suspicious'. Thirty-year-old Margaret B disappeared from her home, in a tiny village in south Tipperary. This is also only the third occasion in a staggering fifty-three-year period that this categorisation appears. I have already touched on the two other two cases, those of Laurence Griffin and Gerry Evans.

★

On 23 June 1989, Earnest Mc. was reported missing. Earnest was suspected, locally, of having been involved in a certain criminal incident. It was believed that his 'suspicious' disappearance had been the result of foul play arising from retaliation over that issue.

Also considered 'suspicious' was the strange disappearance of thirteen-year-old schoolboy Phillip Cairns, from Rathfarnham in Dublin. He was last seen alive during the school lunch break on 23 October 1986. He had left his family home at around 1.30 PM to return to the nearby Colaiste Eanna Secondary School, which he attended. Some six days after Phillip's disappearance, his school bag would be located by two young girls in a laneway near his home, an area that had already been extensively searched by investigating Gardai. This find followed a visit by investigating detectives to Phillip's school, where they addressed the assembled pupils, and asked them to report any suspicious sightings or incidents of which they may have been aware. A number of books were missing from the bag, prompting the suggestion that they had been retained as 'souvenirs' by his abductor.

Phillip was the only son of Alice and Phillip Senior. He had four sisters, Suzanne, Sandra, Helen and Mary, and a younger brother, Eoin. The family have, for the most part, avoided contact with the media, maintaining a dignified and united quest for their missing son and sibling. They did, however, mark the twentieth anniversary of his disappearance by taking part in a media appeal and poster campaign. Alice, in a direct appeal to her son's abductor, asked him or her to 'Please let him go. We just want Phillip back.'

The family would also later engage with best-selling author and investigative journalist Barry Cummins, who featured Phillip's disappearance prominently in one of his books.[13] Phillip's father is quoted as saying that he believed that his son had dropped his school bag as he was being dragged into a car by his abductor and, furthermore, that if the bag had been left in the laneway where it had been located by an innocent person, they would have come forward to help in the search for Phillip. His whereabouts remain unknown to the present day.

The circumstances attending the disappearance in 1990 of Theresa Terry, a forty-three-year-old native of Lancashire, England, were also categorised as 'suspicious'. This is only the sixth time this categorisation appears, and only the second time it was applied to a missing female.

Theresa had arrived in Ireland with her boyfriend Colin in early January of that year. They were part of the 'New Age' movement, and were attracted to the nomadic lifestyle enjoyed by their peers in the south-west of the country. However, as time went on, her family back in England became more and more concerned as to her whereabouts. Enquiries were made with her partner, who did not provide any useful information as to where she might be. He would subsequently return to England and, while serving a prison sentence for an unrelated matter, regularly played games with his fellow inmates, whom he would ask to guess the whereabouts of Theresa's body.

In 1991, Charles Brooke Picard, a native of England residing at Castlegrove, Sneem, in County Kerry, with his wife and children, went missing. He was last seen alive being bundled into the back of a van near his home by armed men. It is suspected that he was shot, and that his body was then disposed of. Charles was believed to have fallen foul of some local drug dealers.

The final month of 1993 would contain a total of three 'suspicious' disappearances, bringing the total number included on our list, which spans a period of seventy years, to ten.

The three cases included, of course, Annie McCarrick, the oldest of the original six disappearances that Operation TRACE were tasked with examining. The other two cases were those of Michelle McCormack, a twenty-three-year-old native of Cork, and her boyfriend, Frank McCarthy, who both went missing from Harrington's Caravan Park, in the picturesque village of Owenahinch, in west Cork. It was generally believed that they had been murdered by a close associate, and possibly buried at sea. They had last been seen alive on 20 July.

Nineteen-ninety-four would see the disappearance of Arelene Arkinson, although, as I have already mentioned, her disappearance possibly occurred outside this jurisdiction. The search for her body continues to the present day.

There was one 'suspicious' disappearance for 1995. Jo Jo Dollard was last seen alive as she attempted to hitch a lift late at night, on the busy Dublin-to-Waterford road, at the village of Moone, in County Kildare. While it was still a common sight to see people attempting to 'thumb' a lift, following Jo Jo's disappearance and the subsequent failure of Gardai to locate her, this practice went into decline. Her disappearance would be the second of the cases to be dealt with by Operation TRACE.

The following year, Tullamore native Fiona Pender would be reported missing on 22 August. Fiona, who was in an advanced stage of pregnancy, was officially last seen alive in the flat she shared with her boyfriend, on Church Street, in the centre of town, early the previous morning. Hers was another disappearance to which it was considered difficult to attribute an external push/pull factor. Her partner (the father of her child) was the only male heir to a wealthy local Protestant farming family. She came from a Catholic lower-middle-class family, and grew up in a local housing estate. Her disappearance was deemed to be 'suspicious', and was another of the cases to be revisited by Operation TRACE.

Another disappearance in 1996, also categorised as 'suspicious', was that of Dublin man Jock Corbally. On 28 February, Jock had been lured to his death by drug dealer Declan Griffin. He had told Jock that he had been asked by a mutual friend to seek his assistance in bringing back a consignment of drugs from Amsterdam. What Jock did not know was that Griffin was acting on the orders of a notorious gangland enforcer and drug dealer, P.J. Judge, known to friends and foes alike as 'Psycho'.

Jock and 'Psycho' were the same age, and had known each other since childhood. He was from Ballygall Parade in Finglas, while Judge was from nearby Ballygall Crescent. Both had begun a life of crime at an early age, but that was where the similarities ended. While Jock was one of the 'ordinary decent criminal' types, Judge began to make a name for himself as a cruel enforcer. The ultimate sadist, he carried out punishment beatings and tortures that became legendary among the criminal fraternity.

In mid 1995, Jock Corbally had been released from prison after serving over two years for an attempted hijack. He discovered that one of his sons owed a drug debt of €800 to Judge, and had been threatened by him. Jock, having known Judge all his life, approached him and asked him to leave his son alone. Judge told him that he would, but only if Jock paid him €1600. Needless to say, this offer was turned down. Judge produced an iron bar and threatened Jock, who took the bar off him and gave him a serious beating. Locals cheered to see this bully getting a taste of his own medicine. Any other person would have taken their beating and conceded that they had lost in a fair fight. However, Judge didn't think that way. He sent out word that Corbally had a month to leave the country 'or else'. To salvage his damaged reputation, he also began a campaign of terror that is talked about to this day amongst the unfortunate heroin addicts whose habits he fed.

When Corbally turned up for the 'meeting' with Griffin, he found that he had walked into a trap. He was surrounded by Judge and a number of his lieutenants in a flat in the Cabra area, and received a savage beating. Not content with this, Judge and two of his most trusted lieutenants, Griffin and John Joe Mooney*, bundled a semi-conscious Corbally into the boot of their car, and drove to a field somewhere near Baldonnell aerodrome. There, Judge took an iron bar from the boot of the car, and began to systematically break almost every bone in his victim's body. Not caring whether he was alive or dead, they then buried what was left of Jock Corbally.

In 1993, I interviewed a criminal who was present in a field at Scribblestown in Finglas when a Judge meted out a similar beating to insurance salesman Michael Godfrey, whom he suspected of having ripped him off in a deal for bad quality cocaine. Godfrey had become involved in a 'get-rich-quick' scheme with Judge. Prior to that, his involvement in crime had been confined to setting up bogus traffic-accident claims. Barely talking above a whisper, my terrified informant told me that the first head-shot had penetrated Godfrey's skull at an angle, and had exited through his forehead. Blinded and crying out in agony, Godfrey had attempted to crawl away on all fours, while pleading with Judge for his life. A laughing Judge had sat upon his back, as if riding a horse, while whipping him with the gun. He then shot him through the temple while advising his henchmen who were present that, in future, this was the correct way of doing things.

★

To date, Jock Corbally's body has not been recovered, leaving him without even the dignity of a burial. It may be some consolation to the family to know that all of those who had tortured Jock themselves suffered untimely deaths. On 8 December 1996, P.J. Judge was shot dead as he sat in the driver's seat of his white Ford Fiesta in the car park of the Royal Oak pub in Finglas. It was rumoured, at the time, that the hit-man was an IRA assassin. It would appear that Judge had, finally, picked the wrong victim. Declan Griffin would be shot dead in a pub on Dublin's south side, on 5 April 2003. At the time of his murder, Griffin was wearing a bullet-proof jacket. Mooney was murdered some months earlier, by coincidence in the Scribblestown area of the city.

Nineteen-ninety-seven would see the disappearances of a further two females being categorised as 'suspicious'. Twenty-three-year-old Ciara Breen would leave her mother's house late at night on 13 February, to keep a date with a local youth. Also in 1997, twenty-seven-year-old Colleen Cronin would be reported missing from her flat by her landlord, at Cecil Street, in Limerick city. Although the circumstances of this case were treated as 'suspicious', it would, unlike Ciara's case, be allowed to 'stand alone', and was not revisited by our task-force. This may have been in part due to the fact that her disappearance did not fall within the same geographic area, the infamous 'Vanishing Triangle', as with the other cases assigned to TRACE.

Indeed, very early that year, the father of an English sex worker who had come to Dublin to work the Rathmines area of the city over the Christmas of 1996, would report her as missing. Cheryl* was thirty years old, and prior to her disappearance had always maintained regular contact with her family. For some reason, her disappearance would be officially categorised as 'voluntary leaving'.

What makes this categorisation of Cheryl's disappearance even more bizarre is the fact that a second English sex worker, Belinda Pereira, who had also come over to Ireland for the lucrative 'Christmas trade', was found, bludgeoned to death, in her apartment in the north inner city. To date, no one has been made accountable for Belinda's murder, although it is almost certainly the case that her assailant was well known to her. The investigation is currently being reviewed by my former colleagues in the Garda Cold Case Unit.

Nineteen-ninety-eight would see a total of six females reported missing. Two of these cases, those of Deirdre Jacob and Wexford girl Fiona Sinnott, would be categorised as 'suspicious', and added to the TRACE caseload. Fiona, the single mother of a two-year-old child, had just escaped from an abusive relationship around the time she went missing. She would be reported as having last been seen as she walked home from a pub in the village of Bridgetown. Unfortunately, unlike Deirdre's case, her disappearance had gone unreported for several days.

★

The TRACE list threw up some amazing categorisations that, by today's standards, would be considered to be highly questionable. There was, for instance, the disappearance of Eva Brennan, a forty-year-old from Terenure, Dublin, who was reported missing on 25 July 1993. She had left the family home after a minor argument. Her disappearance was categorised as a 'possible suicide', a finding that is disputed to this day by her siblings.

There was also the case of Imelda Keenan, a twenty-two-year-old from Mountmellick, who was reported missing by her family in early January of 1994. Imelda's partner, with whom she shared a flat in Waterford city, had not reported her disappearance. The partner subsequently told Gardai that she had left their flat a few days earlier, to collect her unemployment assistance money, and had not returned. She had, he said, also confided in him that she was feeling 'very depressed'. The office where she had gone to collect her money was actually closed throughout that period. Her stated health status was strongly questioned by her immediate family. They had spent a considerable amount of time over the holiday season in her company, and said that there was no evidence to suggest that she was in any way troubled or down. Her disappearance was categorised, though, as a 'possible suicide'. A small monument erected in Waterford, near the spot where she was last seen alive, stands as a reminder to her family and friends of a bright, intelligent girl whose disappearance has never been adequately explained.

In at least one of these disappearances, it was the case that the report that a man's wife had gone missing was only filed by her husband after Gardai, responding to rumours that were circulating widely in the area, called to enquire about her welfare. Her husband told Gardai that his forty-six-year-old wife had a 'tendency' to leave the family home 'occasionally'. The initial report had been made at the local Garda station after concerns as to her whereabouts had been raised by worried friends and workmates. The suggestion that there had been incidences of previous disappearances took them by surprise. Investigating Gardai nonetheless categorised this case as a 'voluntary leaving'.

★

I was astonished, while reading a comprehensive Garda investigation file into the abrupt disappearance of this wife and mother, to discover that her husband had threatened to seek a court injunction to prevent Gardai entering his land to search for her body. This injunction was also intended to stop them asking his children about their mother's disappearance. What I found to be even more surprising was the fact that this disappearance allegedly occurred not in the mid-twenties or thirties, but in the mid-eighties!

The disappearance of persons from our psychiatric institutions who were considered to be mentally ill was a regular occurrence and, by law, had to be reported to the Gardai. These incidents often ended with the patient never being located. Our list suggested that in the year 1971 alone, three in-patients who had been reported missing from a very large psychiatric hospital were never located. The patients, two male and one female, would later be described in official Garda reports as 'left hospital, suffering from mental illness, possible suicide'. The previous year, Gardai had received reports of another in-patient from the same hospital, who had left the complex on a bicycle. The bicycle would later be found abandoned near the seafront, and the disappearance was categorised as 'possible suicide'. Official investigations into how four patients could disappear, without trace, from a secure environment would appear to have been minimal.

Before leaving the TRACE list, I want to briefly mention a few very high-profile missing-person cases that had not been included. As I have already stressed, the criteria used in the selection of cases for inclusion on the list was never explained to us. For instance, it showed that in 1977, two females had been reported as missing. Both, from different parts of the country, were believed to have committed suicide. There was, however, a third female who had not been included, whose whereabouts had not then been established and who, to the present day, has never been located.

On 18 March of that year, seven-year-old Mary Boyle disappeared after she left her grandparents' house at Cashelard, near Ballyshannon in County Donegal, to walk to a neighbour's home, some five hundred yards away. Her uncle Gerry was with her. He would later tell her distraught parents that she had turned back just before reaching the neighbour's house, saying that she would make her own way home. She was never seen again.

Mary had been born in Birmingham to immigrant parents who decided, when she was just two years old, to return to their native Donegal, in order to ensure a better and safer life for Mary, her twin sister, Ann, and their older brother, Patrick.

They moved back to Burtonport, where they began to build a new house for themselves. They had driven to Cashelard on Saint Patrick's Day 1977, to attend an anniversary mass for their uncle Patrick. They stayed overnight, and intended to return to their rented home in Ballyshannon on 18 March.

★

It was almost 5 PM before the adults discovered that little Mary was not out in the yard playing with the other children, as they had believed. Frantic searches were carried out in and around the family farm. The neighbour's farms and out-houses were also checked. Becoming increasingly worried, the Gardai would be notified shortly after 6 PM, and a full-scale investigation was launched. Neighbours and friends combed the area, and Gardai called in the assistance of the army helicopter, based at the nearby Finner Barracks. Despite all the searches, no trace of Mary was found.

A number of theories have been proposed as to the possible cause of Mary's disappearance. One theory centres on the activities of convicted child serial murderer Robert Black. In 1994, forty-seven-year-old Black was convicted of the murder of three children between 1982 and 1986, in various locations in the English Midlands. He had been arrested in the village of Stow in Scotland, in May of 1990, after police received a telephone call from a member of the public who had observed a young girl being dragged into a van. When Black's van was intercepted, his six-year-old victim was found alive, tied up and stuffed into a sleeping bag. She had been sexually abused.

On 28 October 2011, Black was convicted at Armagh Crown Court of the abduction and murder of nine-year-old Jennifer Cardy, who had been taken from near her home at Ballinderry, County Armagh, on 12 August 1981. Her body was discovered by hunters on 18 August at Hillsborough, some fifteen miles away. It was noted that the unfortunate child's wristwatch had stopped at just after 5.30 PM. Just what she had endured in the intervening four hours, at the hands of this brutal paedophile, does not bear thinking about. Evidence of Black's presence in the area had been established by the Police Service of Northern Ireland, who obtained petrol receipts for a delivery van that Black was known to have been driving at that time. The jury took little more than four hours to convict him.

Black has, since his 1994 conviction, been questioned by Gardai about Mary Boyle's disappearance, and has consistently denied any involvement. He has also been questioned about the murder of ten-year-old Sligo schoolgirl, Bernadette Connolly, in April of 1970.

Bernadette had been abducted near her family home at Doorla, Colloney in County Sligo on 17 April 1970. At 3 PM that day, Mary had set out to cycle to a neighbour's house to run an errand for her mother. The two houses were about a mile apart, but it was a journey that was well known to the young girl. Her bicycle and purse were found thrown into a ditch. As with the Boyle family, Bernadette's parents had, some years earlier, returned from Birmingham to their ancestral home in Sligo, to provide a better life for their children.

★

Suspicion had quickly fallen on a Passionist Order priest attached to a local monastery. Emphasis was placed on an alleged sighting in the area of a green van, similar to one owned by the religious order. It would also be suggested that one of the brothers attached to the monastery had, within hours of the first reports of a young girl having gone missing, been transferred to a mission outpost in Africa.

In another development, an English serial sex offender, Robert Reynolds, was arrested and convicted some years later of the abduction and rape of an eight-year-old girl in Castlebar, in County Mayo. Reynolds, when interviewed, denied any involvement in Bernadette's death.

On 4 August 1970 the skeletal remains of Bernadette were found in a bog hole near the town of Boyle in Roscommon, some fifteen miles from her home. Her clothing would be identified by the religious medals pinned on it by her mother to keep her safe. She had been raped and strangled. Some body parts were never located.

Award-winning author and crime editor with the *Sunday World* newspaper, Nicola Tallant, has spent a number of years investigating Mary's disappearance. She has interviewed principal witnesses who provided information at the time of the disappearance. In addition, based on her suggestions, and on what she has been told locally, a number of further searches and forensic 'digs' have been carried out in the vicinity. Her investigations have led her to suggest that the likely suspect for the abduction and murder of Mary Boyle lies 'much closer to the lonely and desolate mountainside where she was last seen'.

The list for year-end 1991 did not include Patricia McGauley, a native of Northern Ireland, who had moved to the Republic of Ireland some years earlier, in search of a new life. Patricia was last seen alive on 12 September 1991. It would later be established that she had been murdered by her husband, Michael Bambrick, in the bedroom of their home at Saint Ronan's Park in Clondalkin, Dublin, on that date. After dropping their children to school, he had returned to the house, and dismembered her body using a hacksaw. He cycled to an illegal dumping area at Lynch's Lane, Balgaddy, in Lucan, with Patricia's body parts wrapped in plastic bags. The disposal of her body took place over two days.

Patricia was one of those who, as it were, fell through the cracks in Irish society. Bambrick told any of their friends who enquired about her whereabouts that she had returned to Northern Ireland. Unfortunately, her disappearance, far from causing an outcry, went virtually unnoticed, especially by those in authority. Even the fact that Bambrick was seen walking through the housing estate where they had both lived, dressed in Patricia's clothing, does not seem to have caused any great concern to those who had known her.

★

The following year, on 23 July, Bambrick met Mary Cummins in Carr's pub, off Francis Street, Dublin. Mary was there with her daughter and a few friends. Bambrick also had his daughter with him. As their children played together, they chatted. Later, they left the pub in each other's company. He brought Mary back to Saint Ronan's Park, where he killed her. The following day, he dismembered her body and, once again, wrapped the body parts in plastic bags. Having learned from his previous venture, he transported the body parts, on this occasion, in a wheelbarrow to Balgaddy, where he disposed of the parts. This meant that he had only to make the one 'run'.

This time, however, Mary's disappearance, unlike that of Patricia, did not go unnoticed. Reports were made to Gardai by family members who were becoming worried by her continued absence. They told Gardai that she had left the pub with Bambrick. Some months after the disappearance, he was questioned in relation to Mary, but stated that they had split up shortly after leaving the pub. Mary's name did not appear on the list as an outstanding missing person at the end of 1992.

In late 1994, an allegation of child sexual abuse was made against Bambrick. There followed a forensic search of his home, in connection with that allegation. Traces of blood from two separate sources were located between the floorboards and along the skirting board in the bedroom. They were, of themselves, not significant enough link him to the disappearances directly. However, in 1995, his luck would run out. In June of that year, he was arrested in connection with a firearms offence. While being interviewed, he admitted involvement in the two deaths, and the dismemberment of the bodies. He would lead Gardai to the spot where he had buried his victims.

His defence was that, at the times of both deaths, they had been engaged in consensual sex, which involved acts of bondage that had gone wrong. Their deaths had been, he claimed, completely accidental, caused by his amateurish efforts at bondage play. This explanation would, unbelievably, be accepted by the courts, and he was allowed to enter a guilty plea to two counts of manslaughter in May of 1996. He was sentenced to eighteen years' imprisonment. Bambrick was released from custody in April 2009, and now lives under an assumed name in Dublin.

In my time at the Garda Street Anti-Vice Unit during the seventies and eighties, I had regularly met Bambrick walking the streets in the Benburb Street area, chatting to the girls who were engaged in prostitution there. We would always 'move him on' when we came across him. Recognised by all of them as dangerous, he was given a wide berth, with the exception of one enterprising soul who used to sell her underwear to him. She certainly, however, did not trust him enough to bring him into any of the nearby back lanes.

Conclusion

Twenty-fourteen marks the sixteenth anniversary of the establishment of Operation TRACE, a unique taskforce that was set up to address a worrying development in a particular area of crime. It was a distinct honour to have served in the tasckforce for almost thirteen years. The work of TRACE is ongoing, and will continue until closure has been obtained in all of the cases. Its continuance is a mark of the seriousness with which each of these cases is considered by the Garda authorities.

This year is a significant anniversary for various other persons for a number of reasons.

(A)   It will be twenty-seven years since the family of Antoinette Smith last saw her alive. A well-earned day off to attend a pop concert would start a nightmare that for them continues to the present day.

(B)   Inga Hauser's parents said goodbye to their daughter as she set out on her journey around Europe twenty-six years ago. Within weeks of her departure they would have the unenviable task of travelling to this country to collect their teenage daughter's body.

(C)   A shopping trip to get some final 'bits and pieces', just days before Christmas twenty-three years ago, would be the last time prison officer Patricia Doherty's children would see their mother alive.

(D)   For Marie Kilmartin's daughter, her search for her birth mother would end in the grim discovery of her death twenty-one years ago this year.

(E)   Annie McCarrick's fascination with the Irish people and their way of life would eventually result in her death. Twenty-one years on, her mother, now widowed, sits alone in her apartment three thousand miles away, hoping that the person who murdered her daughter will return her remains to her.

(F)   Arlene Arkinson has not been seen alive since she attended a dance with her friends twenty years ago this year. Her grieving family would later watch while the convicted rapist who had spent that last night in her company would be found not guilty by a jury of her murder.

(G)   For Jo Jo Dollard, a chance meeting with former friends in a Dublin pub would end with her standing on the side of a quiet country road at midnight, hoping that some 'Good Samaritan' would give her a lift home. Instead, she would place her trust in a complete stranger, and it is now nineteen years since she was last seen alive.

(H) In October 2014, a female came forward and told Canadian Police that her partner had admitted to the murder of Fiona, and gave her the location in which he disposed of her body. At the time of publication, this matter is currently being investigated by Gardai and hopefully will, in time, bring some solace to her mother. The alleged culprit is well known to all of us involved in Operation TRACE.

(I) It is now seventeen years since Ciara Breen's mother tucked her daughter into bed and closed the bedroom door, while telling her how much she loved her. Later that same day, after returning from a medical appointment which confirmed that she had cancer, she would have to call to her local Garda station to report her teenage daughter missing.

(J) In the years prior to her disappearance, Fiona Sinnott had been systematically beaten and abused by a partner for whom she felt nothing but love. It is sixteen years since her disappearance. The failure to disclose, even at this stage, her last resting place is symptomatic of the contempt in which the person she loved held her.

(K) Deirdre Jacob disappeared sixteen years ago, on a day when her every movement was witnessed and monitored by friends and acquaintances. Searches were begun within hours of her last been seen. To date her whereabouts have not been established.

All have left family and friends behind them. These people mark each passing year by honouring their missing loved ones, whose memories they still cherish, and whose loss still gives them pain.

To those who know, I beg, help them.

End Notes

1. Cohen and Felson (1979). 'Social Change and Crime Rate Trends'.

2. *Ibid*.

3. Beaufort, Rossme and Proulx (2007). 'A Descriptive Model of the Hunting Process of Serial Sex Offenders'.

4. Canter, David (2003). *Mapping Murder: The Secrets of Geographical Profiling*.

5. Turvey, Brent (2002). 'Criminal Profiling: An Introduction to Behavioural Evidence Analysis'.

6. O'Drisceoil, Fachtna (2011). *The Missing Postman*. Mercier Press.

7. Ayers and Durm (1993). 'Psychics: Do Police Departments Really Use Them?'

8. Silence, Eddie (2006). 'Do the Police Use Psychics?'

9. Jadwiszczok and Shafer (2013). 'Psychic Defective, Sylvia Browne's History of Failure.'

10. *The Irish Times*, 12 March 2014.

11. Report of The Garda Inspectorate 2007.

12. Joint Committee on Justice Defence and Equality (May 2012).

13. Cummins, Barry (2010). *Missing*. Gill & Macmillan.